A quintessential work of the High Renaissance in Venice, Titian's *Venus of Urbino* also represents one of the major themes of Western art: the female nude. But how did Titian intend this work to be received? Is she Venus, as the popular title – a modern invention – implies, or is she merely a courtesan? This book tackles this and other questions in six essays by European and American art historians. Examining the work within the context of Renaissance art theory, as well as the psychology and society of sixteenth-century Italy, and even in relation to Manet's nineteenth-century "translation" of the work, their observations begin and end with the painting itself and with appreciation of Titian's great achievement in creating this archetypal image of feminine beauty.

Titian's "Venus of Urbino"

MASTERPIECES OF WESTERN PAINTING

This series serves as a forum for the reassessment of several important paintings in the Western tradition that span a period from the Renaissance to the twentieth century. Each volume focuses on a single work and includes an introduction outlining its general history, as well as a selection of essays that examine the work from a variety of methodological perspectives. Demonstrating how and why these paintings have such enduring value, the volumes also offer new insights into their meaning for contemporaries and their subsequent reception.

VOLUMES IN THE SERIES

Masaccio's "Trinity," edited by Rona Goffen, Rutgers University

Raphael's "School of Athens," edited by Marcia Hall, Temple University

Titian's "Venus of Urbino," edited by Rona Goffen, Rutgers University

Caravaggio's "Saint Paul," edited by Gail Feigenbaum, National Gallery of Art, Washington, D.C.

Rembrandt's "Bathsheba with David's Letter," edited by Ann Jensen Adams, University of California, Santa Barbara

David's "Death of Marat," edited by Will Vaughn and Helen Weston, University College, University of London

Manet's "Le Déjeuner sur l'Herbe," edited by Paul Tucker, University of Massachusetts, Boston

Picasso's "Les Demoiselles d'Avignon," edited by Christopher Green, Courtauld Institute of Art, University of London

TITIAN'S
"VENUS OF URBINO"

Edited by
Rona Goffen
Rutgers University

CAMBRIDGE
UNIVERSITY PRESS

PUBLISHED BY THE PRESS SYNDICATE OF THE UNIVERSITY OF CAMBRIDGE
The Pitt Building, Trumpington Street, Cambridge, United Kingdom

CAMBRIDGE UNIVERSITY PRESS
The Edinburgh Building, Cambridge CB2 2RU, UK http: //www.cup.cam.ac.uk
40 West 20th Street, New York, NY 10011-4211, USA http: //www.cup.org
10 Stamford Road, Oakleigh, Melbourne 3166, Australia

First published 1997
Reprinted 1999

Printed in the United States of America

Typeset in Bembo

A catalogue record for this book is available from the British Library

Library of Congress Cataloguing-in-Publication Data is available

ISBN 0-521-44448-9 hardback
ISBN 0-521-44900-6 paperback

CONTENTS

ILLUSTRATIONS

CONTRIBUTORS

DANIEL ARASSE is professor at the Centre d'Histoire et Théorie de l'Art at the Ecole des Hautes Etudes en Sciences Sociales in Paris. Among his recent books are *Vermeer: Faith in Painting* (first published in French in 1993) and *Le Détail: pour une histoire rapprochée de la peinture.*

T. J. CLARK, Professor of the History of Art at the University of California, Berkeley, is a scholar of nineteenth- and twentieth-century art. His recent publications include a book on the American painter Pollock published in German, *Jackson Pollock: Abstraktion und Figuration.* At present, he is completing a book on modernism to be called *Farewell to an Idea.*

CARLO GINZBURG is Professor of History at the University of Bologna in Italy and at UCLA. His numerous publications on the social history and art history of Renaissance Italy include *The Night Battles: Witchcraft & Agrarian Cults in the Sixteenth & Seventeenth Centuries* and an anthology of his essays, *Clues, Myths, and the Historical Method.*

RONA GOFFEN is Distinguished Professor of Art History and Director of the Rutgers University Global Programs. She has published extensively on Italian Renaissance art, including such books as *Giovanni Bellini* and *Titian's Women.* Her eighth book will be *Masaccio's "Trinity,"* published by Cambridge University Press.

MARY PARDO, Associate Professor in the Department of Art at the University of North Carolina at Chapel Hill, has published articles on Giotto, Leonardo da Vinci, Savoldo, and Titian. She is participating in a collaborative project on Leonardo's Codex Urbinas and has recently completed a book, *True Alchemy: Paolo Pino's "Dialogo di Pittura" and the Origins of Venetian Art Criticism.*

DAVID ROSAND is Meyer Schapiro Professor of Art History at Columbia University. His many publications include *Titian,* one of the standard monographs on the artist, and a revised edition of *Painting in Cinquecento Venice: Titian, Venonese, Tintoretto,* published by Cambridge University Press.

PREFACE

The restoration of Titian's *Venus of Urbino* was completed while this book was in production. Thanks to the publication of *La "Venere di Urbino" di Tiziano restaurata,* a "flyer" that includes a brief report by the conservator of the painting, Alfio Del Serra, it is possible to preface our book with a few words about the painting's condition and technique.

Del Serra confirms that Titian painted his *Venus* in oil, with medium impasto. Unfortunately, much of this textured brush work has been flattened by earlier relining(s) of the canvas, a procedure accomplished by past generations of restorers with the use of an iron. That is, earlier restorers had literally ironed Titian's canvas onto its new lining, and in the process, "ironed out" his impasto, removing or diminishing the varied texture of the pigment. (Modern conservators have abandoned this formerly common but ill-advised practice.)

No preparatory drawings are visible in infrared reflectography: It seems that Titian created his forms entirely with the brush. As in other works of the 1530s and 1540s, here too Titian employed a medium weave canvas, lightly applying his preparation in red bole. Pigments employed in the *Venus of Urbino* are also familiar from other works by Titian and his Venetian contemporaries, including the green of the curtain behind Venus's head. This green was painted with a rich impasto of pigment (pure or almost undiluted), brilliant in tone, and finished with a *velatura* of copper green resinate. Copper green resinate almost always darkens or turns brown with age – hence the numerous "brown" trees and fields of grass in Renaissance paintings, all the result of irreversible chemical change. But Titian's green curtain is surprisingly unaltered. Most striking, now that the painting is clean, is the brilliance of Titian's combination of red, white and green – the chromatic triad favored in many earlier sixteenth-century works by Titian himself and by Giorgione, including the *Sleeping Venus* (Fig. 3), the prototype of the *Venus of Urbino.* Transferring the goddess from Giorgione's landscape setting to a domestic interior, Titian substituted his green curtain for Giorgione's grassy field.

Looking at the restored *Venus of Urbino,* one can appreciate not only the color but also the richly modelled folds of Titian's fabric – previously all but obliterated by dirt, so that the material was almost indistinguishable from the screen or wall behind it. Now we can understand and share Giorgio Vasari's enthusiasm for the "finely-woven fabrics . . . very beautiful and well finished" in the *Venus of Urbino.* (Mary Pardo, who examined the painting during restoration, discusses Vasari's text in her contribution to this volume.)

Removal of the discolored varnishes has revealed that a large part of the *Venus of Urbino* is still covered with Titian's original varnish, described by Della Serra as cool gray in color and of exceptional hardness. This enhances the brightness of Titian's whites and the delicacy of his treatment of flesh, notably the light red intonations of Venus's skin (e.g., her knees), which seems warmed by the red of her bed covering. Conservation has thus confirmed the enthusiastic and detailed description of Venus's flesh offered by Crowe and Cavalcaselle, and quoted by David Rosand in his contribution to our volume. The discolored varnishes and overpaintings had also obscured the variations of handling that distinguish, for example, Venus' glittering jewelry from her pink-and-white flesh, or the soft rose petals of her bouquet from the floral pattern of her red bed cover. Here Titian juxtaposed the firm black contours of his floral fabric with nearly amorphous forms, evoking petal shapes to represent his "real" flowers. Sometimes Titian draws edges with a loaded brush, so that contours exist as substance (though much of the impasto has been lost or flattened, as we have seen, one can still recognize this effect in some details of the white sheets). Elsewhere, Titian dissolved contours by dragging a brush laden only with traces of pigment, so that color is subjugated to the weave of the canvas (for example, where the white pillow rests against the red bed cover, or where Venus's fingers disappear into the leaves and petals of her bouquet). Asserting the canvas texture in this way, Titian arouses the beholder's tactile sense, even as he seduces the eye with his brilliant colorist.

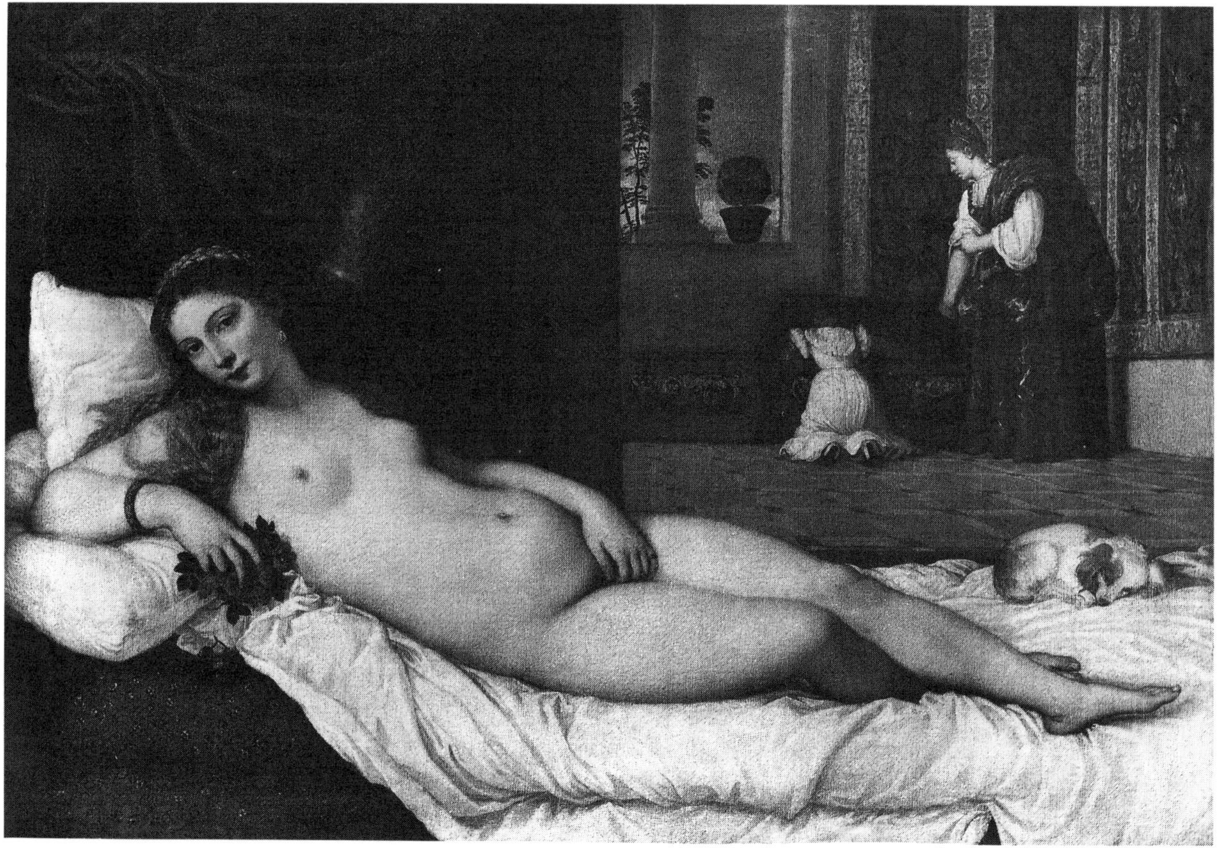

Figure 1. Titian, *Venus of Urbino*. Florence, Galleria degli Uffizi. Photo: Alinari/Art Resource.

RONA GOFFEN

INTRODUCTION

I.

When Edouard Manet wanted to overturn the apple cart of traditional representations of the female nude, he painted the *Olympia* as a refutation of Titian's *Venus of Urbino* (Figs. 1 and 2). Titian's close association with the female nude is not only a modern perception, moreover, nor is it due only to the enthusiasm of his contemporaries for his so-called love poems or *poesie,* paintings characteristically featuring beautiful women.[1] Indeed, Titian's professional investment in paintings of women is so striking that it may be related to his deepest creative impulses.

By the time Titian's *Venus* was delivered to Guidobaldo della Rovere, duke of Camerino (and thereafter of Urbino) in spring 1538, the painter had achieved preeminence not only in his native Venice but also throughout Europe.[2] Indeed, Titian can be described as the first artist to have had an international career (not only occasional foreign commissions). Born about 1488–90 in Pieve di Cadore in the foothills of the Italian Alps, which was then part of the Venetian Republic, Titian moved to Venice itself while still in his teens and there joined the studio of Giovanni Bellini, the greatest – and most successful – painter of the preceding generation.[3] Titian soon established something of a reputation, and in 1508 shared a commission with the slightly older Giorgione to fresco the exterior of the Fondaco dei Tedeschi, the foundation of the German merchants' resident in Venice. Titian was assigned the side wall of the Fondaco and Giorgione the more important façade

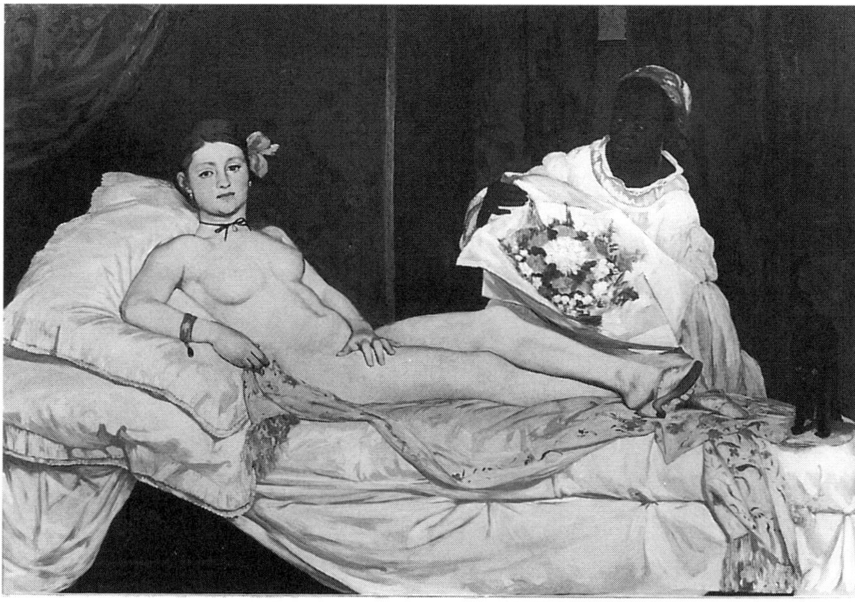

Figure 2. Edouard Manet, *Olympia*. Paris, Musée d'Orsay. Photo: Giraudon/Art Resource.

on the Grand Canal. Representing male and female allegorical figures, the detached frescoes are preserved in the Galleria Franchetti of the Ca' d'Oro in Venice. Having proved himself with this first public commission, Titian was then invited to paint three frescoes for the Confraternity (or lay brotherhood) of St. Anthony of Padua, adjacent to the great Franciscan church dedicated to that saint in his city, called simply "Il Santo." The fresco cycle occupied Titian for one year from December 1510 to December 1511, after which he returned to Venice. There he remained until his death in 1576, except for brief sojourns in various cities (including Bologna, Ferrara, and Mantua) and a longer stay in 1545–6 in Rome, where Michelangelo visited his studio.[4]

Titian's early association with the Paduan Friars may have proved influential in obtaining his next important public commission: the *Assunta* or *Assumption of the Virgin* for the high altar of S. Maria Gloriosa dei Frari, the principal Franciscan church of Venice.[5] The largest panel painting in the world (6.9 meters high) – and one of the most beautiful – the *Assunta* took two years to complete; when it was unveiled in 1518, Titian's primacy was assured. From then on, Titian dominated painting in Venice and eventually in Europe. His influence on the other great masters active in the Venetian Republic, notably Tintoretto, Veronese, and the Bassano (all slightly younger than he), can hardly be exaggerated; similarly, many of his successors elsewhere in Europe, including such giants of Baroque painting as Velazquez and Rubens, were profoundly affected by him. Even before completing the *Assunta,* Titian had been taken up by some of the wealthiest and most influential patrons in Venice and in Padua (then ruled by the Venetian Republic). Among them was the humanist poet Pietro Bembo, who tried to persuade Titian to join the papal court in Rome, an invitation that the painter declined. But after the completion of the *Assunta,* the greatest patrons of Italy and Europe came to Titian. And the greatest of these were certainly the Emperor Charles V and his son, Philip II of Spain.

Titian's first commission for the emperor was a portrait (now lost) painted around the time of Charles's coronation, probably in early 1530. Many other imperial commissions followed, mostly for portraits and religious works, and in 1533 Charles ennobled Titian with the title of "Knight of the Golden Spur, Count of the Lateran Palace and of the Imperial Consistory." Conferring this extraordinary honor on the painter, Charles explained that he was following the example of Alexander the Great – his own predecessor, as it were – and Alexander's favorite painter, Apelles, whom the emperor compared to Titian. Charles recalled that Alexander had allowed only Apelles to paint his portrait, and similarly, the emperor praised Titian as a portraitist. To be sure, complimenting a painter by comparing him to his most famous ancient predecessor had become commonplace by the 1530s: Numerous masters had already been praised as the "new Apelles" or as "Apelles reborn" (*Apelles redivivus*). But when the cliché is repeated by the Holy Roman Emperor in the context of knighting his own "Apelles," it regains all its metaphoric power.

Charles continued to honor Titian with his patronage and with numerous favors, social and financial; and beginning in 1548, the painter worked for the emperor's son Philip as well. First as prince, then briefly as king of England and consort of Queen Mary Tudor ("Bloody Mary"), and finally as king of Spain, Philip became Titian's most ardent patron, both as the commissioner of numerous works and as the eager recipient of paintings representing subjects chosen by the artist himself. Today, conditioned by the modern art market, we are accustomed to the idea that a collector will pay for a work by a particular master, the subject represented being comparatively unimportant. One speaks first of buying a Picasso, for example, and only then of the subject. But this is a very recent development in the history of art, a situation anticipated and indeed encouraged by Titian. Even Michelangelo was given specific commissions by his patrons, the principal works initiated by the artist himself being drawings that he might offer as gifts to his friends. Titian's artistic freedom in his relationship with Philip was unprecedented and perhaps not repeated until modern times. Moreover, probably no painter has been more influential than he – not only in terms of his compositions and figure types (as Manet reminds us) but even more importantly in terms of his painterly brushwork and expressive handling of pigment, his exquisite colorism and treatment of light.

By 1538, then, when Duke Guidobaldo della Rovere received the *Venus of Urbino,* Titian was already world famous. Anyone who was anyone wanted (or already had) a portrait by Titian, and indeed, he managed to portray most of the titled heads of Italy and Europe. In addition to the portraits, Titian's Venetian patrons traditionally preferred sacred works, such as the *Assunta;* clients elsewhere were also interested in secular compositions, which Titian himself described with the literary terms *poesie* or *favole* (poems or fables). Sometimes based on ancient literary sources, sometimes derived from the artist's (or his patrons' or advisors') imagination, these visual "poems" almost always include beautiful women and almost always treat the theme of love. The three canvases executed for the studiolo of Duke Alfonso d'Este of Ferrara between 1518 and 1523 belong to the first category, being visualizations of texts by Philostratus and Ovid (the *Worship of Venus* and the *Bacchanal of the Andrians,* both now in the Museo del Prado in Madrid; and the *Bacchus and Ariadne* in the National Gallery of Art in London).[6] The *Venus of Urbino* illustrates the second category and seems to

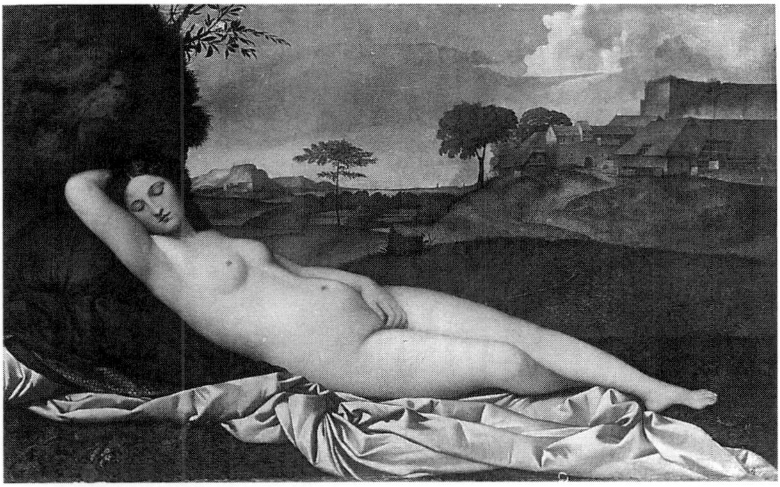

Figure 3. Giorgione, *Sleeping Venus*. Dresden, Gemäldegalerie Alte Meister, Staatliche Kunstsammlungen. Photo: Alinari/Art Resource.

have been conceived without specific reference to any literary source, contemporary or ancient.

Unlike Duke Alfonso's *poesie,* then, the *Venus* has no explanatory text. Rather, it is to be understood in relation to its visual sources: the *Sleeping Venus* of about 1508–10 by Giorgione (Fig. 3), Titian's former colleague at the Fondaco dei Tedeschi; and the ancient *Venus Pudica*, or so-called modest Venus (Fig. 4). Giorgione's *Venus* sleeps in a landscape, while the classical *Venus* stands with her arms before her, trying (in vain) to conceal her nudity from the beholder. Titian's protagonist, however, is awake, reclining on a bed in a sixteenth-century palace. His old master, Giovanni Bellini, had already represented a classicizing nude in a contemporary interior, but she is seated, attending to details of her toilette, and her setting is a neutral location – a domestic setting, to be sure, but a room with no specific clues to its customary use (Fig. 5). Titian's nude, on the contrary, reclines on her bed in a room decorated with marriage chests, called *cassoni,* immediately recognizable to sixteenth-century viewers as bedroom furnishings. No one before Titian had placed a classicizing nude in such a setting, and few artists had ever shown a woman – especially a nude – beholding the beholder so directly. In this regard, the forthright

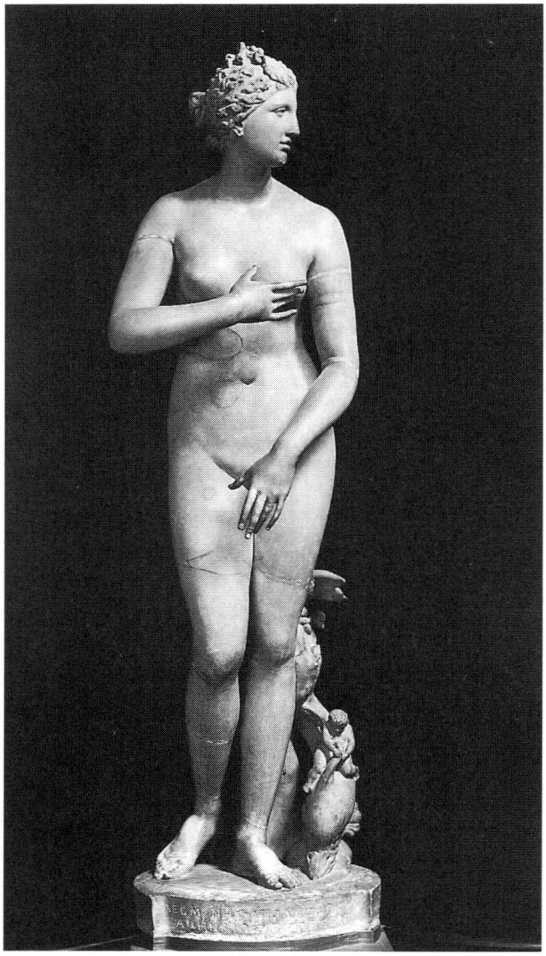

Figure 4. *Medici Venus,* after Praxiteles, *Aphrodite* or *Venus of Cnidos* (*Venus Pudica*). Florence, Galleria degli Uffizi. Photo: Alinari/Art Resource.

glance of the gowned woman in Titian's *Sacred and Profane Love* may be seen as Venus's predecessor (Fig. 9). Similarly, the women of *Sacred and Profane Love* anticipate the type of female beauty represented in the *Venus of Urbino,* although it might be more accurate to say that Titian idealized his models in each case to suit his preconceptions of beauty. Even the palette of the *Venus* recalls that of the earlier work, combining the complementary colors red

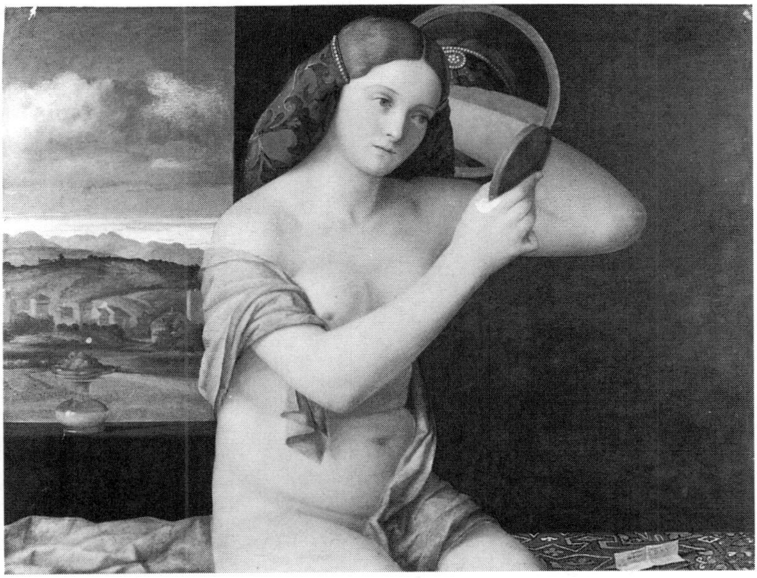

Figure 5. Giovanni Bellini, *Nude with Mirror.* Vienna, Kunsthistorisches Museum. Photo: Kunsthistorisches Museum, Vienna.

and green with white and the flesh tones of the nudes. Indeed, Giorgione's *Sleeping Venus* and numerous other Venetian works of the earlier sixteenth century made use of the same color combination. (Because the green pigments have aged badly in these paintings by Giorgione and by Titian, the original chromatic effects must be restored in the mind's eye.)

The composition of the *Venus of Urbino* also incorporates elements found in earlier works, notably its asymmetry, the juxtaposition of closed and open spaces, and the sudden contrast of large foreground forms with much smaller forms in the background – without any transitional midground. Thus Titian's *Venus of Urbino* purposefully recalls paintings completed as much as twenty-five years before. The *Venus* is in no way retardataire, however; rather, as we shall see in reading the essays in this volume, these recollections of earlier works are relevant not only to the appearance but also to the meaning of Titian's goddess. Moreover, other stylistic elements relate the *Venus of Urbino* to such contemporary works as the *Presentation of the Virgin in the Temple,* which Titian began in

1534 and completed in 1538. Still in situ in the room of the Confraternity of Charity (Scuola Grande della Carità) for which it was painted – the building has been converted into the Accademia Galleries – the *Presentation* is a frieze composition very like the *Venus,* with a similar combination of geometrical, mostly rectilinear, shapes. Titian's brushwork and the definition of form in these works of the mid-1530s may also be distinguished from his handling in the earlier paintings. The more precise, almost prismatic shapes formed by light and shadow in the draperies of the *Sacred and Profane Love* (Fig. 9), for example, and the definition of facial features have become freer and more fluid in the *Venus of Urbino.* Similarly, the coarse weave of the canvas of the later work is exploited together with the loaded brush to blur the contours of things, although Titian also delights in contrasting very precisely defined shapes (such as the printed flowers of the bed cushions) with the most freely painted, amorphous areas of color (such as the nude's flesh or the white sheets and pillows).

A nude woman reclines on a bed. Her pet dog dozes at her feet. In the background, two servants either remove her garments from, or return them to, a *cassone.* The nude's pose derives from that of the ancient *Venus Pudica* (Fig. 4). Unlike the classical goddess, however, this woman does not conceal her breasts but rather uses her right arm to prop herself up on two plump white pillows. The weight shift of the ancient figure's standing *contrapposto* is transformed into an almost spiraling pose of fluid motion in the reclining woman, beginning with the side view of the left leg and foot and culminating with the frontality of the head. Whereas the classical Venus turns her head in profile, away from the viewer, Titian's goddess beholds us directly. As we shall see, her glance is one of her most surprising and problematic features.

The bed sheets are somewhat disarrayed, revealing the red cushions beneath them: a large, brightly lit area beneath the woman's torso and a much smaller triangular area, almost concealed in shadow at the painting's edge below her feet. This red fabric is printed with a floral pattern, a motif that Titian varies throughout the composition. The woman holds real flowers, roses, in her right hand, and some of these have fallen onto the foliate cushion – a seemingly casual juxtaposition of art and nature. The theme is reiterated in the background, where larger foliate motifs decorate the *cassoni* and the wall hangings, while nature provides a myrtle plant on the sill and leafy trees visible through the window. Titian employs these different foliate patterns together with color and light to unify his composition. To be sure, the picture space is constructed and unified according to the traditional precepts of mathematical or one-point perspective (although we shall see that scale relations are purposefully problematic). But even more than space and pattern, Titian exploits color and light – what Venetians call *colorito* – to unite the composition. Thus he repeats the reds and whites of the foreground in the costumes of the maids in the background; echoes the gold of the nude's hair in the wall hangings and especially in the gown slung over one servant's shoulder; and bathes the entire scene in a light-filled air that softens the edges of things both near and far. Space is unified primarily by means of this palpable atmosphere, addressing the beholder's senses through the pleasure of vision itself. Titian's painterly style seduces the eye as irresistibly as the direct glance of his beautiful heroine.

Who is she? Is she an ancient goddess or a modern courtesan? What relationship to the beholder does Titian construct for her? We know who first owned the painting: Guidobaldo II della Rovere, duke of Urbino, from whom the painting takes its traditional title. (Guidobaldo succeeded his father as duke of Urbino in October 1538, a few months after having purchased the *Venus*.) But we do not know whether the duke commissioned the work or what he and his contemporaries thought it represented. These are some (not all) of the fundamental questions regarding the *Venus of Urbino* that the authors of the present book address. Because very few (and very unrevealing) sixteenth-century sources are known, all of us have sought our answers first of all in the primary source provided by Titian – namely, the painting itself. Only she can tell us who she is.

II.

When sex or sexuality is inherent in the (female) subject being described, whether in writing or in images, the (male) author or artist may debase the female, partly in response to the psychological exigencies of guilt. By condemning the female object of desire, the male observer can presumably have his cheesecake and eat it too.

Renaissance literature offers numerous examples of such misogyny, as well as poems and treatises in honor of feminine beauty, perhaps equally if differently misogynistic in the imposition of impossible ideals and idealized generalizations.[7] Misogyny seems to be endemic in Western culture – but in the Judeo-Christian tradition this hatred and mistrust of women have been characterized by a fundamental paradox. Eve, the mother of humankind, was the cause of humanity's downfall; but Mary, her antithesis, was the mother of Christ, the means of redemption. Mary, however, is "alone among her sex," while Eve has innumerable daughters. Are Titian's representations of women misogynistic? Or worse, are they pornographic illustrations, the visual equivalent of the scurrilous writings by his intimate friend, Pietro Aretino?[8]

Pornography may be narrowly defined as the depiction of sexually aroused/arousing females for male delectation and exploitation: The theme is sex as commerce, and the subject is the whore (*porne* in Greek) available to all men.[9] Famously or infamously, Aretino created the modern literary genre almost singlehandedly with his *Sonetti lussuriosi* written in the mid-1520s to accompany Marcantonio Raimondi's engravings after Giulio Romano's *I Modi*. The "modes" of the title refer to sexual intercourse, and only one of the sixteen athletic postures illustrated resembles the "missionary position" endorsed by theologians and physicians for the propagation of the species.[10]

Prostitutes are Aretino's protagonists in *Il Ragionamento della Nanna e della Antonia* (1534), which pretends to record their conversations about their experiences with men. In other words, the poet speaks in the guise of women, and the thrust of much of his "feminine" discourse is the disparagement of men. The same is true of the *Dialogo nel quale la Nanna insegna a la Pippa* – a prostitute's teaching manual, as it were – a condemnation of men written with a female voice. Women ostensibly speak to each other in these works that in reality were addressed to a largely male readership. To be sure, Aretino made women condemn themselves as lascivious, morally corrupt, and pretentious – but they are rarely stupid, although their male victims may often be so. Aretino's fictional prostitutes are exploiters and manipulators of men, not their victims, just as the female protagonists of the *Sonetti lussuriosi* are equal, enthusiastic partners in the sexual escapades of their male partners.

Like other matters related to sex and gender, pornography must be considered in its cultural context, as Paula Findlen has argued.[11] Twentieth-century people may assume that pornography is inherently misogynistic and exploitive of women, but it is probably anachronistic to apply our modern disapprobation to sixteenth-century images and texts. Admittedly, "not every culture distinguishes the erotic from the pornographic," as Findlen warns.[12] But it seems to me that such a distinction applies to sixteenth-century Venice, or more precisely to such pornographic writings as Aretino's *Sonetti lussuriosi,* as opposed to such erotic images as many of Titian's women, including the *Venus of Urbino.* The erotic involves mutual emotion, not just (sexual) activity; the pornographic is merely genital. Titian's erotic art may involve or inspire affection, respect, or empathy for the subject. Unlike the pornographic women (and men) in the illustrations for *I Modi,* Titian's women are never mere body without individuality.

There are other, concomitant differences between Aretino's self-proclaimed whores and Titian's imaginary women. Aretino's prostitutes are probably incapable of reading the volume of Petrarch that they consider a standard accessory of their dress or home furnishings. Yet, while twitting their intellectual pretensions, Aretino acknowledges their cleverness and mocks the gullibility of their male prey. In this regard, Aretino's women may be understood as a reversal or perhaps a parody of Titian's: The former pretend to have the culture that the latter undeniably possess in such images as Venus with a musician (Fig. 13).

Prostitutes may have posed for at least some of Titian's women, as he himself suggested; and Titian certainly enjoyed the company of courtesans, as Aretino informs us.[13] For many historians, these facts have led to the generally unstated and entirely dubious assumption that Titian's personal proclivities can explain his art. This simplistic equation is tantamount to saying that because Titian frequented courtesans, the female subjects of his art must perforce be such women (or worse): that the quotidian details of his biography explain his life's work. Similarly, to argue that Titian's "beautiful women" are prostitutes or courtesans because his models may have subsidized their incomes in this way is equally beside the point. A prostitute may pose for a nude or indeed for any other character and provide the appearance – but not the morality or the identity – of the painted subject. Only in the case of portraiture is the viewer instructed to identify model with subject; yet even then, as the portrait of *Isabella d'Este* reminds us, one individual may be represented by another. The person whose likeness is depicted acts as the proxy of the one whose name and identity are applied to the image.[14]

The fundamental question regarding Titian's women is not whether they are goddesses or whores but rather *how* Titian represents them and how, in turn, this representation may define the role of the beholder. The modern beholder's (sometimes prurient) response to the image is (wrongly) considered proof of Titian's meaning. Such conscious or unconscious projection should not be confused with historical analysis. While Aretino might speak as a woman to damn women – and men – Titian might assume a female voice to speak on their behalf. The result of Titian's psychological acuity is seen in images as diverse as his tragic rapes of Lucretia and his erotic rapes of Danae: The former invite compassion for the victim; the latter arouse the viewer's sexuality – male or female – in response to the *mutual* pleasures of the lovers.

Because sexuality and gender identity are bound to society, understanding Titian's women requires understanding his time and place.[15] The psychological, political, social, and economic situation of women in sixteenth-century Venice – contemporary philosophical, theological, and medical views of women – all colored Titian's interpretation of women. By proposing to consider a broad sociological context for Titian's art, I do not mean to imply that his women should be interpreted as history book illustrations of life in sixteenth-century Italy. Yet the one cannot be understood without reference to the other, any more than Titian's sacred images can be understood without knowledge of the Bible, Catholic theology, and the lives of the saints. Because every human being is defined in part by gender and is (or was, until modern times) the result of sexual intercourse, it is easy to assume that understanding of Titian's nudes comes naturally, that no special knowledge is required or perhaps even desirable for their comprehension.[16] This is wishful, lazy thinking, in part the result of a confusion between sex (gender) and sexuality. Doubtless it is impossible to examine such intimate and fundamental matters with complete disinterest; and admittedly, the very questions posed and the methodological stances taken predetermine, to some extent, the results. Nonetheless, the contextual approach to Titian's women is warranted, not to say required, by historic and aesthetic responsibility to a great master.

Other critics have posited a different but equally reductive analysis of Titian's images according to the dynamic of active male beholder and passive female object – an exploitation to which we moderns are particularly sensitive.[17] But, to repeat Susan Gubar's rhetorical question, "Does a genre produced primarily by and for men necessarily demean women and alienate or exclude the female spectator/reader?"[18] And can we be certain that this confrontation of male subject/female object is necessarily implicit in all such images, the inevitable concomitant of the display of nude women? Although some degree of voyeurism may be inherent in the act of viewing per se, whether the subject is male or female, this would have been mitigated in the Renaissance imagination by the belief in the magic of images.[19] An image may hear, speak, and see; and undeniably, Titian's *Venus of Urbino* seems to see us, to return or to compel our gaze. Doing so, she implies reciprocity – and the force of her gaze empowers her. To be sure, Titian's definition of the female emphasizes her sexuality, defined (perforce?) with reference to the masculine other, even though the male presence is merely invoked.[20]

Manet understood that the *Venus of Urbino* asserts the presence of a male beholder (who becomes a "paying customer" in the *Olympia*), and like Titian, Manet invites the actual viewer to identify with that beholder – or rather, the female gaze proffers the invitation. Whatever else a sixteenth-century viewer may have perceived in the *Venus of Urbino,* surely he understood that the painting addressed him. But educated viewers would also have understood something else about the painting, which Manet likewise recalled: the traditional association of the beautiful (nude) woman with beautiful art. Representing the beautiful female nude, the artist represented his own genius. Thus Apelles, the great artist par excellence, had demonstrated his genius by painting a nude portrait of Campaspe, the mistress of his patron Alexander the Great. The painting convinced Alexander that the artist was better able to appreciate Campaspe than he himself – and so he rewarded Apelles for the picture by the gift of its model. (We recall that

Titian compared himself and was compared by others to Apelles.) The story thus suggested both the master's canonical choice of subject and his prize: The successful creation of the beautiful woman's image will be rewarded by possession of the woman herself, the incarnation of beauty. Thus sculpted Galatea becomes flesh in Pygmalion's embrace. At the same time, the artist may presume to surpass nature in the creation of the beautiful woman, as Praxiteles did when he combined the best features of many women to represent one more perfect than any of them. Like his mythological counterpart Pygmalion and like his younger contemporary Apelles, Praxiteles possessed his primary model – in this case, his mistress Phryne, whose body provided the basis for his female anthology.[21]

The ancient and Renaissance conception of the beautiful woman as the archetypal image of beautiful art is related in turn to misogynistic conceptions of the very structure of the universe. As David Summers has explained, according to "Aristotle (and legions after him) . . . things are unions of matter and form" – but these two constituents are not equal. Matter, perceived as female, is amorphous until shaped by masculine form; inferior matter is related to the physical or material, and superior form is associated with the soul.[22]

Aristotle's ideas were remarkably persistent. Their relevance to the two kinds of creativity – that is, to human generation (male semen brings breath and form to female matter) and to art (which Aristotle himself invoked in explaining nature) – still endured in Titian's day and long thereafter.[23] Thus, according to traditional Western views of conception, a child, including the Christ Child, is inherent in the paternal seed, the mother supplying only the matter and environment for gestation. Innumerable depictions of the so-called Homunculus Christ represent this idea in scenes of the Annunciation. As the Archangel Gabriel addresses Mary, God the Father dispatches both the Holy Spirit and the Homunculus Christ to her. The homunculus body is already perfectly formed and complete.[24]

A Renaissance person did not need to be an Aristotelian philosopher to know these things: The gendered view of human generation and of artistic creation had become common knowledge. In Christian thinking, moreover, the two kinds of creativity are linked in the familiar metaphors of God as father of humankind and as the artist-creator who sculpts Adam and designs the world. In the Renaissance discourse concerning art and its making, the power of the equation of the great artist and God the Creator is taken as a given, and with it, the analogy of artistic creativity and fatherhood, including, of course, the fatherhood of God.[25] That is to say, in the sixteenth-century reversal of this metaphor, the mortal artist is extolled as divine creator.[26] Aretino's much-quoted encomium of Michelangelo, "more than angel, divine" ("più che Angelo, Divino"), alludes to the same equation. But in their day, or rather beginning with Leon Battista Alberti (if not before), art theoreticians extended the analogy to the fundamental elements of style, namely, *disegno* (design or drawing) and *colorito* (the application and expressive use of color).[27]

Disegno was considered, by Central Italians at least, to be primary and essential – hence masculine – as Leonardo da Vinci reminds us by advising aspiring artists to trace the contours of cast shadows. Color, on the contrary, was considered to be secondary and feminine: It is mere decoration, inessential to the comprehension of form. Worse still, color may be linked to deception, like the color of women's cosmetics that can impart a charming and seductive blush to an ashen cheek. Disegno is intellect and reason; colorito is pleasure and emotion – and potential danger – for the men who bought and made most Renaissance paintings and who theorized about them.

To be sure, misogyny was no mere theory for Renaissance people but a reality of daily life. The subjugation of women was an undeniable fact of sixteenth-century Italian culture, perhaps a "pan-cultural fact," as anthropologist Sherry Ortner has argued.[28] From this point of view, the answer to Joan Kelly's rhetorical question, "Did Women Have a Renaissance," is a resounding "no."[29] But this "no" must be nuanced by emotional realities as compelling as legislation and treatises and theology, albeit admittedly more difficult to reconstruct. Titian's women may be seen as illustrations of these otherwise largely invisible realities. Even if we assume that Titian was to some degree misogynistic, like most Renaissance people, nonetheless his art demonstrates profound sympathy for his female subjects. Indeed, Titian's contemporaries appreciated this, just as they perceived elements of his style to be feminine and yet praiseworthy. Titian's "feminine" coloristic style may be explained in part as the visualization of this sympathy.

Titian was then not a pornographer, either high- or lowbrow. For the sake of argument, however, if one wishes to retain that much-repeated estimation of his art, the "pornography" may also be explained in terms of Titian's identification with his subject, comparable in a sense to Aretino's speaking with a female voice. Even pornographers and misogynists have mothers, and inevitably "masculine self-definition evolves through a process of agonist differentiation from the mother," as Susan Gubar explains. Thus "If we read pornography this way" – and likewise, if we look at Titian's women this way – "we would interpret female characters and their fates in the narrative . . . as portraits of the male artist's fears about himself, fears over which the work seeks to triumph. By re-creating in his own image the woman who created him, by repossessing through fantasy the woman who had to be relinquished, by punishing the woman whose separateness was itself experienced as a punishment, and by eroticizing the woman whose eroticism was taboo, the pornographer converts his greatest trauma into his greatest thrill."[30] Thus, whether his women are pornographic and misogynistic or exalted and sublime, Titian's subject is himself.

III.

Four of the six chapters in the present book – those by Daniel Arasse, Rona Goffen, Mary Pardo, and David Rosand – deal specifically with the *Venus of Urbino,* considered from different points of view, offering complementary rather than conflicting interpretations of Titian's work. The first and last chapters do not deal with the *Venus* per se but with closely related issues. The book begins with Carlo Ginzburg's classic study of sixteenth-century erotic prints, first published in Italian some twenty years ago. Ginzburg elucidates the popular visual context of Titian's work, relating his imagery to Italian translations of ancient texts and elucidating his debt to these texts and to their illustrations. Finally, because the *Olympia* has indelibly altered our view of the *Venus,* the last chapter is T. J. Clark's incisive stylistic and sociological analysis of Manet's work in relation to its sixteenth-century source. Directly or indirectly, the chapters by both Ginzburg and Clark have influenced the authors of the four Venus chapters. Rosand's contribution is in part an analysis of perceptions of the *Venus,* that is, its *Rezeptionsgeschichte;* Goffen's chapter may be characterized primarily as visual analysis in the context of social history; Arasse's chapter is a psychological reading of the *Venus* and her pictorial space; and Pardo's is a reading of the physical surface of Titian's painting – its facture – in relation to Renaissance art theory, notably Alberti's textile analogies.

These authors reject the overly positivist, reductionist approach (as it seems to us) of such scholars as Hans Ost in Germany and Charles Hope in England (although Ginzburg may be read as endorsing their ideas in part). Hope has been the most vigorous proponent of the view that Titian's women, including those with recognizable mythological identities, are to be understood as "soft core pornography," seen as indistinguishable from erotica.[31] Hope recognizes little if any difference between such paintings as the *Venus of Urbino* and "pin ups."[32] Similarly, according to the Italian scholar Roberto Zapperi, "the painting known today as the *Venus of Urbino* simply shows a nude woman lying on a bed."[33] Ost, Hope, and Zapperi are reacting in part to what they consider to be Erwin Panofsky's overinterpretation of Titian's nudes as Neoplatonic images of the senses, an explanation that the present authors likewise reject.[34] None of our chapters offers a single or simple answer to the question of the *Venus,* and none espouses only this or that theoretical point of view. Rather, each chapter is flexible and pragmatic in regard to the questions asked and the means employed to answer them. Indeed, this methodological flexibility may be seen as a virtue shared by all six essays in this volume: Titian's painting is never made to fit a preconceived theory; rather, theory is adapted to the painting.

The four chapters dealing with the *Venus of Urbino* are related in other ways as well. In addition to the influence of Ginzburg and Clark, which has already been mentioned, readers will recognize the impact of David Rosand's essay (previously published elsewhere) on the other three contributions, namely, those by Arasse and Pardo (whose chapters were written for this book) and by Goffen (an essay first published in 1994 and emended for this book). At the same time, Goffen, Pardo, and Rosand were all much influenced by an earlier essay by Arasse – which he himself has by and large ignored in his present study. When, as the volume's editor, I first read his new contribution, the one included here, I was struck by the remarkable coincidence of our thinking about the *Venus,* and if I did not know otherwise, I would have imagined that he and I had cooperated in writing our chapters. The "cooperation," so to speak, was telepathic if unintentional, but as editor of the volume, I was reluctant to abbreviate either argument. I hope that readers will not be bored by the reiteration of similar ideas and will take the exchange represented by all four Venus chapters as a demonstration of productive scholarly symbiosis.

To be sure, no volume on such a masterpiece as the *Venus of Urbino* can be all-inclusive or exhaustive (a colleague once suggested to me that the definition of a masterpiece is precisely that it is inexhaustible, always revealing new aspects of itself). But it is hoped that in offering disparate considerations and various methods of analysis, the present book will both increase understanding and invite further discussion of its subject.

NOTES

1. For the literary terms *poesia* (plural, *poesie*) and *favola,* which Titian used to describe some of his paintings, see Rosand, "*Ut Pictor Poeta,*" pp. 533 and 534*n*14. He suggests that the development of these kinds of subjects starting in early-sixteenth-century Venice was related to the publication of such illustrated books as the *Metamorphoses* and the *Hypnerotomachia Poliphili.* Titian was not the first artist to use these terms; Paul Holberton cites Jacopo de' Barbari's use of the word *poesie* in 1502: "historie, ovvero poesie." See Holberton, "Antique and Other Figures," p. 41. For the earlier history of the word's use by men of letters, see the *Vocabolario degli Accademici della Crusca,* v. 3 (Florence, 1733), s.v. "poesia," with references to Dante and Boccaccio; and Salvatore Battaglia, Giorgio Bárbari Squarotti, et al., *Grande dizionario della lingua italiana* 13 (UTET, Turin, 1986), pp. 708–9, s.v. "poesia."
2. For a concise and sensitive introduction to the artist, see Rosand, *Titian.* See also the catalogue raisonné by Wethey, *The Paintings of Titian, Complete Edition,* 3 vols., and the catalogues of several major exhibitions recently devoted to Titian: Maria Grazia Bernardini, ed., *Amor Sacro e Amor Profano;* Laclotte and Nepi Scirè, eds., *Le siècle de Titien;* and *Titian, Prince of Painters.*
3. See Goffen, *Giovanni Bellini.* Titian's birthdate is uncertain, but modern scholars doubt the claims of his contemporaries that he was 100 years old at the time of his death in 1576.

4. The rivalry between these two giants of sixteenth-century art is discussed at length in my book, *Titian's Women.* Both Lodovico Dolce and Giorgio Vasari described the visit; Vasari accompanied Michelangelo to Titian's studio in 1545, but Dolce based his account on Titian's recollections of the meeting. See Roskill, *Dolce's "Aretino",* pp. 110–11, which is page 14 of the *Dialogue,* called *L'Aretino,* first published in 1557; and Vasari-Milanesi 3: 574–5 (first published in 1568).
5. For the Scuola murals, see Goffen, "Wives and Mothers"; and for the *Assunta,* see idem, *Piety and Patronage,* pp. 73–106.
6. In addition to the bibliography cited in note 2, see Cavalli-Björkman, ed., *Bacchanals by Titian and Rubens.*
7. This and large parts of the following paragraphs appear also in the Introduction to my *Titian's Women.* Chastel, *Art et Humanisme,* pp. 297–8, notes that poems and treatises (in praise of beauty) multiply rapidly beginning in the early sixteenth century. He cites as an example Ariosto's description of the fairy Alcina in *Orlando furioso,* 7: 11ff. Chastel finds the painters' discourse to be more sensual than the poets'; but the fashionable vocabulary always celebrates feminine beauty in terms of Neoplatonism, and representations of Venus reclining or Venus with a musician seem to take this into account. For misogyny as "any essentialist definition of woman, whether negative or positive," that is, whether couched as condemnation or encomium, see Bloch, *Medieval Misogyny,* p. 7 and passim.
8. For an interpretation of the painter's "embarrassing" association with the notorious author and the nature of their friendship, see Gregori, "Tiziano e l'Aretino," pp. 271–306; see pp. 282–3, 285 for Titian's portraits of Aretino; and p. 294 for his first published mention of a work by the artist (a lost *St. John the Baptist*) in a letter dated October 8, 1531. More recently on the writer, see Di Monte, Mozzetti, and Sarti, "Pietro Aretino 1991," pp. 139–61.
9. Dworkin, *Pornography,* pp. 199–200, 202, and passim. As Dworkin explains, the *porneia* were the lowest, vilest class of whores: Pornography is writing about these women. I am not concerned here with homosexual pornography, and I am well aware that pornography resists precise definition, notwithstanding the *Oxford English Dictionary.* Paula Findlen summarizes the problem, "acknowledging that it is impossible to be sure exactly *what* is defined *as* pornography when writing its history." Yet the effort is warranted, Findlen continues, because "The history of pornography charts changing attitudes toward male and female bodies. . . . To define Renaissance pornography is . . . to define the intersections of sexuality, politics and learning – the constitutive elements of the culture itself." See Findlen, "Humanism, Politics and Pornography," pp. 53–4 and passim; see also Gubar, "Representing Pornography," p. 713 and passim.

10. The engravings were probably printed and first circulated in 1524. Aretino apparently wrote his sonnets in 1525. A counterfeit edition of the sonnets, illustrated with woodcuts after the engravings, was printed shortly thereafter, probably in Venice in 1527. This has been recently republished; see Lawner, *I Modi;* note her introduction, pp. 3–56; and Talvacchia, " 'Figure lascive,' " pp. 277–80. For an incisive discussion of Aretino's sonnets in their social context, see Findlen, "Humanism, Politics and Pornography," pp. 65, 69–71, 95–102. The Italian texts of the counterfeit edition of 1527 are partially reproduced in Lawner, *I Modi* (her primary concern was to illustrate the woodcuts, and the ends of several poems are sometimes cut from the page). For the complete texts, edited by Alcide Bonneau in 1882, republished with an introductory essay by Guillaume Apollinaire, see Aretino, *Sonetti lussuriosi e pasquinate,* with the sonnets numbered differently than in Lawner.
11. "Humanism, Politics and Pornography," pp. 49–108.
12. Ibid., p. 53.
13. See his letter to Alfonso d'Este, duke of Ferrara, quoted in Goffen, *Titian's Women,* chapter 3, part 1, at n. 66.
14. For the portrait of *Isabella d'Este* (*Isabella in Black*) in Vienna, Kunsthistorisches Museum, see Wethey 2:95–6, cat. 27; see also Ferino-Pagden et al., "*La Prima donna del mondo*", pp. 86–97, on portraits of Isabella, and pp. 111–12, cat. 50, on Titian's portrait in Vienna. At her request, Titian based Isabella's portrait on an earlier work by Francia, now lost; and by her own admission, the result was more beautiful than she herself had ever been. In addition to consulting the earlier portrait, Titian presumably used a flesh-and-blood model.
15. On the constructionist–essentialist debate regarding human sexuality – that is, whether it is a "construct" of society and therefore variable or whether "humans are differentiated at an individual level in terms of erotic attraction . . . in all cultures" – see Boswell, "Concepts, Experience, and Sexuality," pp. 67–8 and passim. Boswell explicates the second point of view, although, of course, he acknowledges historical differences, e.g., the fact that "marriage and parenthood were not thought to depend on erotic attachment" in pre–modern Europe (p. 71).
16. See Caulfield, "Sexuality in Human Evolution," pp. 343–63. As she explains (p. 343), the issue concerns a nature vs. nurture argument. Is human sexuality explained as a genetically programmed, male-dominant mode and adaptive because it ensures that males will continue to impregnate females? Or is sexuality "socially constructed," hence mutable? Caulfield's answer, with which I agree, is that human sexuality involves much more than reproduction, and "in every society has deep symbolic meaning" (p. 353); the "[d]istinctive aspect of human sexuality is the cultural or

symbolic component" (p. 355). Thus Caulfield denies the so-called law of nature that decrees a dominant/submissive mode in sexual intercourse. The penetration of the male organ into the female body, which implies to some that men are natural aggressors and females sexual recipients, can also be accurately described (as in some cultures) as the vagina's engulfing the penis; see p. 357 and p. 363*n*23.

17. Much of this kind of criticism is borrowed from writing about film, notably Mulvey, "Visual Pleasure and Narrative Cinema," esp. pp. 57–68, on "Woman as Image, Man as Bearer of the Look." For the dynamic of masculine/active/beholder and feminine/passive/object in earlier fifteenth-century art, see Simons, "Women in Frames," pp. 4–30. On the presumed physical and emotional "availability" of women in later Venetian images, see Rogers, "Sonnets on Female Portraits," pp. 291–305; idem, "The Decorum of Women's Beauty," pp. 47–88; and Junkerman, "*Bellissima Donna.*"
18. Gubar, "Representing Pornography," p. 715.
19. On the distinction between scopophilia (Freud's term for looking as a source of pleasure), which may be fetishistic, and voyeurism, which may be associated with sadism, see Mulvey, "Visual Pleasure," pp. 59, 64. On the magical powers of images, see Goffen, "*Nostra Conversatio in Caelis Est,*" pp. 220–1; and Trexler, "Florentine Religious Experience," pp. 7–41.
20. M(ichelle) Z. Rosaldo warns that "we will never understand the lives that women lead without relating them to men," i.e., it is unproductive to study the female in isolation. See Rosaldo, "The Use and Abuse of Anthropology," p. 396.
21. Phryne also posed for Apelles. Similarly, according to Lucian, a group of artists may (in theory) collaborate in the creation of a surpassingly beautiful woman, each master creating that part of her to which his talent is best suited; see Richter, *The Sculpture and Sculptors of the Greeks,* pp. 156–7.
22. Summers, "Form and Gender," p. 254 for the quotation, p. 255 for the paraphrased explanation of matter and form.
23. Ibid., p. 257 and passim.
24. The Homunculus Christ often holds his cross: his predestined death is, of course, bound to his Incarnation. See Lorenzo Veneziano's *Annunciation* of 1371, the central panel of his polyptych with Saints John the Baptist and Gregory (right) and James and Stephen (left), illustrated in Moschini Marconi, *Gallerie dell'Accademia,* p. 13; and in Scirè Nepi, *Treasures of Venetian Painting,* pp. 34–5, with an illustration in color.
25. For Galen's assertion that the female organs provide only a safe haven for conception and gestation, and for Renaissance embryology, see [Galenus], *Galen on the Usefulness of the Parts of the Body,* vol. 2, pp. 620–

80, which is books 14 and 15 of *De usu partium* "on the reproductive tract"; Adelmann, *Marcello Malpighi and the Evolution of Embryology,* vol. 2; Boylan, "The Galenic and Hippocratic Challenges to Aristotle's Conception Theory," pp. 83–112; Irwin, "Embryology and the Incarnation," pp. 93–104; Laqueur, "Orgasm, Generation," p. 5; and Siraisi, *Avicenna in Renaissance Italy.* Such views, however, are not universal. The Bamana of Western Africa, for example, believe, on the contrary, that artistic creativity is essentially female rather than male. See Sarah Brett-Smith, *The Making of Bamana Sculpture: Creativity and Gender* (New York and Cambridge, England, 1995).

26. For this Renaissance analogy, see Summers, "Form and Gender," p. 261; and idem, *Michelangelo and the Language of Art,* pp. 473–4, n. 38.

27. As Jacqueline Lichtenstein explains, Ludovico Dolce insisted "on the necessary distinction between color as it comes out of a tube, *color* [or *colore*], and color as it is worked by the artist, *colorito*"; see *The Eloquence of Color,* p. 152, citing Dolce's *Dialogo della pittura intitolato l'Aretino* of 1577, ed. Barocchi, *Trattati* 1:184. For the gendered discourse of art, including *disegno* and *colore,* see ibid., chapter 6; the review of the French edition of this book by Fort, "In Defense of Color," pp. 75–81; Summers, "Form and Gender," pp. 269–70, n. 23, with bibliography; Fermor, "Movement and Gender," pp. 129–36, 197; Reilly, "Writing Out Color," pp. 77–99, rpt. as "The Taming of the Blue," pp. 87–99; and Sohm, "Gendered Style in Italian Art Criticism."

28. Ortner, "Is Female to Male as Nature Is to Culture?," pp. 67–87, p. 67 for the quoted phrase.

29. This seminal essay, first published in 1977, is included in Kelly, *Women, History & Theory,* pp. 19–50.

30. Gubar, "Representing Pornography," p. 737, citing Nancy Chodorow and Walter Ong. For the infant's differentiation from the mother, see also Mahler, passim.

31. See Hans Ost, "Tizians sogenannte 'Venus von Urbino' und andere Buhlerinnen," pp. 129–49; Hope, "Problems of Interpretation," pp. 111–24; and idem, *Titian,* p. 82.

32. For Titian's women as "pin-ups," as Hope calls them, with little purpose beyond titillation, see his *Titian,* p. 62.

33. Zapperi, "Alessandro Farnese, Giovanni Della Casa and Titian's *Danae* in Naples," p. 163.

34. Panofsky, *Problems in Titian,* pp. 109–71.

1 CARLO GINZBURG

TITIAN, OVID, AND SIXTEENTH-CENTURY CODES FOR EROTIC ILLUSTRATION

One of the characters in Terence's *The Eunuch,* the young Chaerea, disguised as a eunuch, slips into the house where the young woman he loves dwells. (The scene has already taken place off stage: Chaerea is describing it to his brother.) The girl is preparing herself for the bath. The eyes of both fall upon a picture of the meeting of Jove and Danae hanging on the wall: "The subject was the story of Jove's sending down a shower of gold into Danae's bosom." The youth exults at the thought that soon he would be imitating the greatest of the gods, he "whose thunder shakes the highest realms of heaven," by seducing the maiden: "Was I a mere manikin, not to imitate him? Imitate I would, and like nothing better" (Fig. 6).[1]

This passage was cited frequently by Saint Augustine to demonstrate the evil effects of lascivious pictures. Through him it passed into the debate over images that burst out in the Catholic church in the sixteenth century. The theologian Johannes Molanus cited Terence's verses and Augustine's indignant comment in a chapter entitled "In Pictures One Should Beware of Anything that Provokes Lust" in his treatise *De picturis et imaginibus sacris* (1570). Almost thirty years earlier, the Dominican controversialist Ambrogio Catarino Politi had done the same in his *De cultu imaginum* (1542), but with different intent: to demonstrate by way of analogy the

Reprinted from *Clues, Myths, and the Historical Method,* tr. by John and Anne C. Tedeschi (Johns Hopkins University Press, Baltimore, 1989, with permission of the publisher).

efficacy of sacred images through the reaction of the young Chaerea to the representation of the love of Jove and Danae.[2]

The passage from *The Eunuch* and its sixteenth-century success pose, implicitly and succinctly, a series of closely linked problems, some familiar to us. Here, I shall try to list them.

1. I will begin with the most general: how does an erotic image function? The answer (it has been said) varies depending on whether the sexual act is or is not represented directly. In the first case, the beholder identifies himself with the figures performing the act. (It should be observed that the audience to which the erotic pictures are directed is exclusively masculine, for obvious historical reasons: what is being suggested thus is an identification with the male protagonist.) In the second, the beholder sees in the depicted figures (generally nude women, for the reason just stated) the partners in an imaginary sexual relationship. In both cases, the role of the spectator is essentially that of a *voyeur*.[3] But there are also intermediate variants on this theme. In the portrayals of love between Jove and Danae the sexual act is indeed represented, but in a symbolic way (Jove appears in the form of a shower of gold): this allows young Chaerea to substitute himself mentally for Jove in Danae's bed and at the same time to identify himself with the god himself. The voyeurism of the beholder acquires a narcissistic charge: through coitus Chaerea – an ordinary man, a man of no consequence, a "manikin" – becomes the equal of the great Jove, who makes the heavens tremble with his thunder.
2. The psychological process that I have described takes on different forms depending on the relationship established between the reality in which the viewer participates and the reality portrayed in the erotic image. This relationship is conditioned by the codes – cultural and stylistic – in which the image is formulated. The two realities may be either homogeneous or heterogeneous; in the latter case there may be a *tendency* towards the base (the comic or vulgar) or towards the more refined (the tragic or the sublime).[4] We know only the cultural, not the stylistic, code of the painting mentioned by Terence (even though we can surmise it with a certain approximation).[5] The effect in any case was a turning upward: by means of an exalted

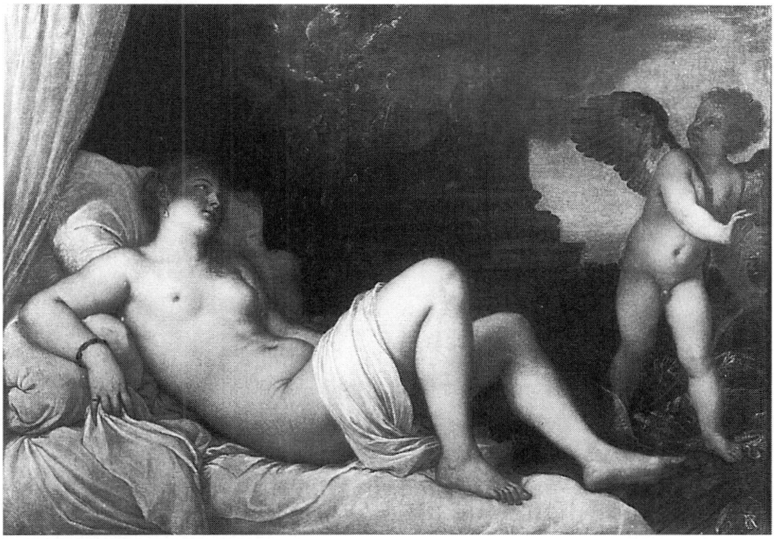

Figure 6. Titian, *Danae* (Farnese *Danae*). Naples, Gallerie Nazionali di Capodimonte. Photo: Alinari/Art Resource.

code such as the mythological, Chaerea could aspire to identify himself with the mighty Jove.

3. The question of the level (high, medium, low) of the codes employed in erotic representations shifts the discussion from the beholder to the work itself. What is an erotic image? In a strict sense, it is one which proposes deliberately to excite the viewer sexually.[6] The painting seen by Chaerea was presumably such a one (the scene takes place in the house of the courtesan Taide). But the purpose behind the image is frequently difficult to decipher. A broader definition should thus include also those images that, beyond their author's intentions, end up assuming, perhaps over a period of time, an erotic charge in the eyes of the public.

During the sixteenth century, the question of erotic images, that is, whether they were intended as such or not, increasingly preoccupied Catholic authorities, as the previously mentioned writings of Politi and Molanus attest. Two different but closely connected phenomena (in a certain sense the first was only an aspect of the second) contributed to this concern: on the one hand, a determination to exert as broad a control as possible over sexual life; on the other, an awareness that images could serve in the campaign to reestablish sundered or weakened links with the faithful, although in some cases it was actually a matter of forging connections that had never existed. These goals were only in part a reaction to the Protestant polemic against sacred images. Even more decisive was the growing awareness of the important function of pictorial representations, *idiotarum libri,* in propaganda efforts directed towards masses, who were overwhelmingly illiterate. Indicative is the recurrent appeal to positions that had been expressed by Gregory the Great.[7] Even if elements in this campaign differed greatly from those of the past and were occurring in an environment in which the spread of printing had greatly altered the relationship with the written word and images, comparisons could be made with attempts to proselytize barbarians made in the High Middle Ages.

In the eyes of such a clear-headed theologian as Politi, the common denominator between erotic and sacred images was *efficacy.* The former stimulated sexual appetite, the latter, religious sentiment. They were directed, however, to different audiences, at least in some respects. In sixteenth-century Italy we can distinguish, schematically, two iconic circuits (let us call them that): one, public, widespread, and socially undifferentiated, and the other, private, circumscribed, and socially elevated. The first contained statues, frescoes, canvases, and panels of large dimensions – objects exhibited in churches and public places, accessible to all. The latter consisted of the above, as well as paintings and panels of small dimensions, gems, and medals preserved in the homes of an elite of lords, prelates, nobles, and, in some cases, merchants. To be sure, this is a simplistic distinction, warped, moreover, by the growing diffusion of printing: it suffices to mention the widespread circulation of sacred images in commonplace settings.[8] Nevertheless, the identification of two iconic circuits, one public, the other private, seems useful, at least in a preliminary evaluation, for the question of erotic images that interests us here.

The only intentionally erotic images admitted to the public sphere were in fact the "immoral images" exhibited, as Gillio wrote, "in brothels and taverns."[9] Unfortunately, we do not know the iconography which inspired them or the stylistic currents to which they were related. We have more information, instead, on the unintentionally erotic images, especially those of a sacred character: the case reported by Vasari of the pious women troubled by a painting of Saint Sebastian by Bartolomeo[10] was probably not so unusual. The Counter-Reformation campaign against the nude had as its chief goal a sweeping removal of images that possessed even a slight erotic potential. This led to the decision to discourage such scriptural subjects as the drunkenness of Noah, David and Bathsheba, Susanne and the Elders.[11]

Intentionally erotic images, inaccessible to the masses with the exception mentioned, could be found in great numbers in the private iconic circuit of the elite. In the overwhelming majority of cases they were couched in a culturally and stylistically elevated code, the mythological, whether they represented ancient images or images expressly painted or carved by contemporary artists. Sixteenth-century erotic fantasy discovered in classical mythology a ready-made treasury of themes and forms able to be instantly comprehended by such an international clientele as the patrons of Titian's "poems." Even a current more closely tied to genre painting, Venetian courtesan portraiture, frequently disguised itself under a thin mythological veil (Fig. 7).[12]

In the course of the sixteenth century, ecclesiastical attacks on even representations of this type grew in intensity. In his *Disputatio . . . de cultu et adoratione imaginum* (1552), Politi accused prelates who possessed depictions of mythological subjects, whether ancient or modern, of downright idolatry. He was unmoved by the excuses of "corrupt" men who alleged that they collected and preserved these pictures "not for the purpose of revering or adoring them, but for the enjoyment of the spectacles and in memory of the ancients, as a demonstration of the skill of the artist." These churchmen were told that they would have done better if they had destined for the poor the money they poured into works of this kind. Gregory the Great had proceeded very differently when he had the pagan idols destroyed: and to think that Platina felt he had to exculpate him by denying the fact! But, to be sure, a man drunk on pagan culture, as Platina was, could not but revere these things, Politi observed, that through spiritual eyes are not held in esteem. Images of false gods, in fact, lead not only to idolatry but also to lust in the beholder who gazes on "the naked limbs of Venus or Diana . . . and the salacious gestures of Satyrs, and the shameful and drunken furies of Bacchus and the Bacchantes."[13]

However vague and allusive, Politi's polemic cannot help but call attention to Titian's paintings on mythological themes, which included, alongside the bacchanals, the Venuses, the Dianas, also the "Danae" painted in Rome and then copied many times,[14] obviously to satisfy specific orders placed by the artist's highly placed clients. Thanks to the condemnation by Augustine, the scene of love between Jove and Danae, as we have seen, came to be considered in the sixteenth century the very prototype of the image created to excite the beholder sexually.

But is it correct to say that these mythological paintings of Titian's are "intentionally erotic"? In recent decades various scholars, influenced by Panofsky's iconological approach, have replied in the negative, discerning in them a number of symbols and arcane allegories of a philosophical character. Panofsky's posthumous book on Titian has given the most authoritative support possible to this position.[15] The following pages are intended to reopen the discussion, especially in regard to certain assumptions implicit in iconological studies devoted to Titian.

First of all, we cannot ignore that contemporaries viewed Titian's mythological "poems" as explicitly erotic paintings. And the artist himself would have agreed. Titian's letter to Philip II has been frequently cited. After recalling the "Danae where one could see everything from the front," he promised to send another "poem," one of "Venus and Adonis," in which it would be possible to view, "just to vary things," "the other side."[16] But we should also look at what Ludovico Dolce, a friend and great admirer of Titian's, wrote to Alessandro Contarini about this second painting:

> The Venus has her back turned, not for any artistic deficiency but to demonstrate double the art. Because in turning her face towards Adonis, straining with both her arms to retain him, and half-seated on a soft fabric of peacock-blue, she demonstrates in every way certain sweet and lively sentiments, and such that they cannot be seen except in her; the miraculous shrewdness of that divine spirit [Titian] is also revealed that in her intimate

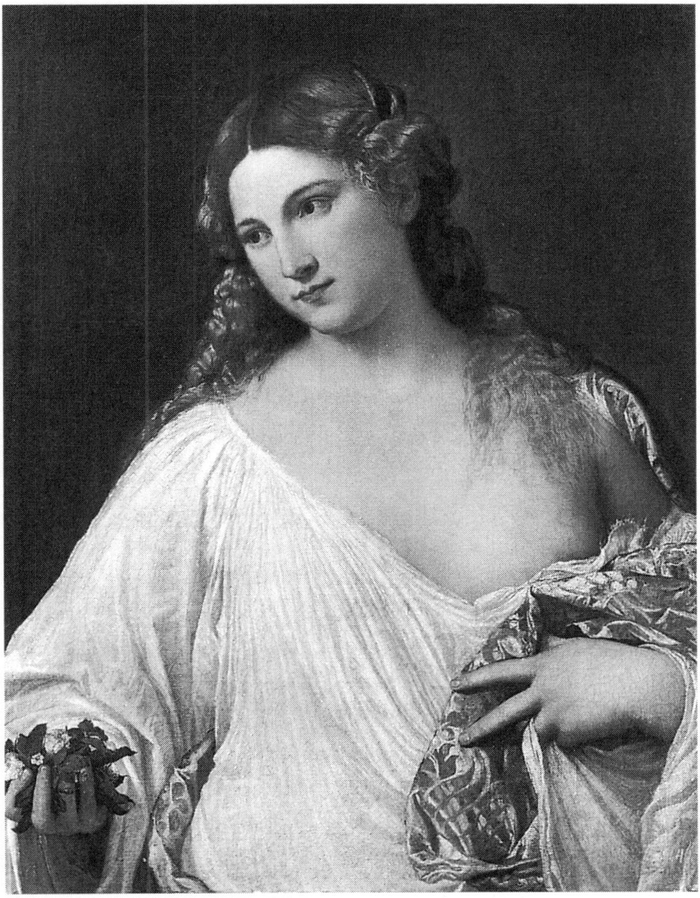

Figure 7. Titian, *Flora*. Florence, Galleria degli Uffizi. Photo: Alinari/Art Resource.

parts we recognize the creases on the flesh caused by her seated position. Why, it can in truth be said that every stroke of the brush is one of those strokes that nature executes with its own hand. . . . I swear to you, sir, that there is no man so keen in sight or judgment, that seeing does not believe her alive; nor anyone made so cold by the years, or so hardened in his being, who does not feel a warming, a softening, a stirring of the blood in his veins. It is a real marvel; that if a marble statue could by the stimuli of its beauty so penetrate to the marrow of a young man,

> that he stained himself, then, what must she do who is of flesh, who is beauty personified and appears to be breathing?[17]

As we see, aesthetic evaluation in terms of realism imperceptibly surpasses the appreciation, which is exceedingly explicit, of the painting's capacity to stimulate erotically. This may explain why this letter has been generally ignored in the literature on Titian and why a renowned scholar even felt he should quote it only in a censored form.[18]

One might object, however, that this evidence does not exclude the possibility of a second layer of meaning in the image, containing the symbols and learned allusions dear to iconologists. But can the existence of this secondary stratum be demonstrated? In the case of the mythological "poems" painted by Titian in his late maturity, the answer is no. The conflicting interpretations recently offered over the *Abduction of Europa* are a good example. M.L. Shapiro has identified the textual "source" of that painting not in Ovid, as had always been thought, but in a Horatian ode (*Carmina* 3.27). This led to the attempt to read a complicated set of Stoic symbols into the painting. The seemingly wildly erotic image of Europa being dragged off by the bull was actually thought to conceal a more complex message: the depiction of surrender to passion condemned by the Stoics. The fish and the dolphins swimming alongside Europa, the cupids who escort her, were embodiments, in fact, of the passions of the soul: fear, joy, desire, pain. The monstrous fish is the symbol of fear, the dolphin of joy, first because Moschus in his poem *Europa* speaks of "joyous" leaps by dolphins, second because Titian's dolphin is of a silvery color and Horace, in another ode, declares "the silver house laughs" ("ridet *argento* domus"); one of the flying cupids symbolizes desire, and the other pain, as his distraught expression demonstrates "rather fittingly," together with "the rather angular outline of his form that should be compared with the soft roundness of both *Joy* and *Desire*."[19]

Fortunately, arguments of this kind have been promptly rejected. Another scholar, D. Stone, Jr., has shown beyond the shadow of a doubt that the "source" for the *Abduction of Europa* is neither Ovid nor Horace, but rather an Alexandrian romance that Titian may have read in F. A. Coccio's vernacular version.[20] From the imaginary painting minutely described by Achille Tazio, Titian took, in particular, Europa's position on the bull: "The young woman was seated on his back, but not the way a man sits on a horse, but side-saddle, with both feet dangling on the right and with the left hand clasping one of the horns." (The iconographic oddity of this pose did not escape Panofsky, *Problems in Titian,* p. 166.) It is possible, then, to identify a text behind the painting, one that in this case was followed scrupulously. But it is a purely descriptive text, lacking in symbolic, Stoic, or Neoplatonic overtones. To Shapiro's typically iconological question, "Is the Stoic program there to veil the pagan nudity?"[21] we can reply negatively, because the presence of a "program" tied to Stoicism cannot be demonstrated. There remains Europa's nudity: veiled or, better, exalted by the "brilliant white robe" of which Achille Tazio's vernacular version speaks and which Titian did not fail to reproduce in his painting. How far can we go with a conclusion of this sort, which in the particular case of the *Abduction of Europa* appears unquestionable?

Not Ovid, then, but a vernacular translation of an Alexandrian romance. And yet we know that Titian found in Ovid the inspiration for most of his mythological "poems," for those paintings, in other words, which in the eyes of contemporaries had, as we have seen, an essentially erotic character. Panofsky has spoken of an exceptionally deep attachment for Ovid on Titian's part – an Ovid read and scrutinized to the last detail of the text.[22] But of the text – or of the translation?

According to Panofsky, Titian "felt free to use all kinds of visual models, ancient or modern, while yet, on the whole, remaining independent of the specific tradition which flourished all around him in countless illustrated editions, translations and paraphrases of the *Metamorphoses.*" In several cases, in fact, Titian would not have hesitated to detach himself from this tradition and return directly to Ovid's original text. But Panofsky's amply illustrated thesis is, actually, untenable. In refutation, it can be demonstrated that (1) Titian did not know Latin; (2) he read the *Metamorphoses* only in translations; (3) his innovations with respect to the iconographic tradition should be traced to the vernacular versions, and not to the Ovidian text. If all this is true, he was not a humanistic painter, as has often been maintained, but one tied closely to the contemporary vernacular culture of the *poligrafi.*[23]

. . . Titian was unable to understand a text by a Latin author without the assistance of a vernacular version.

It is unnecessary to insist on the importance of this point, first of all because sixteenth-century translations, as we know, were anything but faithful renderings. Usually they were reworkings, often abridged or expanded. . . .

It is well known that Titian freely borrowed the most varied figurative materials. Contemporary paintings, ancient statues, and even, as in this case, more or less crude illustrations taken from Ovid translations ended up being reshaped and fused in a language that was his alone. We are also well aware that the stimuli for this extraordinary inventiveness could be literary as well as figurative. But the present demonstration that Titian used only vernacular texts provides us with a picture of his education and culture that differs considerably from the customary one.

But what does all this have to do with my original question concerning erotic representations in the sixteenth century? To answer we need to return to my earlier contrast between the two iconic circuits, the public and the private: the first, broad and socially undifferentiated; the second, restricted and socially of high rank. As I cautioned, it is a schematic distinction, one that would soon be disturbed by the advent of printing. Thanks to this invention, a public whose contours are still a little blurred but which included, at any rate, elements from the lower classes (artisans and even peasants) came into contact not only with the printed page but with the images that frequently accompanied it. The existence of relatively inexpensive, often illustrated books suddenly expanded, in both a quantitative and qualitative sense, the patrimony of words and images available to these social groups. The presumably enormous repercussions of this phenomenon are beginning to be investigated only now.[24]

As for the question under examination here, we can only guess at the enrichment of the erotic imagination provoked by such images. . . .

A survey, unfortunately still in its initial stages, of manuals for confessors and penitents printed in Italy between the end of the fifteenth and the close of the sixteenth century yields a preliminary, not unexpected result. Up to 1540, roughly, avarice is the sin discussed at greatest length, by far; lust follows. About this date that process of control and thoroughgoing repression of sexual life that we are accustomed to attribute, as far as Catholic countries are concerned, to the Counter-Reformation began to take hold. Why did tensions typical of a society in which commerce played such an important (even if not prevalent) role become secondary to those connected with the sexual life? And why, more or less around this time, did similar forms of control spring up even in Protestant countries, foremost in Calvin's Geneva?[25] In a final analysis, all this probably can be explained by the demographic strains emerging in European society,[26] even when the control exercised by the authorities, whether lay or ecclesiastical, took different forms depending on the political and religious situations.

But the study of confessionals suggests another, less obvious motive for reflection. The minute analyses of the sin of lust concentrate on the senses of touch and sound well into the sixteenth century. Sight is hardly mentioned. The social occasions that abet the transgression of the commandment "Do not fornicate" are principally dancing and singing. To make "cantiones vel sonetos . . . lascivia turpia et inhonesta ad provocandum" is a mortal sin, wrote Bartolomeo Caimi in his confessional.[27] He did not warn against immoral images, simply because their diffusion must have been minimal or nil, except among the upper classes. Only later in the century did sight emerge slowly as a prominent erotic sense, immediately after touch. In the still unwritten history of the senses, due weight will have to be given to this eroticization of sight in respect to hearing, tied to such specific historical circumstances as the diffusion of the printing press and the increased circulation of images.[28]

Nude Dianas and Venuses, nymphs and bacchantes, even if to a limited degree, now fell under the gaze of a public much larger than the prelates and nobles so scathingly condemned by Politi about mid-century. More time had to pass before erotic representations would replace the culturally elevated mythological canon with that middling one, whether realistic or comic, of genre painting. Meanwhile, that refined and complex world of pagan divinities recreated by humanists was being translated by the illustrators of printed books into frequently humble and rudimentary forms – except when that process took an opposed direction, as in the case of Titian's *Andromeda*. But the circular journey traveled by erotic images in the sixteenth century remains to be explored. Indeed, not only Philip II in his private chamber, but many anonymous readers of the vernacular *Metamorphoses* must have projected, as with Terence's Chaerea, their own most intimate fantasies into the amorous deeds of the ancient gods.

NOTES

1. Terence, *The Eunuch,* in *Terence with an English Translation by John Sargeaunt,* Loeb Classical Library (Cambridge, Mass., and London, 1929), 1:293, 295.
2. See D. Freedberg, "Johannes Molanus on Provocative Paintings: *De historia sanctarum imaginum et picturarum,* Book II, Chapter 42," *Journal of the Warburg and Courtauld Institutes* 34 (1971): 242, n. 24. F. Orlando alludes to the passage in Saint Augustine, but in a different context: "Su teoria della letteratura e divisione del lavoro intellettuale," *Strumenti Critici,* no. 29 (February 1976), p. 115.
3. See J. L. Connolly, Jr., in *Woman as Sex Object: Studies in Erotic Art, 1730–1970,* ed. T. B. Hess and L. Nochlin (New York, 1972), p. 1, and the piece by Nochlin, ibid., pp. 9 ff.
4. See I. Calvino, "Considerazioni sul sesso e sul riso," *Il Caffè* 17, no. 2 (1970): 3–5. The classical and medieval distinction between various stylistic levels is accepted here in E. Auerbach's sense (*Mimesis: The Representation of Reality in Western Literature* [Princeton, 1953]).
5. See the Pompeian fresco reproduced by W. S. Heckscher, "Recorded from Dark Recollection," in *De artibus opuscula XL: Essays in Honor of Erwin Panofsky,* ed. M. Meiss (New York, 1961), fig. 5.
6. In contrast, I would define as pornographic those illustrations which are intended exclusively to arouse the spectator sexually.
7. See Freedberg, "Johannes Molanus," p. 233.
8. This distinction is based principally on P. Burke, *Culture and Society in Renaissance Italy, 1420–1540* (London, 1972), pp. 144, 158, passim.
9. See Freedberg, "Johannes Molanus," p. 241, n. 15.
10. See G. Vasari, *Le vite,* ed. G. Milanesi (Florence, 1879), 4:188.
11. P. Barocchi, "Un 'Discorso' sopra l'onestà delle immagini di Rinaldo Corso," in *Scritti . . . in onore di Mario Salmi* (Rome, 1963), 3:173–91.
12. See J. S. Held, "Flora, Goddess and Courtesan," in *De artibus opuscula XL,* pp. 201–18.
13. A. Catarino Politi, *Disputatio . . . de cultu et adoratione imaginum* (Rome, 1552), pp. 142–43.

14. H. Tietze, "An Early Version of Titian's Danae: An Analysis of Titian Replicas," *Arte Veneta* 8 (1954): 199–208.
15. E. Panofsky, *Problems in Titian, Mostly Iconographic* (London, 1969).
16. *Raccolta di lettere sulla pittura, scultura ed architettura* (Rome, 1757), 2:22.
17. *Raccolta* (Rome, 1759), 3:259–60.
18. The truncated passage is in R. Pallucchini, *Tiziano* (Florence, 1969), 1:140–41.
19. M. L. Shapiro, "Titian's 'Rape of Europa,' " *Gazette des Beaux Arts* 77, no. 1225 (1971): 109–16. The previously formulated hypothesis of a derivation from "such more recondite authors as Moschus" is rejected by Panofsky (*Problems in Titian,* p. 165) in favor of the traditional Ovidian theory, on which more below.
20. D. Stone, Jr., "The Source of Titian's *Rape of Europa,*" *Art Bulletin* 54 (1972): 47–49. (And see now, following a similar line of interpretation, but with the addition of new elements, P. F. Watson, "Titian's 'Rape of Europa': A Bride Stripped Bare," in *Storia dell'Arte,* no. 28 [1976], pp. 249–58.)
21. Shapiro, "Titian's 'Rape,' " p. 114. Note that Stone does not exclude (with excessive prudence in my opinion) the Stoic implications proposed by Shapiro.
22. Panofsky, *Problems in Titian,* pp. 140–41.
23. It does not seem to me that all the implications of the relationship between Titian and Aretino have been exhausted. On the significance of the latter's literary success, see the perceptive comments by C. Dionisotti, *Geografia e storia della letteratura italiana* (Turin, 1967), pp. 193–94. On the sixteenth-century *poligrafi,* see the useful work by P. F. Grendler, *Critics of the Italian World (1530–1560): Anton Francesco Doni, Nicolò Franco, and Ortensio Lando* (Madison, 1969).
24. For one attempt, see my *Cheese and the Worms: The Cosmos of a Sixteenth-Century Miller* (Baltimore, 1980).
25. See E. W. Monter, "La sodomie à l'époque moderne en suisse romande," *Annales: E.S.C.* 29 (1974): 1023–33, esp. p. 1030.
26. D. Herlihy offered some interesting observations on the subject at the Venetian roundtable in September 1976.
27. B. Caimi, *Interrogatorium sive confessionale* (n.p., 1474), unpaginated.
28. See the stimulating remarks by L. Febvre, *Le problème de l'incroyance au XVI siècle: La religion de Rabelais* (1942; Paris, 1968). The subject of a "history of the senses" was proposed by Marx in a famous page of the Parisian *Manuscripts.*

[The present article was reprinted (without the illustrative material, owing to editorial oversight) in the proceedings of the conference *Tiziano e Venezia*

(Venice, 1980). In that volume see the contributions by C. Hope and H. Zerner, who discuss themes treated here. On vernacular versions of Ovid I should have cited B. Guthmüller, "Die literarische Uebersetzung im Bezugsfeld Original-Leser am Beispiel Italienischer Uebersetzungen der Metamorphosen Ovids im 16. Jahrhundert," *Bibliothèque d'Humanisme et Renaissance* 36 (1974): 233–51. See also, by the same author, "Ovidübersetzungen und mythologische Malerei: Bemerkungen zur *Sala dei Giganti* Giulio Romanos," *Mitteilungen des Kunsthistorischen Instituts in Florenz* 21 (1977): 35–68 (brought to my attention by Carlo Dionisotti). On Dolce's dedication to Titian, discussed above, see the clarifications by Dionisotti, "Tiziano e la letteratura," in *Tiziano e il manierismo europeo,* ed. R. Pallucchini (Florence, 1978) (but his entire essay is important). In the same volume see also the contribution by M. Gregori, "Tiziano e Aretino." A. Chastel, following Dionisotti, has insisted on the significance for Titian of vernacular versions of Ovid: "Titien et les humanistes," in *Tiziano Vecellio,* Atti dei convegni dei Lincei, 29 (Rome, 1977), pp. 31–48. A. Gentili takes a different position (*Da Tiziano a Tiziano* [Rome, 1980], pp. 173ff.) and argues against my interpretation. I have corrected an error in the name of Achille Tazio's translator and specified that the reference to Titian's *Danae* applied to both versions. For the rest, however, it does not seem to me that Gentili grasped the sense of my argument, which intended to deny not Titian's capacity for invention (imagine!), but simply his direct dependence on Ovid's text, assumed by Panofsky. The attempts to devaluate the importance of the quite clear passage in Dolce's dedication are doomed to fail.]

2 DAVID ROSAND

"SO-AND-SO RECLINING ON HER COUCH"

Titian's *Venus of Urbino* (Fig. 1), one of the most familiar images in Western art, has come to stand for both the sensuality and the classicism we ascribe to the culture of the High Renaissance, its low as well as its high life.[1] More recently, it has become the locus of critical debate over ways of perceiving and understanding the imagery of the past, our modes of response and interpretation. That conflict has inevitably colored our perception of the picture, forcing certain issues to the fore. Any attempt at an *explication de tableau* therefore involves a declaration, however tacit, of methodological principle – or, at least, a certain methodological self-consciousness.[2] It is in this spirit that I would like to consider the interpretive challenge posed by the lady on the couch.

VICTORIAN VISIONS

But is she – a lady, that is? That question has come to loom large in consideration of the painting. Whatever its validity or relevance, the question itself serves to locate the picture with a certain historical – or historiographical – exactness. For our view of this Renaissance image is hardly a direct one; rather, it has been screened by intervening events, and one in particular of the mid-nineteenth century: Manet's *Olympia* (Fig. 2), which was so conspicuously inspired by Titian's picture, and the scandal that at-

Earlier versions of this essay were published as "Venereal Hermeneutics" and as " 'So-And-So Reclining on Her Couch.' "

tended its public exhibition in 1865. Whatever the desired focus of our historical vision, it is impossible for us to ignore this occlusion. Manet's pictorial commentary has affected our sense of the interpretive possibilities inherent in its Renaissance model.

Indeed, our consideration of Titian's painting may legitimately begin in the nineteenth century, when the picture's reception becomes increasingly problematical. The *Venus of Urbino* has long been a highpoint on the tourist's obligatory rounds of the galleries of the Uffizi, and, by way of introducing some of the basic hermeneutic problems surrounding the picture, I offer as an opening text the response of one such observer, an American traveler abroad. Upon entering the Uffizi, he reports, you

> proceed to that most-visited little gallery in the world – the Tribune – and there, against the wall, without obstructing rag or leaf, you may look upon the foulest, the vilest, the obscenest picture the world possesses – Titian's Venus. It isn't that she is naked and stretched out on a bed – no, it is the attitude of one of her arms and hand. If I ventured to describe that attitude, there would be a fine howl – but there the Venus lies, for anybody to gloat over that wants to – and there she has a right to lie, for she is a work of art, and Art has its privileges.

Our American tourist then makes his contribution to the dossier on the picture's *Rezeptionsgeschichte:* "I saw young girls stealing furtive glances at her; I saw young men gaze long and absorbedly at her; I saw aged, infirm men hang upon her charms with pathetic interest." And he concludes his outburst by reconciling himself to the power of the aesthetic and taking one final stab at historical explanation:

> There are pictures of nude women which suggest no impure thought – I am well aware of that. I am not railing at such. What I am trying to emphasize is the fact that Titian's Venus is very far from being one of that sort. Without any question it was painted for a bagnio and it was probably refused because it was a trifle too strong. In truth it is too strong for any place but a public Art Gallery.

This splenetic account of a visit to the Uffizi is by Mark Twain, from *A Tramp Abroad* (published in 1880).[3] It was professionally inspired by what in a Renaissance context we might call a *paragone,* a comparison between the visual arts and literature – more specifically, between the moral courtesy extended to each by society, by Victorian society. "Art," the author observes in his opening attack, "is allowed as much indecent licence to-day as in earlier times – but the privileges of Literature in this respect have been sharply curtailed within the past eighty or ninety years."[4]

Mark Twain's satiric outrage at the blatant nakedness of Titian's lady on the couch, then, is a kind of oblique First Amendment defense. But the issues it raises – or, better, exemplifies – go to the heart of more traditional debates in visual hermeneutics. How, indeed, are we to read this picture? How should we respond to this image of the female body? Can our response be validated in any way? Can we speak of intention? If so, whose? The culture's? The artist's? The picture's? If the questions seem obvious, the answers are less so.

The problems begin with the painting itself, for critics do not readily agree on just who or what is being depicted. Nor is recourse to the scant historical documentation of much help. One immediate question concerns the identity of the young woman herself. Is this "Venus" in fact a Venus? Or is she one of the celebrated courtesans of Venice, a *cortigiana onesta,* or merely a common whore, a *cortigiana meretrice,* called up from the *calli* to pose for the painter friend of the infamous Pietro Aretino?[5] Some art historians have taken this as the central question, that which contains *in nuce* all the others; in the identity of the painter's model, they assume, lies the resolution of the entire interpretive challenge.[6] For all its obvious interest and relevance, the question itself, however, merely displaces the issue – or, worse, confounds it by the simplistic confidence of its own positivism, the prosaic literalism of its historicizing pretension.

As a more direct introduction to the painting, we might adduce another nineteenth-century text, published only three years before Mark Twain's. This is the description of the *Venus of Urbino* by Crowe and Cavalcaselle in their classic *Life and Times of Titian* (1877):

> Lying as nature shaped her, with her legs entwined, at the foot of a deep green hanging, on a muslin sheet, that covers a ruby tinged damask couch, her left arm reposes on her frame, her

> right supporting her on cushions, whilst the hand is playing with a chaplet of flowers. We may fancy her to have bathed and to be waiting for the handmaids, who are busy in the room, one of them having raised the lid of a chest and taken a dress out, whilst a second stoops to select another. Meanwhile a little dog lies curled up on the couch. . . .
>
> Not after the model of a Phryne [the Athenian courtesan said to have posed for Apelles], nor yet with the thought of realizing anything more sublime than woman in her fairest aspect, did Titian conceive of this picture. Nature as he presents it here is young and lovely, not transfigured into ineffable noblesse, but conscious and triumphant without loss of modesty.[7]

We recognize the inevitable passage of description into interpretation. Unlike the American tourist, the Victorian art historians have no difficulty with the license claimed by Art. It is exactly such license that permits their indulgent participation in Titian's painting, that allows them to enjoy publicly the charms of his Venus – "if," as they themselves wonder, "Venus be an appropriate name." Their account of the picture brings it to a more licit life than did Mark Twain's. "What the painter achieves," they continue,

> is the representation of a beauteous living being whose fair and polished skin is depicted with enamelled gloss, and yet with every shade of modulation which a delicate flesh comports; – flesh not marbled or cold, but sweetly toned; and mantling with life's blood, flesh that seems to heave and rise and fall with every breath. Perfect distribution of space, a full and ringing harmony of tints, atmosphere both warm and mellow, are all combined in such wise as to bring us in contact with something that is real, and we feel as we look into the canvas that we might walk into that apartment and find room to wander in the grey twilight into which it is thrown by the summer sky that shows through the coupled windows.[8]

With delicate avoidance of the all too obvious focal point of the composition – so aggressively acknowledged in Mark Twain's analysis of the picture – the Victorian critics manage to sublimate the sensual in the aesthetic with a decorousness that we can only admire for its self-control. And their aesthetic prophylaxis returns us to a fundamental question: Just what kind of painting is this directed display of female flesh?

A QUESTION OF GENRE

Ironically, perhaps, the first (and only) serious effort to locate the significance of Titian's picture historically, to articulate its iconography and set it within a specific social context, was in effect the by-product of scholarship on Manet. To understand the meaning of *Olympia,* Theodore Reff quite naturally felt obliged to come to terms with its inspiring image.[9] Against the provocation of a tableau of a French *courtisane,* a brazen pictorial gesture calculated to *épater le bourgeois,* Titian's nude was recognized as a model of domestic virtue. The *Venus of Urbino* was seen as a marriage picture, the goddess of love characterized by her surrounding attributes as the protectress in particular of marital love. She holds a bunch of roses, and on the window ledge in the background a myrtle plant, in perpetual bloom, is pointedly silhouetted against the glowing sky. These floral symbols, traditionally associated with Venus, combine to define the very special kind of love she here represents: the fruitful passion of licit love, not the quickly sated and sinful lust of the body but the permanent bond of conjugal affection. The little dog curled up at her feet in contented slumber overtly signifies the ideal of marital fidelity – its trusting nature having become so much more poignant for us in light of its feline transformation in Manet's painting. The enframed background scene of maids at an open *cassone,* a wedding chest, offers a naturalistic anecdotal comment on the symbolism of the main motif that would seem to confirm the social significance of the image.[10]

Although Crowe and Cavalcaselle had their doubts and, as we shall see, more recent critics were certain she was not, from Vasari on most commentators have automatically identified Titian's nude as a Venus.[11] Indeed, as late as the early nineteenth century, the values inherent in such an identification were still apparent. Stefano Ticozzi quite naturally read the action of the two maids in the background as going to the *cassone* for the garments necessary to hide such beauty from profane eyes.[12] Hardly signaling a revival of Neoplatonism in the early nineteenth century, Ticozzi's reading essentially repeats a conventional language of response to such imagery – which we understand immediately in a more hieratic picture like Botticelli's *Birth of Venus*.[13] Throughout the long Renaissance tradition, images, however supposedly "straightforward" their subject matter, were meant to be interpreted.

Other aspects of the *Venus of Urbino,* as well, seem to confirm its generic status as a marriage picture. Before considering them, however, we must acknowledge one potentially embarrassing issue. If Titian's canvas was indeed painted to celebrate a marriage, then whose wedding was it? And this returns us to its history. We assume that the painting was acquired in 1538 by Guidobaldo II della Rovere, then duke of Camerino and subsequently of Urbino. On March 9, 1538, Guidobaldo wrote to his agent in Venice that he was most anxious to take possession of two paintings still in Titian's studio, a portrait of himself and a picture of a nude woman ("il ritratto mio e la donna nuda").[14] Unfortunately, the duke was short of funds and proposed to borrow from his mother, Eleonora Gonzaga. The duchess was agreeable and wrote to her son on April 14 that she was having the portrait sent to him (three days earlier, it was reported as not yet finished).[15]

The following month, on May 1, Guidobaldo was still anxious to obtain the other picture, the nude woman, which remained in the painter's shop and which the duke feared Titian might sell to someone else. By May 9 the picture was still undelivered, and the reason seems to have been that Titian, for his part, was rather anxious about payment; at least, the ducal agent reported his guarantee to the painter that his master was good for it.[16] Exactly when Guidobaldo finally possessed his "donna nuda" the extant documents do not reveal.[17]

On the basis of this archival situation, two major objections to an epithalamic interpretation of the *Venus of Urbino* have been registered: first, that the Venus of Urbino is no Venus – since the letter of March 9 refers to her only as a naked woman. Second, that this painting of 1538 cannot possibly be a marriage picture – since Guidobaldo's marriage (to the ten-year-old Giulia Varano of Camerino) occurred four years earlier, in 1534. Moreover (the argument runs), if the picture had been specifically commissioned by Guidobaldo, then it is unlikely that he would have so feared losing it to another buyer.[18] The highly circumstantial nature of these objections pretends to a certain historical verifiability, appealing to the supposedly unproblematic truth of documents. In any event, I propose to shift the ground of the debate by offering the picture itself as the essential document, allowing it to testify on its own behalf.

What kind of picture is the *Venus of Urbino?* Format and iconography – that is, shape and subject: the horizontal rectangle of its field and the reclining female nude (which may be said to generate the format) – both relate the canvas to a larger group of pictures, including others by Titian himself. Most famously, of course, Titian's *donna nuda* represents a variation on an invention by Giorgione, the *Sleeping Venus* in Dresden (Fig. 3) – "das Prototyp dieser Art Liebesbilder," as Giovanni Morelli recognized in returning the picture to the painter.[19] Evidently painted for Girolamo Marcello, in whose house it was seen in 1525 by Marcantonio Michiel, the Dresden picture was actually completed by Titian. Michiel records "the canvas with a nude Venus sleeping in a landscape with Cupid" as by the hand of Giorgione, but he notes explicitly that "the landscape and Cupid were finished by Titian" (Fig. 19).[20]

Although the Cupid is no longer visible, X-radiography has confirmed its original existence at the feet of the goddess, holding a symbolically loaded little bird. Jaynie Anderson has elegantly demonstrated the epithalamic nature of this imagery, tracing the motif of the sleeping Venus back to classical literature, Claudian in particular.[21] Within the ancient tradition of epithalamia, Venus is found at rest in her sacred landscape; roused by Cupid, she prepares herself for the mortals' wedding where she will serve as *pronuba,* the patroness of marriage. The wedding of Girolamo Marcello and Morosina Pisani took place on October 9, 1507, and it is plausibly suggested that Giorgione's canvas was commissioned for that occasion.

Commissioned, but evidently not delivered. It would seem likely that the painting was still incomplete when Giorgione died in the plague of 1510. Like other pictures presumably left behind in his studio, the *Sleeping Venus* was brought to completion by a surviving artist.[22] Marriage pictures, we might infer, did not always arrive on time.[23]

A quarter of a century later, Titian recalled his Giorgionesque intervention in the *Venus of Urbino*. He awakened and domesticated Giorgione's dreaming pastoral deity. Brought indoors, this nude stresses less her classical poetic pedigree than her contemporary social function. And her blatant address to the viewer, inviting by sight as well as touch, reinforces even as it complicates that dimension of the image in the world. Although Giorgione had reinvoked an antique type of Venus – as well as Ariadne – reclining in a landscape, the distended female nude had already found her natural pictorial field in the Quattrocento: in the painted panels inside the lids of *cassoni,* those trousseau chests whose decorations often celebrated uxorial virtue or dynastic generation (Fig. 8).[24] It is precisely the furniture format of those panels that is recalled in another painting by Titian, one that can be documented to a particular marriage.

This is the painting generally known as *Sacred and Profane Love* (Fig. 9). Although it too has had to withstand more than its share of scholarly attention, at least here we are certain of the picture's patronage and purpose, for two coats of arms affirm the joining of two families.[25] The more prominently displayed, above the fountain spigot in the relief of the transformed sarcophagus, is that of Nicolò Aurelio. More discreetly hidden, inlaid within the silver bowl, are the arms of the Bagarotto family of Padua. Niccolò Aurelio, then secretary to the Venetian Council of Ten, was married to Laura Bagarotto in May 1514.[26]

Confirming the Neoplatonism of the received title, Erwin Panofsky has given the *Sacred and Profane Love* its canonical interpretation.[27] His reading, however, has hardly gone unchallenged. Recently, the debate over the exact nature of the iconography of the picture has reached a particularly feverous pitch, as serious scholars – in what can only be described as anti-Panofsky hysteria – have vehemently argued against any philosophical, especially Neoplatonic, dimension to the painting. Insisting on what they call "straightforward" interpretation, these critics reject the reading of the image as a representation of twin Venuses, terrestrial and celestial, or, as described in the early seventeenth century, "Beltà disornata e Beltà ornata." Instead, they prefer a more prosaic path. Forced by the presence of Cupid into acknowledging the identity of the nude figure, at least, as Venus, they see the clothed beauty as the bride herself; the painting is thus to be retitled "Laura Bagarotto at the fountain of Venus."[28] The extraordinary acuity – not to say fantasy – of physiognomic perception necessary to distinguish between these two faces is, I confess, beyond my powers,

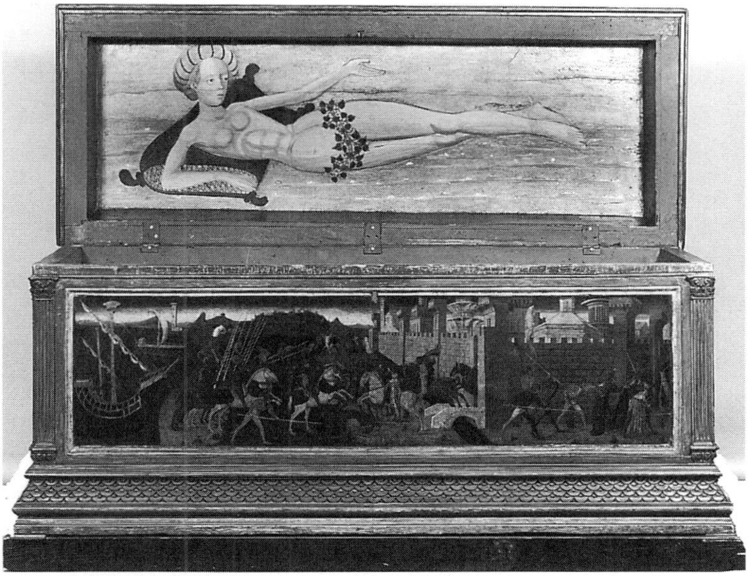

Figure 8. Florentine School, Painted Cassone, c. 1465–70. New Haven, Yale University Art Gallery. Photo: Yale University Art Gallery, New Haven.

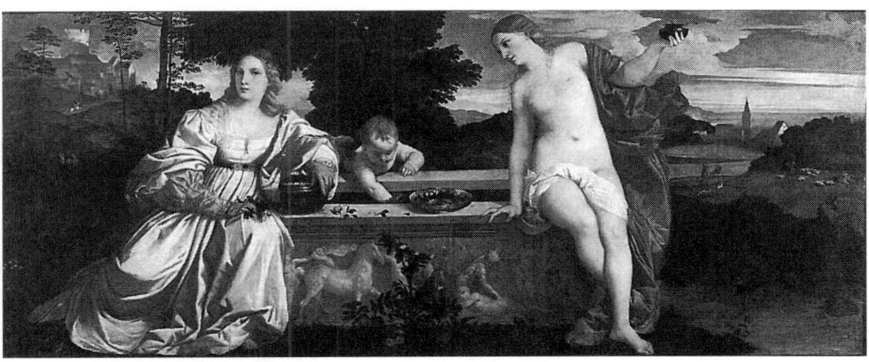

Figure 9. Titian, *Sacred and Profane Love* (after restoration). Rome, Galleria Borghese. Photo: Soprintendenza per i Beni Artistici e Storici di Roma.

especially since their features grace any number of *belle donne* in Titian's work of this period. To call this *beltà ornata* a portrait of Laura Bagarotto is as wishful as the nineteenth-century recognition of the *Venus of Urbino* as a portrait of Eleonora Gonzaga, duchess of Urbino and mother of the patron.[29]

At this point in my argument, without rehearsing the long history of interpretations of the *Sacred and Profane Love,* I wish only to emphasize the format of the field.[30]

GENERIC AUTONOMY

Titian's *Sacred and Profane Love* and, even more pertinently, Giorgione's *Sleeping Venus* affirm the existence of one pictorial category directly relevant to an understanding of the *Venus of Urbino:* the marriage picture – or, to use Morelli's more open term, *Liebesbild.* Without totally subscribing to what E. H. Gombrich, following E. D. Hirsch, has called "the principle of the primacy of genres,"[31] I want to stress the significance of such a category and what we might term its impulse toward autonomy. Although created within a specific context, to serve a particular social function, the category eventually liberates itself from the restrictions of historical circumstance to assert its own generic independence, its existence as a recognizable formal type per se. But it carries with it as well the meanings, actual or potential – however vestigial or attenuated – generated by its origin.

The *cassone* panel of the Quattrocento preserved the social context of the image by setting it in furniture that would continue to fulfill a social function. As an easel picture, such as Giorgione's, the image of Venus gained a certain independence and, we might say, flexibility of function. Whatever its originating cause, its continued existence and significance necessarily became, over time, less dependent on that cause. So, too, the image-type itself came to enjoy a meaning and an appeal beyond the socially legitimizing marital context. A "marriage picture" might be painted without a marriage. (Such generic independence notwithstanding, we can hardly rule out the possibility that the *Venus of Urbino* may indeed have been commissioned on the occasion of the wedding of 1534.)

There is another genre of picture that is equally relevant to this interpretive problem, one that is, however, more difficult to fix

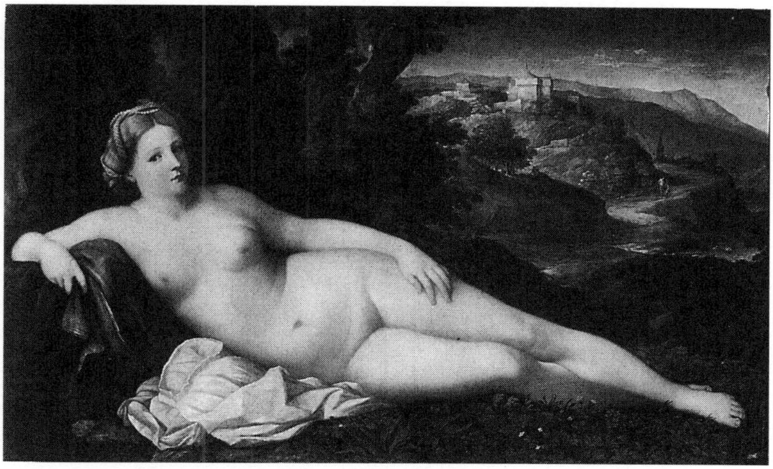

Figure 10. Jacopo Palma il Vecchio, *Reclining Nude in Landscape*. Dresden, Gemäldegalerie. Photo: Alinari/Art Resource.

with such apparent documentary clarity. This comprises pictures of beautiful women, usually coming down to us without name or title, in various states of deshabille. The highest example of the type is Titian's own *Flora* (Fig. 7), who so identifies herself by the flowers she offers.[32] Flora was both goddess and courtesan, and hers was one of the names adopted by Venetian courtesans when they entered the profession. Another name that appears frequently among the sixteenth-century lists of courtesans in Venice is Laura – ironic homage to the idolized Petrarchan *madonna*.

In this light, we can hardly accept the reading of Giorgione's *Laura,* displaying herself before the floral declaration of her name, as the portrait of a good Venetian matron.[33] Palma Vecchio, to judge by the number of extant works, seems to have made a specialty of this type of imagery – "fantasy pieces" ("quadri di fantasia"), as Crowe and Cavalcaselle called them – thereby thinking to absolve such pictures of any charges of social irresponsibility (Fig. 10).[34] Even the aged Giovanni Bellini was called upon to contribute (Fig. 5). Whether or not his lady at her toilet is a Venus or the portrait of someone's *favorita,* whether or not she is susceptible of allegorization as Vanitas, her primary appeal is clear.[35] On a basic level – that is, on the first level of Erwin Panofsky's synoptical table of interpretation – the "object of interpretation" is "primary or natural subject matter." And the "equipment [necessary] for interpretation," to stay with Panofsky's outline, is "practical experience (familiarity with objects and events)."[36]

Crowe and Cavalcaselle faced the hermeneutic problem with their usual Victorian tact. Wondering whether Titian's Flora was "one of those ladies of light fame who survived to be copied by Rubens under the name of courtezan," they concluded that "The lover of art may now say it is a matter of little consequence. The 'Flora,' if nothing more, is a lovely ideal which ranges far above the realms to which her earthly lot would seem to bind her."[37] And the moral generosity of these art historians – however patronizing its tone – inflected critical response, once again, into aesthetic sublimation: The delicate sensuality of their description, its loving attention to detail, pays full tribute to the effect of Flora on her admirers.

Not quite so delicate is the more recent verdict of a contemporary English art historian: "The implication is that these pictures [the *Flora* and the *Venus of Urbino*] were for the most part mere pin-ups, and that the girls were seen as little more than sex objects."[38]

It is true that in one of the very few early references we have to a picture like the *Venus of Urbino,* a reclining nude by Savoldo in the house of Andrea Odoni, the invaluable Marcantonio Michiel locates it in the bedroom over the bed: "La Nuda grande destesa da drietto el letto."[39] The location of Savoldo's picture hardly diminishes its cultural position. Rather, it would seem to confirm its higher talismanic function: To conceive a child under the sign of Venus increases the chance, presumably, of generating beauty. And we might imagine a similar location and function for Lotto's *Venus and Cupid* (Fig. 11).

This power of images was acknowledged in a tradition from antiquity through the Renaissance. A century earlier Leon Battista Alberti had recommended that the bedroom of the master of the family and his wife there be hung only images of "dignity and handsome appearance; for they say that this may have a great influence on the fertility of the mother and the appearance of future offspring."[40] And in the early seventeenth century, Giulio Mancini summarized the function of such "lascivious pictures" in the bedroom, "because once seen they serve to arouse one and to make beautiful, healthy, and charming children."[41]

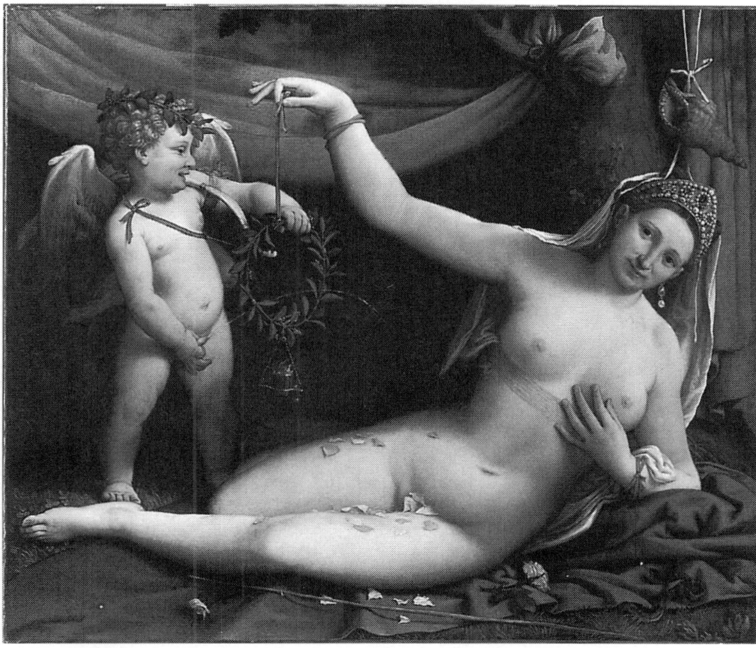

Figure 11. Lorenzo Lotto, *Venus and Cupid.* New York, Metropolitan Museum of Art. Photo: Metropolitan Museum of Art, New York.

Whatever its ostensible source in the antique *Venus Pudica* (Fig. 4), the gesture of the Venus of Urbino, even more than that of her Giorgionesque prototype, hardly serves the cause of modesty. It was just this gesture that Mark Twain could not bring himself to describe for fear "there would be a fine howl."[42] The Venetian Venus rather calls attention to her genitalia, and that focus is still more precisely fixed by the central vector of the hanging curtain in the *Venus of Urbino* – part of the tectonic grid against which her curves are so deliberately measured.[43] Compared to Titian's nude, the manual self-protection of Manet's Olympia seems determinedly chaste. The Venetian woman's gesture, not covering but rather stimulating, as Rona Goffen has recently suggested, confirms the licit nature of sexuality in these images; its invitation is to love within marriage, its allusion to the generative function of such love – the procreation, ideally, of beauty.[44]

To call these images "mere pin-ups" can only strike us as a

rather perverse form of Venus envy. Worse than just a flippant response from the twentieth century, an easy way of accommodating a complex past to what can only seem a simplistic present, it represents a willful act of critical irresponsibility, a failure to confront the very hermeneutic issues it pretends to resolve with such casual aplomb. Such reduction of meaning is predicated on a vacuation of the possibilities of meaning from the image, a denial of its cultural resonance. To deny a Renaissance picture of a nude woman her mythological garb is indeed to turn her out into the streets. It is also to deny the complexity and vitality of Renaissance culture, especially its appropriation of the classical as a way of dealing with the present. And yet this argument claims to found itself on a close reading of the documents.

With regard to the *Venus of Urbino,* this means the correspondence of Guidobaldo II della Rovere and his attempt to acquire the painting he apparently ordered some time before 1538 but was having some difficulty affording. His reference to "la donna nuda" is really quite adequate descriptively, and yet this has been read as an indication of the picture's non-subject: "It is surprising," we are told, "that Guidobaldo should have referred to the picture merely as 'la donna nuda' if he really meant 'la Venere'."[45] So runs the argument. But such efficient references, like those in inventories or in Marcantonio Michiel's notes, were hardly meant to be interpretive epitomes; they were, rather, functional identifying labels, indications of pictures seen. And "the nude woman" affords a most satisfactory description of the "object of interpretation." The reference is to its "primary or natural subject matter" – the base level of Panofsky's synoptical table – and represents the beginning not the end of interpretation.

GENERIC TRANSFORMATIONS

Guidobaldo's "donna nuda" leads us back to the question of pictorial genre and the conception of such pictures. Another letter and another painting expand the discussion. The letter, written from Venice on September 20, 1544, by Giovanni della Casa to Cardinal Alessandro Farnese, is filled with sarcastic allusions to members of the Farnese circle as well as to a number of paintings by Titian. Among the latter is one, nearly finished, being done for the cardinal himself, "una nuda," to which della Casa devotes special attention. Anticipating with relish the impact it will have on a certain member of the curia, he then compares it explicitly with the *Venus of Urbino.* The nude now on Titian's easel, he writes, makes that of the Duke of Urbino seem like a Theatine nun. Onto this nude body Titian joked about attaching the head of a well-known Roman courtesan and Farnese favorite (Camilla Pisana) – presumably when he himself arrived in Rome, which would be the following year (October 1545 to May 1546). The painter was in fact most anxious to please the Farnese, for he was hoping to guarantee a benefice for his son Pomponio; his jesting offer to add the features of a *favorita* might well have been an especially appreciated gesture. Della Casa concludes his comments with praise of the painter's personality and recommends him most highly to the cardinal.[46]

The painting in question is the *Danae* (Fig. 6), part of the Farnese collection now in the Gallerie di Capodimonte in Naples.[47] Here there is no doubt about its subject matter: The shower of gold and the presence of an encouraging Cupid confirm the identity of the heroine in the tower, ravished by Jupiter in his gilded potency. This nude is more actively engaged than her Urbinate cousin; turned into her own narrative situation, she manifests a richer sensuality. Titian's brush has moved closer to its role as tactile surrogate, giving us a lusher feast of flesh. Whether or not she makes the Venus of Urbino seem like a Theatine nun, Giovanni della Casa's comparison was hardly fortuitous. As X-radiography of the Naples canvas has revealed, Titian constructed this composition on the basis of the earlier design (Fig. 12). Beneath the final version we find the essential structure of the *Venus of Urbino,* recognized most notably in the background opening and the kneeling maid at the *cassone.*[48]

It was Titian's practice to preserve compositional inventions in this way, maintaining a record of a completed painting in the form of a newly begun canvas, blocked in (*abbozzata*), a sketch awaiting further realization.[49] In the course of realizing a second redaction, he might significantly modify it, and the old composition would evolve into a new variation of the theme. How far this particular canvas had evolved when della Casa saw it in 1544 is difficult to say, but we may imagine that it still acknowledged its origins in – if not as – the *Venus of Urbino,* thus inspiring the writer's salacious comparison. Titian brought the canvas *in medias res* to Rome, where he finished it in the studio provided for him in the Belvedere – the site of one of the great encounters of art history, according to Vasari: There Michelangelo visited the Venetian painter, saw the *Danae,* and upon leaving, offered his grudging praise of Titian along with his critique of painters in Venice.[50]

Whether or not Giovanni della Casa saw a composition already representing the rape of Danae in Titian's studio in Venice, it is clear from the final painting that the nude he did see was fully capable of being inflected into such a mythological narrative. Indeed, thanks both to della Casa's letter and to the confirming X-rays, we can follow just such a transformation: The receptive object of our attention, "la donna nuda" of the *Venus of Urbino,* becomes the more responsive objective of Jupiter's passion. That declension – from passive to active, from iconic to narrative – attests at once to the potentiality of meaning in such images, as the two related paintings in effect comment on and define one another.

"La donna nuda," we may say, exists as a foundational structure, a generic sign latent with a range of significance – from *una Venere mondana,* goddess of base passion, to the celestial deity of divine love. And the Neoplatonic hierarchy of Venuses articulated just such a range of possibilities. Indeed, the usefulness and appeal of the scheme lie precisely in its ability to accommodate that range of experience, from low bestial lust to the highest spiritual aspiration to union with the divine.

We need not ascribe to Titian any profound commitment to Neoplatonism to recognize how much he profited from the hermeneutic potential of the system. His long series of variations on the basic Giorgionesque invention of the reclining Venus may be read as a commentary on that potential (Fig. 13). While these later compositions, eventually including serenading courtiers, complicate the basic theme in fascinating ways, that complexity builds on the kinds of hierarchies and alternatives we have been discovering – between high and low values, communal and personal, the sacred and the profane, the licit and the libidinous.[51] Within the spread of these extremes lies what we may call the arena of interpretation: a hermeneutic space whose boundaries are defined by a complex of coordinates – historical, cultural, critical, phenomenological – a space filled with potential, latent with possibilities of meaning.

We can see, then, just how the *Venus of Urbino* functions within

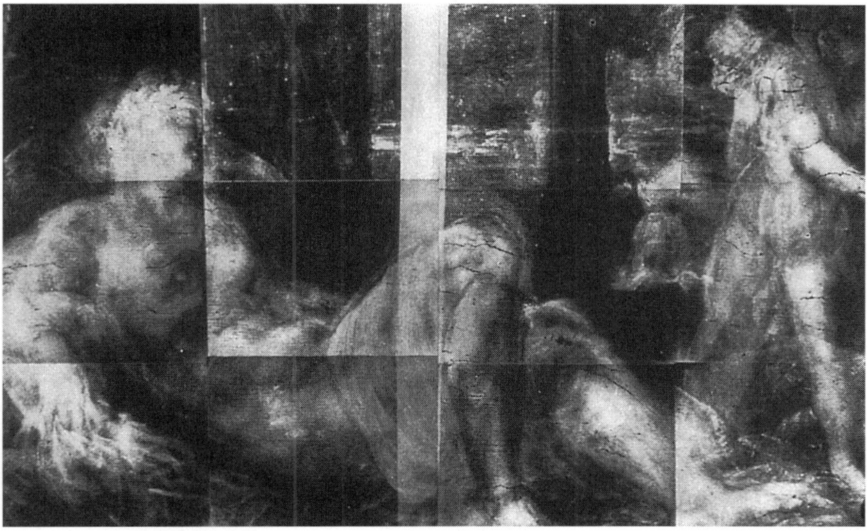

Figure 12. Titian, *Danae* (Farnese Danae), X- radiograph. From Ludovico Mucchi, "Radiografie di opere di Tiziano," *Arte veneta* 31 (1977).

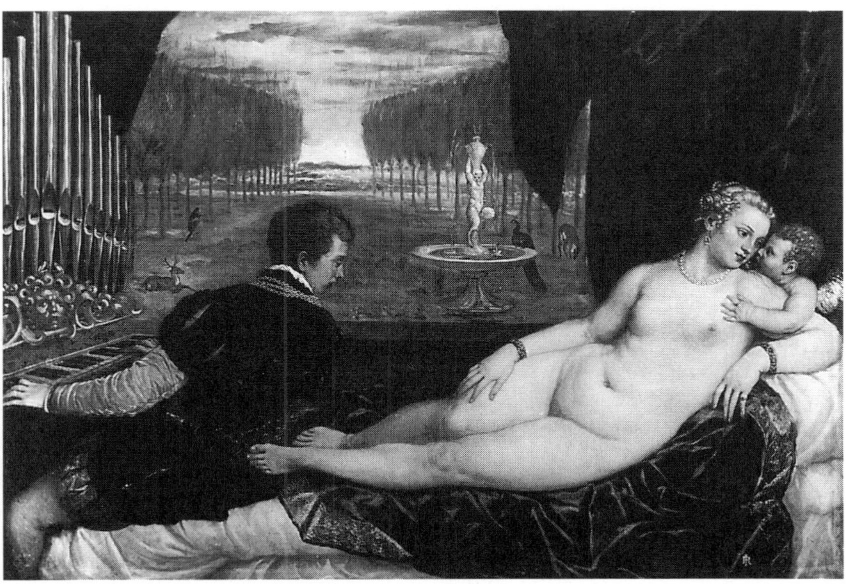

Figure 13. Titian, *Venus and Cupid with an Organist*. Madrid, Museo del Prado. Photo: Alinari/Art Resource.

such an arena, how it depends upon and exploits that potential. The picture operates on an equivocal scale of values, and from that very ambivalence derives its richness of experience. The image's direct appeal is blatant: a naked woman offering herself – Panofsky's "*primary* or *natural* subject matter." And yet she is clothed in cultural convention, as the disingenuously frustrated Mark Twain had to acknowledge. A nude woman, in painting, was seen as a Venus as easily and naturally as the lover or sonneteer saw his beloved as a Laura – and it is worth recalling that Vasari had no trouble in recognizing the divinity of Titian's naked lady ("una Venere giovanetta"). Generic expectation conditions vision and interpretation. This would be the second level of Panofsky's synoptical table: "*secondary* or *conventional* subject matter, constituting the world of *images, stories* and *allegories*."

VENEREAL HERMENEUTICS

But we are not dealing with a simple hermeneutic algebra of nude = Venus. In paintings like this one such elementary symbolic equations hardly do justice to the situation. This is no emblem; it is not in an allegorical mode – as is, for example, Bronzino's more obviously programmatic complex of Venus and Cupid with modifying attendants (Fig. 14).[52] Rather than a mystery to be unriddled, decoded, it represents an invitation to participation, an invitation that engages the imagination on several levels.[53] Indeed, it is out of the interplay of intellectual response and sexual fantasy, of social function and private satisfaction, that the possibilities of meaning in the *Venus of Urbino* emerge.

At the third and highest level of Panofsky's table the object of interpretation is "*intrinsic meaning* or *content,* constituting the world of *'symbolical' values.*" On this level we move beyond analysis to seek in "specific *themes* and *concepts*" the expression of "*essential tendencies of the human mind.*" We tend to assume that such iconological reach is upward, toward the higher spiritual level of a hierarchy, from the literal through the moral and allegorical to, finally, the anagogical sense. All of these senses are, of course, historically circumscribed.

Taking advantage of Panofsky's notion of "essential tendencies," however, I would like to suggest an additional, somewhat different

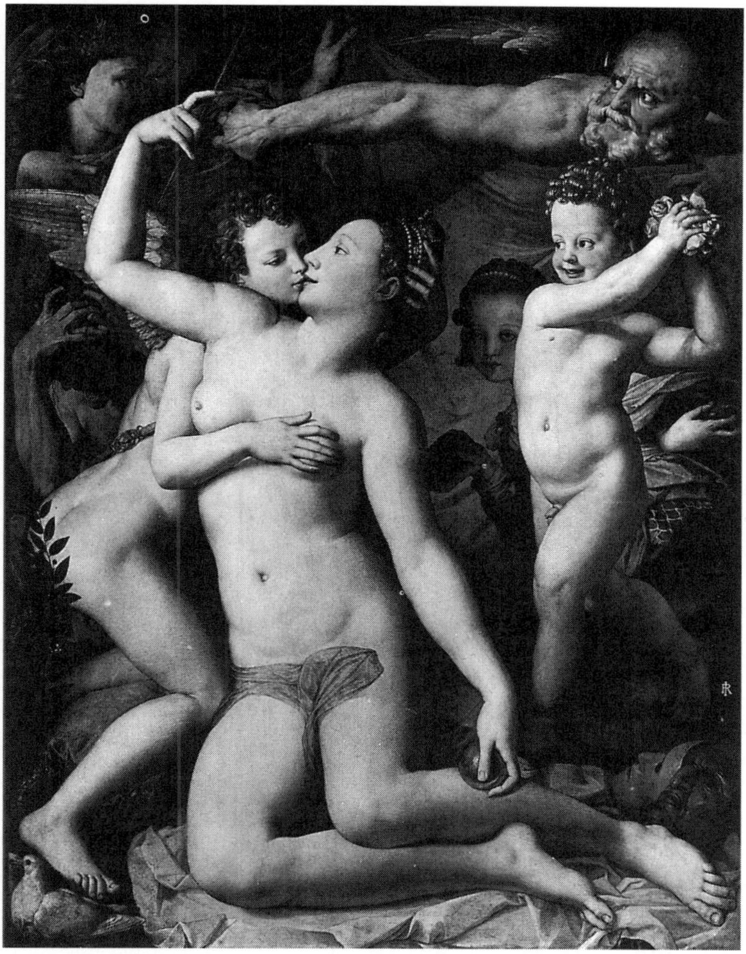

Figure 14. Agnolo Bronzino, *Allegory with Venus, Cupid, Folly, and Time.* London, National Gallery. Photo: Alinari/Art Resource.

dimension or direction for our search for meaning: toward the artist and the act of painting itself. What did it mean to Titian to paint such an image? Addressing that question, Paul Valéry could conclude: "When Titian arranges a purely carnal Venus, softly stretched out . . . in all the fullness of her perfection as goddess and subject for paint, it is obvious that, for him, to paint meant to caress, a conjunction of two voluptuous sensations in one supreme act in which self-mastery and mastery of his medium were identified with a masterful possession of the beauty herself in every sense."[54] Nor is this merely a twentieth-century perception imposed upon the past. We can recast it into more historical terms. One late-sixteenth-century witness describes the painter's total absorption in the human subjects of his art: "when he wanted to draw or paint some figure, and had before him a real woman or man, that object would so affect his sense of sight and his spirit would enter into what he was representing so that he seemed conscious of nothing else."[55] The concept itself is a Neoplatonic commonplace, involving especially the lover and the object of desire: "The lover is moved by the beloved object as the senses are by sensible objects; and they unite and become one and the same thing." That is the way it was formulated toward the beginning of the sixteenth century by Leonardo da Vinci, hardly a committed Platonist.[56]

Vision and desire, representation and possession: These are terms of a psychosexual dynamics of painting that we know best and acknowledge more readily in the art of a modern master like Picasso. But they are no less valid for picture-making in the past. The phenomenology of painting, the act of projecting another being onto canvas, implicates a level of meaning that must demand our attention. It is on this level that viewer and artist meet most directly, for we do assume, in some basic sense, that what we project into the image, or read out of it, is what the artist put into it. To ignore that encounter is to deny a fundamental dimension of meaning, that which is both historically based – in that it represents past moments of creation – and most essentially available to us.[57]

My title, "So-And-So Reclining on Her Couch," is taken from another text of our own time, by our most pictorial poet, Wallace Stevens. More completely and satisfying than Panofsky's platonizing synoptical table, Stevens's poem addresses the several dimensions of the hermeneutic situation – the reality and ideality of the image, the necessary intervention of the viewer, the absence and presence of its maker, being itself in the world of "things as they are" – and from their tensions and contradictions it defines the possibilities of response and interpretation. I recommend it to art historians in particular as a lecture with slides:

"So-And-So Reclining on Her Couch"

On her side, reclining on her elbow.
This mechanism, this apparition,
Suppose we call it Projection A.

She floats in air at the level of
The eye, completely anonymous,
Born, as she was, at twenty-one,

Without lineage or language, only
The curving of her hip, as motionless gesture,
Eyes dripping blue, so much to learn.

If just above her head there hung,
Suspended in air, the slightest crown
Of Gothic prong and practick bright,

The suspension, as in solid space,
The suspending hand withdrawn, would be
An invisible gesture. Let this be called

Projection B. To get at the thing
Without gestures is to get at it as
Idea. She floats in the contention, the flux

Between the thing as idea and
The idea as thing. She is half who made her.
This is the final Projection, C.

The arrangement contains the desire of
The artist. But one confides in what has no
Concealed creator. One walks easily

The unpainted shore, accepts the world
As anything but sculpture. Good-bye,
Mrs. Pappadopoulos, and thanks.[58]

NOTES

1. Wethey, *Titian* 3:203–4, cat. 54; Gregori et al., *Tiziano nelle gallerie fiorentine,* pp. 125–35, cat. 30, with further bibliography.
2. Cf., most recently, Freedberg, *Power of Images,* pp. 13–21 and passim.

3. Twain, *A Tramp Abroad,* p. 357.
4. In this respect, I wonder if Leo Steinberg, who properly notes the displacement of response in this passage, is not a bit too harsh in his indictment of the author of *Huckleberry Finn;* see "Art and Science," pp. 10–11.
5. On the topic in general, see Larivaille, *La vie quotidienne;* Lawner, *Lives;* and *Il gioco dell'amore.* See also Cozzi, "La donna, l'amore e Tiziano," pp. 47–63.
6. Cf. especially Hope, "Problems of Interpretation," pp. 117–20, and Ost, "Tizians sogenannte 'Venus von Urbino,' " pp. 129–49.
7. Crowe and Cavalcaselle, *Titian, His Life and Times* 1:389–90.
8. Ibid., pp. 390–1.
9. Reff, "Meaning of Titian's Venus of Urbino," pp. 359–66. On Manet's picture and the social problematics of interpretation, cf. Reff, *Manet: Olympia,* and Clark, *Painting of Modern Life,* pp. 77–146 (excerpted in the present volume).
10. Charles Hope's attempt to discredit any symbolic association of the attributes in the *Venus of Urbino* seems arbitrary and forced, and historically naive ("Problems of Interpretation," p. 118). The same floral attributes, myrtle and roses, plus a fertilizing Cupid, characterize Venus in another epithalamic painting, a remarkable picture by Lorenzo Lotto recently acquired by the Metropolitan Museum of Art in New York (Fig. 11). Instead of the dog, clinging ivy around the tree behind Venus symbolizes commitment and fidelity. See Christiansen, "Lorenzo Lotto and the Tradition of Epithalamic Paintings," pp. 166–73.
11. Vasari, 7:443: "una Venere giovanetta a giacere, con fiori e certi panni sottili attorno molto belli e ben finiti."
12. Ticozzi, *Vita dei pittori Vecellj di Cadore,* pp. 168–9: "vanno da un cassone traendo le vesti che devono nascondere ai profani sguardi tanta beltà."
13. For readings of Botticelli's picture in a Neoplatonic key, cf. Wind, *Pagan Mysteries,* pp. 128–40, and Gombrich, "Botticelli's Mythologies," pp. 72–5.
14. Gronau, *Documenti artistici urbinati,* p. 93, doc. XXXI.
15. Ibid., p. 93, docs. XXXII, XXXIII.
16. Ibid., p. 94, docs. XXXV, XXXVI.
17. The immediately subsequent correspondence indicates that Guidobaldo continued to have difficulties paying Titian for pictures; see, in particular, his letter of July 30, 1539 (Gronau, *Documenti,* p. 95, doc. XLII).
18. These objections have been voiced most forcefully by Hope, "Problems of Interpretation," pp. 117–20.
19. Lermolieff [Morelli], *Kunstkritische Studien,* p. 289. *Liebesbilder* are "love pictures" (editor's note).
20. "La tela della Venere nuda, che dorme in uno paese cun Cupidine, fu de

mano de Zorzo da Castelfranco; ma lo paese e Cupidine furono finiti da Tiziano" (Michiel, *Notizia,* p. 169). Further on the picture: Pignatti, *Giorgione,* pp. 111–12, cat. 23.

21. Anderson, "Giorgione, Titian and the Sleeping Venus," pp. 337–42.
22. The other notable example is *The Three Philosophers* in Vienna (Pignatti, *Giorgione,* pp. 107–8, cat.. 19). Describing the canvas in the house of Taddeo Contarini in 1525, Michiel observes that it was begun by Giorgione and finished by Sebastiano del Piombo (*Notizia,* pp. 164–5).
23. For the moment I pass over alternative reconstructions of the situation, such as that suggested by Anderson: namely, that Titian (then presumably not more than nineteen years old) was called in to assist Giorgione because the older master had his hands full with official commissions in 1507.
24. These recumbent female nudes were usually paired with male counterparts; see Schubring, *Cassoni,* nos. 156, 157, 184, 185, 289, 290. We observe the conflation of these couples into single horizontal fields in late Quattrocento images such as Botticelli's *Mars and Venus* (London, National Gallery of Art) and the similar composition by Piero di Cosimo (Berlin-Dahlem, Staatliche Museen), which may indeed be marriage pictures; see Gombrich, "Botticelli's Mythologies," pp. 66–9; also Wind, *Pagan Mysteries,* pp. 89–91. Further on *cassoni* paintings, see Gombrich, "Apollonio di Giovanni," pp. 11–28; Callmann, *Apollonio di Giovanni;* Witthoft, "Marriage Rituals," pp. 43–59.
25. See Wethey 3:175–9, cat. 33.
26. For the details of this politically complicated union, see Wethey 3:177 and, more fully, Goffen's essays "Titian's *Sacred and Profane Love* and Marriage" and "Titian's *Sacred and Profane Love:* Individuality and Sexuality."
27. Panofsky addressed the picture several times in the course of his career: *Hercules am Scheidewege,* pp. 173–80; *Studies in Iconology,* pp. 150–60; *Problems in Titian,* pp. 110–19.
28. Cf. Hope, "Problems in Interpretation," pp. 115–17, and *Titian,* pp. 34–6; also Fry, "In Detail: Titian's *Sacred and Profane Love,*" pp. 34–9.
29. For a corrective as well as the most satisfying reading of the social conditions and construct of this painting, see Goffen's essay in this volume.
30. I have commented on the implications of the essential dialogic structure of the composition and the significance of that structure as a guide to meaning – the two beauties standing to each other as terms of an equation – in Rosand, "Panofsky, Tiziano e le strutture pittoriche."
31. Gombrich, "Introduction: Aims and Limits of Iconology," p. 5.
32. Wethey 3:154–6, cat. 17; also Rosand, *Titian,* p. 82, pl. 11.
33. The nature of the problem is manifest in the equivocal commentary in Campbell, *Renaissance Portraits,* pp. 6–7 and pl. 17. For fuller consider-

ation, see Anderson, "Giorgionesque Portrait," pp. 153–8. On the character herself, see Held, "Flora, Goddess and Courtesan," pp. 201–18.

34. Crowe and Cavalcaselle, *Titian* 1:391. "Un quadro de fantasia" is how the imperial ambassador described a painting Titian executed for Charles V in 1545, presumably the "figura di Venere" mentioned by Titian himself in a letter of December 8, 1545 (Wethey, *Titian* 3:197). On Palma's "molti ritratti di Dame con ornamenti e vesti all'antica," "many portraits of ladies with ornaments and garments in the ancient manner" (Ridolfi), see Rylands, *Palma Vecchio,* pp. 89–110.
35. Bellini's painting is discussed, with specific reference to its sensuous appeal and in the context of Titian's art, by Goffen, *Giovanni Bellini,* pp. 252–7.
36. Panofsky, *Studies in Iconology,* pp. 14–15 – slightly modified in idem, "Iconography and Iconology," pp. 40–1. For further comment on the hierarchy of this interpretive scale, see my forthcoming paper, as in note 30.
37. Crowe and Cavalcaselle, *Titian* 1:271.
38. Hope, "Problems in Interpretation," p. 119.
39. Michiel, *Notizia,* p. 160.
40. "Ubi uxoribus conveniant, nonnisi dignissimos hominum et formosissimos vultus pingas monent; plurimum enim habere id momenti ad conceptus matronarum et futuram spetiem prolis ferunt" (Alberti, *De re aedificatoria* IX.iv, vol. 2: 805). The English translation is from Alberti, *On the Art of Building,* p. 299. The two sixteenth-century Italian translations are worth quoting for their directness: "Ammoniscono che si dipingano belle faccie de huomini ove concorrono le mogli con li mariti à generare. Il che molto importa che le matrone faccino belli figliuoli" (*I Dieci libri de l'architettura,* Venice, 1546, p. 200). "Ma nelle camere dove i padri delle famiglie hanno a dormire con le lor' moglie, avertiscasi che non vi si dipinga se non volti di huomini, o di Donne bellissimi, & honorati, & dicono che questo importa grandemente quanto allo ingravidare, delle Matrone, & quanto alla bellezza della futura progenie" (*L'Architettura,* Florence, 1550, p. 334).
41. Mancini, *Considerazioni sulla pittura* 1:143; translation in Freedberg, *Power of Images,* p. 3, who cites similar passages back through Saint Augustine to the ancient medical writer Solinus.
42. In a letter of 1864, Swinburne anticipated the American's response, but with less ambivalent enthusiasm: "As for Titian's Venus – Sappho and Anactoria in one – four lazy fingers buried dans les fleurs de son jardin – how any creature can be decently virtuous within thirty miles of it passes my comprehension." The passage is cited by Freedberg, *Power of Images,* p. 345.

43. For a sensitive structural analysis of the picture, see Arasse, *Tiziano: Venere d'Urbino*.
44. Goffen, "Renaissance Dreams," pp. 683–706, esp. pp. 697–701. Observing that Giorgione's Venus "denotes not the act of love but the recollection of it," S. J. Freedberg then suggested, in a note, "that this is the interpretation of Giorgione's placing of the left hand, quite different in meaning from its presumable antique source in the *Venus Pudica* type" (*Painting in Italy,* p. 85 and p. 476*n*25).
45. Hope, "Problems in Interpretation," p. 118.
46. Della Casa: "ha presso che fornita, per commession di Vostra Signoria Reverendissima, una nuda, che faria venir il diavol adosso al Cardinale San Sylvestro; et quella che Vostra Signoria Reverendissima vide in Pesaro nelle Camere del Signor Duca d'Urbino è una teatina appresso a questa; et vole appicciarle la testa della sopradetta cognata, pur che'l benefitio venga. Verrà a Roma et per tutto, et non è giuocco sì strano, che non sia per farlo, e petitione di questo benefitio. Et senza burla, è valente persona et affettionatissima servitore di Nostro Signore et di Vostra Signoria Reverendissima, et io glielo raccomando quanto posso più efficacemente." The letter was republished and discussed by Hope, "Neglected Document," pp. 188–9.
47. Wethey 3:132–3, cat. 5.
48. The X-rays were taken and published by Mucchi, "Radiografie," pp. 297–304. Mucchi did not recognize the relationship of the Naples *Danae* to the *Venus of Urbino,* and the significance of his X-radiography has unfortunately gone unnoticed; cf. the entry on the painting in the recent exhibition catalog, *Titian,* pp. 267–9, cat. 40, which fails even to mention Mucchi's publication.
49. See the still fundamental study of Titian's workshop practices by Tietze-Conrat, "Titian's Workshop," pp. 76–88.
50. Vasari 7:447. Tietze, "Early Version of Titian's Danae," pp. 199–208, suggested that Titian carried an unfinished canvas with him to Rome to be brought to completion there; although his attribution in this particular case is unconvincing, Tietze's intuition regarding Titian's practice has proved quite accurate.
51. I have commented on the motives and implications of Titian's thematic variations in "*Ermeneutica Amorosa:* Observations on the Interpretation of Titian's Venuses," pp. 375–81; for a different reading of the situation, cf. Hope, "Problems in Interpretation," pp. 111–24.
52. On Bronzino's picture, see Panofsky, *Studies in Iconology,* pp. 86–91; cf. also Levey, "Sacred and Profane Significance," pp. 30–3, as well as the most recent interpretive contributions: Cheney, "Bronzino's London *Allegory,*" pp. 12–18; Bosch, "Bronzino's London *Allegory,*" pp. 30–5;

and Barolsky and Ladis, "The 'Pleasure of Deceits,' " pp. 32–6 – whose "ludic" reading of the picture still depends on its composite structure of visual and literary conceit.

53. Our task is not a "game of unriddling the mysteries of the past," as Gombrich formulates it in his essay on "Aims and Limits of Iconology" (in *Symbolic Images,* p. 21). Rejecting the very idea of levels of meaning, Gombrich would restrict us to a search for a presumed "dominant meaning, the intended meaning or principal purpose of the picture" (pp. 15–16).

54. Valéry, "The Nude," p. 48.

55. Persio, *Trattato dell'ingegno dell'huomo,* p. 98: "[il] gran Titiano padre del colorire; il qual, secondo ho udito di sua bocca, & di quegli cho sono ritrovati presenti a' suoi lavori, quando volea disegnare o colorir alcuna figura, tenendo avanti una donna o un huomo naturale, cotal oggetto cosi movea la vista corporale di lui, & il suo spirito cosi penetrava nell'oggetto di chi ritirava, che facendo vista di non sentire altra cosa, che quella, veniva a parere a' circostanti d'esser andato in ispirito." We owe our awareness of this important passage to Hope, "Problems of Interpretation," p. 170.

56. Richter, *Literary Works of Leonardo* 2:249, no. 1202.

57. I have discussed some of these issues in *Meaning of the Mark.*

58. *Collected Poems of Wallace Stevens,* pp. 195–6. Copyright 1947 by Wallace Stevens. Reprinted by permission of Alfred A. Knopf, Inc.

3 RONA GOFFEN

SEX, SPACE, AND SOCIAL HISTORY IN TITIAN'S *VENUS OF URBINO*

Because human biology is unchanged between Titian's time and our own, art historians have often assumed that sexual behavior is likewise immutable, and that the comportment of Titian's people (especially his women) is understandable in terms of modern expectations. But "much of what we take to be natural," as semioticians remind us, "is in fact cultural" – and that includes Titian's perceptions of sexuality.[1] Whatever else may have changed between Titian's time and our own, however, two things have remained the same: Men and women still get married; and when they can afford to do so, they commemorate the event with pictures. All modern wedding photos are essentially the same; they fulfill societal expectations precisely by reiterating the expected pattern. But the disparity of Renaissance wedding pictures is such that almost no two seem alike, and often as not, this appears to have been due as much to the patrons' wishes as to the artist's imagination.

Titian's *Sacred and Profane Love* is a case in point, a marriage picture that resembles no other example of its genre (Fig. 9).[2] Titian was commissioned to paint the canvas around 1514, to honor the wedding of the Paduan noblewoman Laura Bagarotto and the future grand chancellor of Venice, Nicolò Aurelio. The *Sacred and Profane Love* is identified as a marriage picture by the costume of the so-called Profane Love, traditional for a Veneto

A slightly different version of this essay was first published as "The Problematic Patronage of Titian's *Venus of Urbino*" in the *Journal of Medieval and Renaissance Studies* 24 (1994).

bride: white gown, belt, gloves, roses, the myrtle wreath (*myrtus coniugalis*), and hair loose on the shoulders. Her red sleeve and slipper are also appropriate, red being another bridal color in Renaissance Venice, particularly among the nobility. (The dress was originally red, overpainted white by Titian.)[3] The same marital context also explains her lidded vessel: Sixteenth-century Venetian brides received symbolic wedding gifts in such silver caskets.[4]

If Titian indeed replicated the bride's gift and her gown, did he also portray their owner? Although some art historians see a likeness here, I suggest that this idealized beauty is not a portrait in the sense of a purposeful record of individual appearance – or at least not the appearance of Laura Bagarotto. The nameless woman who actually posed for the *Sacred and Profane Love* also posed for the *Flora* of about 1515 in Florence (Fig. 7), and the same generic, Titianesque type had already appeared in the Paduan *Miracle of the Speaking Infant* of 1511.[5] If it were the bride herself whom we see clothed, moreover, it would also be the bride whom we see nude; and this seems unthinkable in light of sixteenth-century Venetian mores. When a bride is shown nude in Renaissance marriage pictures, she is generally represented by a "body double," a model or an ideal of the artist's imagination, not an actual likeness of the bride herself.[6]

The woman commonly known as "Profane Love" is then more appropriately called a bride, but the traditional name for the nude is in fact correct. As her antique lamp confirms, she is "Sacred" or "Celestial Love."[7] These two figures represent the same individual, albeit in different conditions or states of being. As bride, crowned with myrtle, she holds Venus's roses and the gift presented by her husband at their marriage; and as wife, nude yet chaste, she turns to the bride as though to exhort her(self) to the Love symbolized by her lamp. Even without this traditional attribute, however, the purity of Sacred Love is evident in every aspect of her appearance and demeanor, whereas her companion could seem wanton to a modern viewer unaware that she is gowned as a bride, hence chaste by definition, this virtue being foremost in any Renaissance recitation of her desired qualities.[8] Nonetheless, to a modern observer, it may seem that one is asked to take this bride's chastity on good faith, because Titian has made her sexy while apparently doing nothing to reassure us about her virtue. But this interpretation ignores the historical and cultural context of sex and sexuality; in other words, it assumes that behavior is natural and hence unchanging, that Titian's understanding of sexual matters was the same as our own. And that is untrue, as the *Sacred and Profane Love* demonstrates.

For Titian, female chastity and sexuality are not antagonistic but sympathetic, interactive aspects of the bride's character. Visualization of the bride's sexuality is tantamount to her empowerment as a female, and Titian magnifies this power by two means: her posture, a vigorous seated *contrapposto,* and her forceful glance. Her addressing the beholder – namely, her husband – directly in this way is neither brazen nor submissive, as historians have assumed. On the contrary, believing in the magic of images – that images may hear, speak, and see – Renaissance people understood that such a glance suggests reciprocation, here signifying marital consent and love communicated through sight because the eyes are the windows of the soul.

Although the image addresses him, however, the husband himself is absent, and the only male figure is a winged boy. The putto (or Cupid himself) encourages the water to flow from the metal spout that has transformed an ancient sarcophagus into a fount, and the spout is adjacent to the new husband's coat of arms. The general sexual significance of all this is particularly appropriate to the wedding commemorated here, the first marriage for the groom but the second for his bride. The sarcophagus-fountain commutes the sterility of her widowhood into the fecundity of remarriage, a theme reiterated by the preternaturally large rabbits in the landscape behind her.

What the *Sacred and Profane Love* demonstrates, then, is that sexy women and more or less overt allusions to sexual reproduction may be represented in a Renaissance marriage picture; that a woman's glance may assert her awareness and individuality while expressing love of her beholder; that a bride may even be shown nude, although she is likely to be impersonated by a "body double"; and that such models may indeed represent brides in their marriage pictures, whether clothed or nude. In other words, a Renaissance woman's wedding picture need not represent her own features, and it certainly need not conform to twentieth-century standards of bridal decorum.

Lorenzo Lotto's *Venus and Cupid* of the 1520s in the Metropolitan Museum is identified as a bride by her veil and crown, and her fecundity is visualized by the remarkably carnal shell suspended above her (Fig. 11). Cupid leers at her while ejaculating or urinating, which is its symbolic equivalent, taking aim so that the liquid penetrates a marriage wreath: Procreation is thus literally enframed by matrimony.[9] Representing the bride as Venus, Lotto evokes a dual tradition. The identification of the beloved with the goddess of love is a trope familiar from ancient times. Less familiar to us, however, although a commonplace in the Renaissance, is the evocation of the ancient goddess in medical texts on human reproduction.[10] In other words, both poets and gynecologists cite Venus, and in this regard, Lotto's imagery, which startles modern viewers, is consistent with sixteenth-century perceptions of marital love and generation. It is, of course, unthinkable that a modern couple would publicize their marriage in such a way – or even with the comparatively tame *Sacred and Profane Love;* unthinkable that the *New York Times* would publish either picture among its wedding announcements. But what Titian and his contemporaries took to be natural in their marriage imagery we recognize to be cultural.

As we have seen, the heroines of the *Sacred and Profane Love* and Lotto's *Venus and Cupid* are identified as brides by their garments, including Venus's bridal crown and veil. Even today brides are often identifiable by their dress, but otherwise, a contemporary woman's marital status is not apparent from her clothing. A medieval or Renaissance woman's marriage, on the contrary, would be marked by her acquisition of a wardrobe reflecting her change of status from maiden to matron and her transition from her father's household to that of her husband. Part of the financial settlement of a marriage typically earmarked funds for this worthy purpose.[11] A woman's clothing was thus specifically associated with matrimony in medieval and Renaissance Italy, from the beginning of her marriage to its end, when her husband's kinsmen were expected to provide her widow's weeds, while also possibly confiscating what was left of her *corredo* or trousseau as part of the estate. (A Renaissance man's dress, on the contrary, was determined by age or office but was unrelated to his marital status.)

This bridal context explains one of the most idiosyncratic details of Titian's *Venus of Urbino,* consigned to Duke Guidobaldo II della Rovere of Urbino in 1538: the two servants who are either remov-

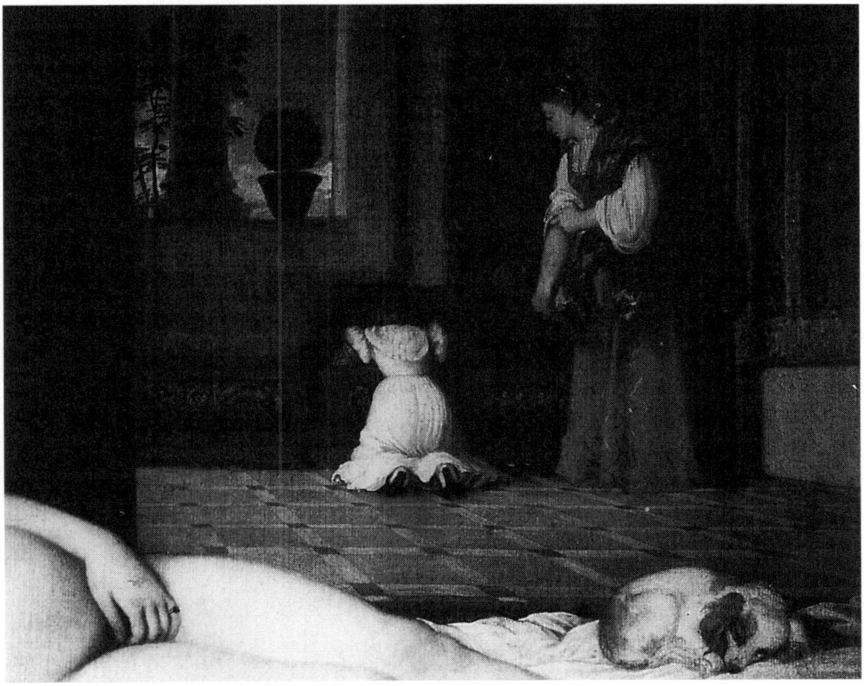

Figure 15. Titian, *Venus of Urbino,* detail of background. Photo: Scala/Art Resource.

ing or replacing a gown in a *cassone* or greatchest (Figs. 1, 8, 15).[12] That is, I suggest that Venus's garment implies her *corredo.* Similarly, the *cassone,* or rather the two *cassoni* – because these greatchests were always made in pairs – also refer to matrimony. *Cassoni* were traditionally commissioned by the bridegroom or his kinsmen on the occasion of his wedding and were intended for the storage of clothing, particularly his wife's trousseau.[13] To be sure, unmarried women, including courtesans, also had to put their clothing somewhere – but evidently not in *cassoni.* The detailed inventories of the estate of the "sumptuous courtesan" Julia Lombardo, compiled in Venice in 1542, list numerous storage chests of various dimensions – "casse, casele, casselete," for example – but no *cassoni,* and (more to the point) there are no matched pairs among the specified chests.[14] Titian's twin *cassoni* are then purposeful signifiers, to be understood as signs of matrimony, the furniture equivalent of the bouquet of roses and the myrtle plant, plants that were then and still remain familiar bridal attributes, used as such also in the *Sacred and Profane Love* and in Lotto's wedding picture.[15]

To these various references to marriage we may add the dog that dozes at Venus's feet. Surely this is "Fido," unless Titian was being uncharacteristically perverse in all this matrimonial iconography. Such a dog may sleep because the person who has just entered is not an intruder, he is the master of this household.[16] And the dog himself suggests that the household in question was indeed that of the duchy of Urbino, for the same spaniel (or a littermate) dozes on the table next to Eleonora Gonzaga della Rovere, the duke's mother, in Titian's portrait of 1536–8.[17] To be sure, no one can say to whom Fido belonged – whether he was actually a household pet of the della Rovere court(s) or Titian's own puppy, readily available to pose. But I think one can say with some certainty that Titian would not have been so gauche as to represent the duchess's painted canine companion in another composition for the same household if it could be considered inappropriate and offensive to do so. Surely Titian, by the 1530s an experienced courtier, would have been incapable of such an impropriety. Even were the dog his own and not the della Rovere's pet, its dozing in two works meant for the same household implies some connection between them. Evidently Venus's household is also located in the duchy of Urbino.[18]

Despite these various referents, however, most scholarship calls the *Venus* "pornography for the elite," as Orest Ranum and others would have it, a courtesan whose impersonation of the goddess "fooled no one."[19] But given all the accoutrements of matrimony, why this stubborn modern reluctance to recognize Titian's protagonist as a bridal Venus? The answer lies in the figure of Venus herself, for unlike the nude *Sacred Love,* her characterization apparently belies all the inanimate references to marriage and indeed to her own divinity, overwhelming their mute testimony with her own potent sexuality. Simply put, this woman seems far too sexy to be chaste.

Titian's heroine lacks classical propriety, the demeanor expected (by modern critics, at least) of an ancient goddess. In particular, her alert intelligence may seem inimical to divinity and, for that matter, to chastity (Fig. 16). Renaissance people, however, did not necessar-

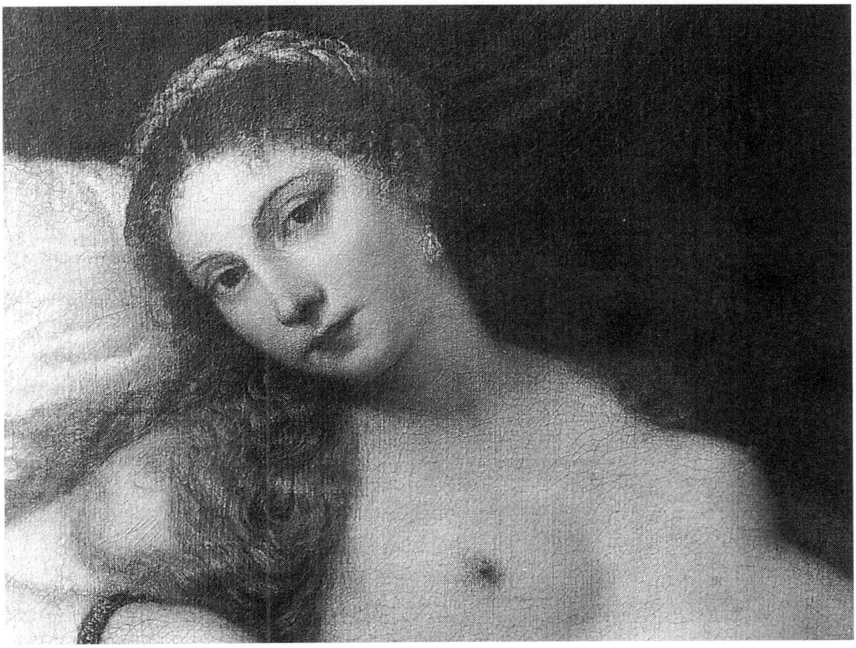

Figure 16. Titian, *Venus of Urbino,* detail of face. Photo: Alinari/Art Resource.

ily share the modern assumption that Venus must be diffident to retain her divinity. Botticelli's Venus, for example, remains entirely alert while Mars sleeps, overcome by their recent sexual encounter (Fig. 17).[20] That these mythological beings obey common laws of human biology does not in the least deprive them of their classical identities. Not coincidentally, this painting has been identified as a marriage picture – and the composition alludes to yet another marriage picture, Aëtion's lost *Nuptials of Alexander and Roxana,* known to the Renaissance through Lucian's ekphrasis in the *Herodotus.*[21] To be sure, the Florentine Venus does not look at us; she turns her eyes toward her beloved – which is precisely the dynamic of Titian's *Venus,* although now the object of the goddess's desire is before her, not within the picture. We have seen that the bride of the *Sacred and Profane Love* addresses her beholder with comparable forthrightness. Although books on comportment might counsel ladies to look down, Titian's women offer different advice, appro-

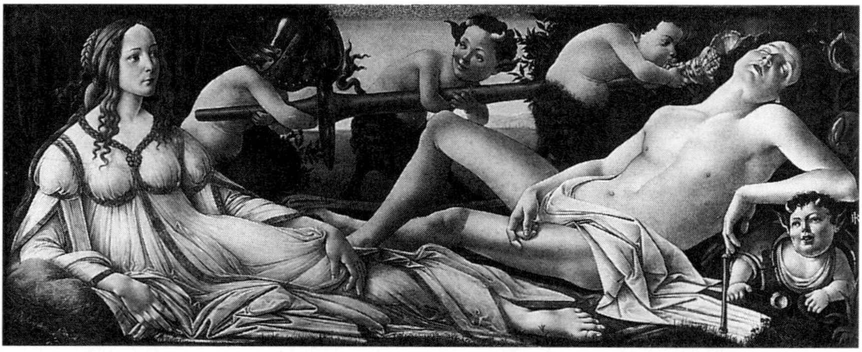

Figure 17. Sandro Botticelli, *Venus and Mars*. London, National Gallery. Photo: Alinari/Art Resource.

priate to the conception of matrimonial consent.[22] To be sure, their gazes may also be characterized as "unambiguous sexual invitation," as one art historian would have it,[23] but the invitation is germane to the matrimonial context and in no way promiscuous. The critics' presumption of impropriety is a misconception that Manet's *Olympia* popularized (Fig. 2).[24]

When Edouard Manet transformed the *Venus of Urbino* into the *Olympia* (1863), he did more than rename her; he also redefined his subject's morality. Even without seeing the painting, French people could understand this from the title alone, "Olympia" being a traditional name of ill repute. Manet's protagonist is undeniably a prostitute. Available to all comers and surrounded by explicit references to her trade, Olympia receives her next customer – by implication, the beholder. But is this true of her Venetian predecessor? In a domestic setting and without Cupid or other explicitly mythological paraphernalia, let us grant for the moment that she may be a goddess or a mortal. If mortal, and even if a courtesan or mistress, she is presented with clear indications of social status – pearls, two servants, a gown, the dog, and a well-furnished bedchamber – not an isolated, rumpled bed, a hissing cat, and a maid with the unseen intruder's floral offering. And these trappings confirm what each woman reveals about herself in her expression and gestures: Olympia is cynical, reluctant, exhausted; Titian's woman is confident, intelligent, alert – and welcoming. To see the *Olympia* as "the

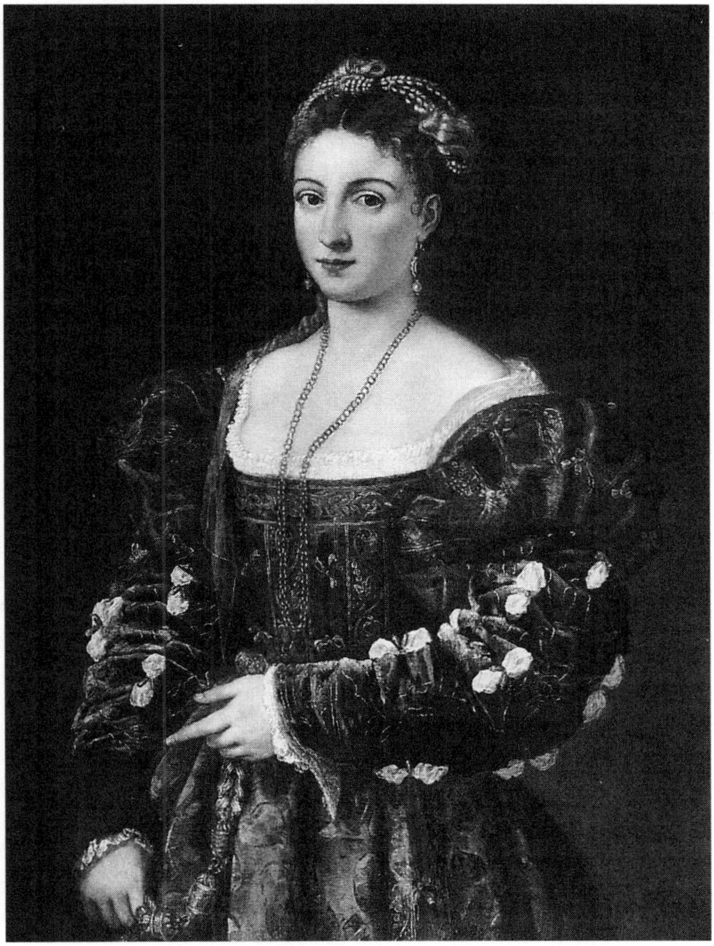

Figure 18. Titian, *La Bella.* Florence, Galleria degli Uffizi. Photo: Alinari/Art Resource.

closest parallel to" Titian's *Venus,* as Charles Hope suggests, is to ignore 400 years of social history and of art history.[25]

Looking closer to home in order to explain Venus's seeming lack of classical propriety, scholars have also observed that the same model appears in another painting acquired in 1536 by the duke's father: Titian's *La Bella,* described in Urbinate sources as the "woman in a blue dress" (Fig. 18).[26] The painting was acquired by

Francesco Maria della Rovere in 1536, two years before the *Venus* was dispatched to his son and successor, Duke Guidobaldo. The critics' implication is that her reappearance in the *Venus of Urbino* somehow demonstrates her immorality or at least her mortality. This reasoning is specious. The anonymous woman's representation in *La Bella* and in other works of the mid-1530s, such as the Vienna *Woman with Fur,* is clearly unrelated to the meaning of any of these compositions.[27] Rather, it is nothing more than testimony to her having been employed by Titian as a model during those years – just as he had employed another anonymous beauty some twenty years earlier to pose for the *Sacred and Profane Love,* the *Flora,* and the mother of the *Speaking Infant.* The actual identities of these models have been lost to history, although they may well have been prostitutes, given that such women often combined modeling with the oldest profession; and for all we know, they may indeed have been employed by Titian also in this sense. But even were that the case, it is not germane to their characterization in art. In Titian's art, the anonymous beauty becomes a mythic being; she becomes Sacred and Profane Love or Venus herself; or indeed she becomes, as Elizabeth Cropper has suggested in another context, the very embodiment of beauty, the beautiful woman as the synecdoche of beautiful art, as in the aptly named *Bella.*[28] And in this process, her historical identity is taken from her: Her own biography is irrelevant.

Admittedly, there does seem to be some basis in historical fact for the modern critic's skepticism regarding the character of Titian's protagonist. The trouble starts with the first owner of Titian's masterpiece, Guidobaldo II della Rovere, who referred to the painting as "la donna nuda," "the nude woman," in letters of March 9 and May 1, 1538, to his ambassador in Venice, Gian Giacomo Leonardi.[29] Most art historians have taken the duke's terse phrase to be a definition of Titian's subject, and they see confirmation in the woman's bold demeanor. But just as there is another way to interpret her glance, there is also another way to read this text, and that is with the realization that della Rovere needed only a two-word reference to identify the painting to his agent. Indeed, della Rovere's pithiness is characteristic of such informal letter writing and of many contemporary legal documents (such as contracts and inventories), which are more concise than precise in their references to art in part because both reader and writer could refer to the object itself. Not every contemporary observer, moreover, was so succint as the duke. For Giorgio Vasari, who saw Titian's painting in the *guardaroba,* a room (or rooms) in the ducal apartments of Guidobaldo's palace at Pesaro, the subject was in fact a "young Venus, reclining, with flowers and certain fine fabrics around [her], [which are] very beautiful and well finished."[30] Whereas the duke had mentioned the painting only briefly in order to instruct his agent, Vasari was providing a professional's description of Titian's work in a published biography addressed to a cultivated audience. To be sure, each writer was correct in describing Titian's subject: She is both a "nude woman" and "a young Venus" – the one being tantamount to a pithy yet accurate account of the other. But as a fellow artist's description of Titian's composition, Vasari's title has particular authority. Yet in the absence of Cupid and other traditional mythological accoutrements, what made Vasari think that *this* woman is Venus? The answer is that for Vasari, as for other informed viewers, confirmation of her identity is found primarily in her pose – a pose adapted from Giorgione's *Sleeping Venus* (Fig. 3).

More than twenty-five years separate Giorgione's invention from Titian's emendation, and he changed the prototype in two conspicuous ways: *Venus* is now indoors, and she is awake. Asleep, Giorgione's Venus seems demure in comparison with Titian's sentient, responsive heroine. As we have seen, that is one reason why critics believe in the divinity of the former while doubting that of the latter. The other reason is the presence of Cupid, painted out in 1843 and now visible only in X-ray (Fig. 19).[31]

Giorgione's Cupid and the landscape were "finished by Titian," as we know from Marcantonio Michiel's contemporary description; and it seems that it too was a marriage picture, commissioned by the Venetian nobleman Girolamo Marcello to honor his marriage in 1507.[32] Giorgione conflated two or three ancient types in the *Dresden Venus,* combining the modest or *pudica* gesture invented for a standing Venus and the sleeping posture of classical characters, reclining with one arm flung over the head (e.g., the Vatican *Ariadne*). While the action of the right arm to indicate sleep was employed for numerous figures in ancient and Renaissance art, however, the *pudica* gesture of the left arm was more restricted in

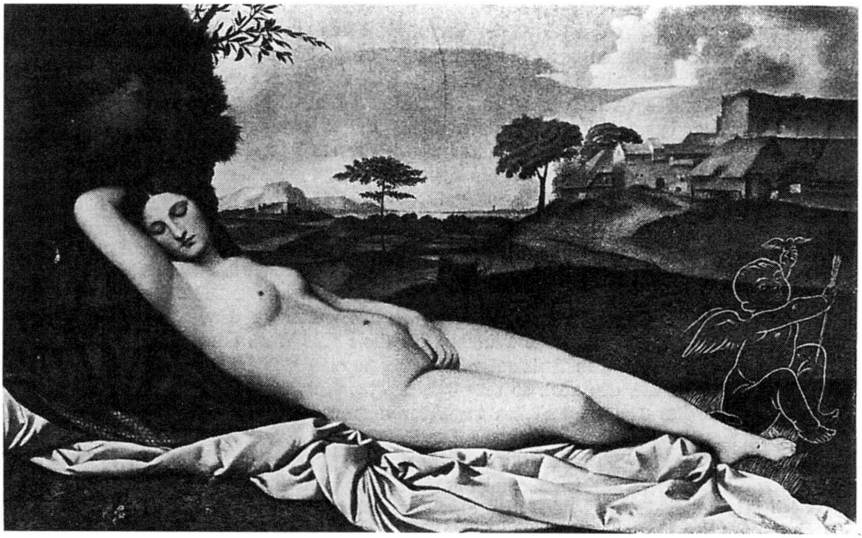

Figure 19. Giorgione, *Sleeping Venus,* Reconstruction based on X-radiograph. Photo: Venice, Museo Civico Correr.

its use, perhaps because this gesture had a name and a history. As readers of Pliny know, the pose was conceived by Praxiteles for the *Aphrodite of Cnidos* (Fig. 4). Supposedly surprised by a worshiper as she steps from her bath – the statue was apparently set in a pool of water – the goddess conceals herself as best she can, placing one arm across her breast and the other over her pudenda: She is literally modest or ashamed (*pudica*) but provocative at the same time.[33]

Ever since Praxiteles's day, his invention has been associated primarily with Venus, as in Botticelli's *Birth of Venus* – although not exclusively with her, as we shall see. Giovanni Bellini, whose brother Gentile owned an antique *Venus,* adapted the pose for his seated *Nude with Mirror* (Fig. 5).[34] Her identity is uncertain for some of the same reasons that confuse us about Titian's *Venus of Urbino,* namely, the absence of traditional mythological attributes – unless we count the mirrors as such – combined with the explicit modernity of her setting. In this regard, Bellini's *Nude,* signed and dated 1515, is the primary antecedent of Titian's conception. Significantly, it too was most likely a marriage picture: Suffice it to say

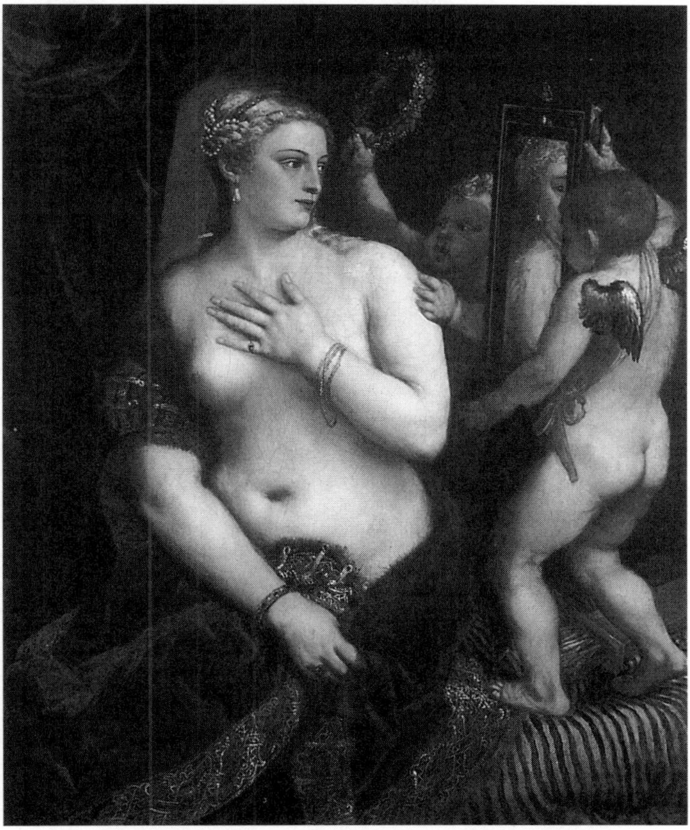

Figure 20. Titian, *Venus with the Mirror.* Washington, D.C., National Gallery of Art, Andrew W. Mellon Collection. Photo: National Gallery of Art, Washington, D.C.

that her snood is the kind of head covering worn only by married women in Renaissance Venice.[35]

Like Bellini, Titian also adapted the *pudica* pose for half-length figures – for example, the repentent, hence modest, *Mary Magdalen* now in the Pitti. This is evidently the Magdalen that Vasari admired in the *guardaroba* of the duke of Urbino in Pesaro, where the *Venus of Urbino* was likewise displayed.[36] Titian repeated the pose for half-length nude or partially nude beautiful women, such as the Washington *Venus with a Mirror,* painted about 1555 (Figs. 20, 21).[37] But more significant in relation to Titian's understanding of the

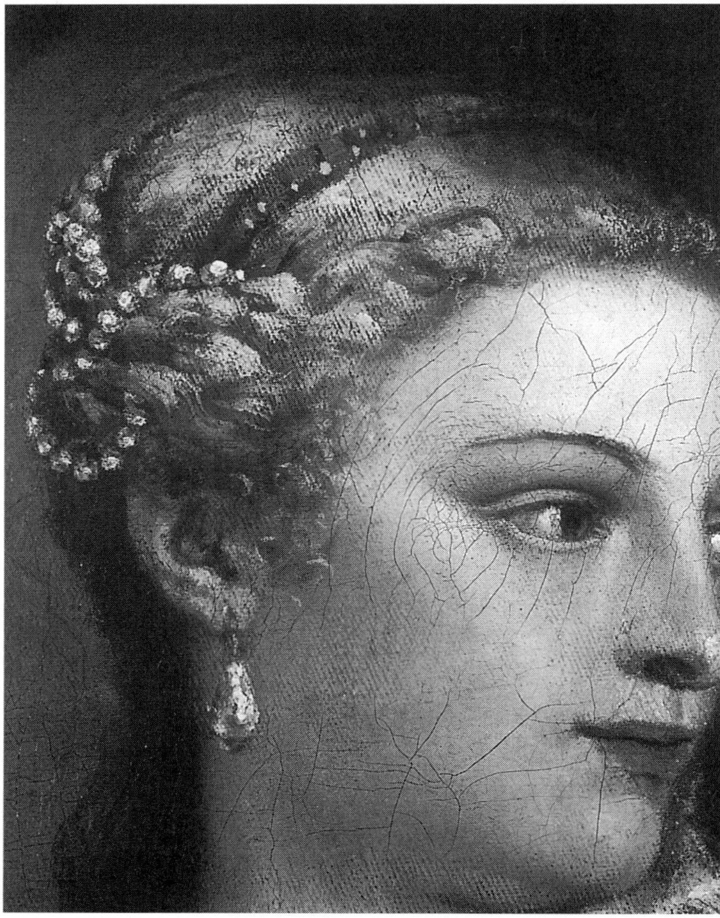

Figure 21. Titian, *Venus with the Mirror,* detail. Washington, D.C., National Gallery of Art, Andrew W. Mellon Collection. Photo: National Gallery of Art, Washington, D.C.

classical pose are those instances when he did *not* use the *pudica,* although one might well have expected him to do so: in the *Venus and Cupid with Partridge* (c. 1532–3), now in restoration at the Uffizi, and in the "Venus and the Musician" series – that is, in all the compositions otherwise reminiscent of the *Venus of Urbino* (Figs. 13, 22).[38] Yet even in the *Venus of Urbino* Titian departed from the venerable prototype in two significant ways. The first is

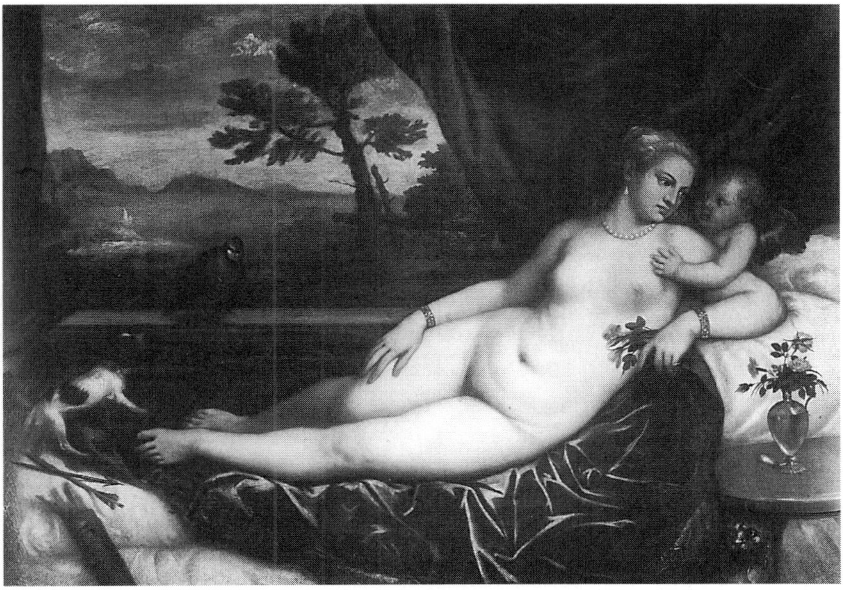

Figure 22. Titian, *Venus and Cupid with Partridge.* Florence, Galleria degli Uffizi. Photo: Alinari/Art Resource.

straightforward: Venus does not cover her breast with her right arm but rather props herself up on the pillows while clutching a bouquet of roses. The second variation, however, is problematic: Unlike the ancient *Venus pudica,* she does not merely conceal, she caresses herself (Fig. 23). The only precedent for this that I know, and at any rate the most conspicuous one, is the *Dresden Venus;* and it's surely not coincidental that Manet also changed this detail, so that *Olympia*'s hand bars access to herself.

Many observers are reluctant to acknowledge that the goddess's gesture is an action, not a passive concealment, although both Giorgione and Titian clearly show her fingers contracted, not extended, as in the ancient prototype and indeed as in other medieval and Renaissance depictions of the *pudica,* including the examples mentioned here. Other observers who acknowledge the caressing gesture of the *Venus of Urbino* see it as confirmation of the woman's *immodesty,* an implication of lasciviousness. There is, however, a different way to interpret this action, one that is consistent with sixteenth-century mentality.[39] Under normal circumstances, this kind of self-caress was unequivocally condemned by medieval and Renaissance theologians and physicians. But they endorsed it in one particular situation, based on a mistaken view of gestation: From Galen's time on, the woman's so-called emission was generally believed relevant to conception. And conception – or its possibility – was the primary justification for sexual intercourse, according to church teaching. In order to achieve this desideratum, female masturbation was deemed acceptable and sometimes necessary.[40] Indeed, every medical treatise I have consulted, from Galen (d. 201), the unrivaled ancient authority, to Gabriele Falloppio, professor of anatomy at Padua in the mid-sixteenth century (d. 1562), to Ambroise Paré, his greatly influential French contemporary, makes the same recommendation, explicitly or by implication.[41] Doing so, the physicians may evoke Venus in their obstetrical texts, as was mentioned in relation to Lotto's picture (Fig. 11).[42] And they commonly offer another piece of advice that may be pertinent to the Venuses by Giorgione and Titian.

All medical authorities agreed that the right side of the human body was warmer than the left, thanks largely to the location of the liver. The right side of the body, the dexter, like the right side of everything else, was thus considered superior to the left, the sinister. All authorities likewise agreed that the male was superior to the female and that his superiority derived from biological warmth, in contrast to her inherent coldness. Consequently, the physicians concluded, the woman wishing to conceive a male child should turn to her right side during or immediately after intercourse.[43] The future father, similarly, should provide seed from his right testicle, although this is admittedly harder to control.[44] Art historians have considered many formal and iconographic reasons to explain why Titian's later variations of the reclining female nude have all turned to recline on their left sides (Figs. 13, 22). But an additional explanation may be that the implications of fertility and gestation, evoked by the pose of the *Venus of Urbino,* were no longer relevant to these later compositions.

Be that as it may, one might well conclude that all this medical information is amusing but irrelevant; and I do not wish to insist too much on the possible obstetrical significance of the Dresden and Urbino Venuses. Yet the fact remains that all of these suggested

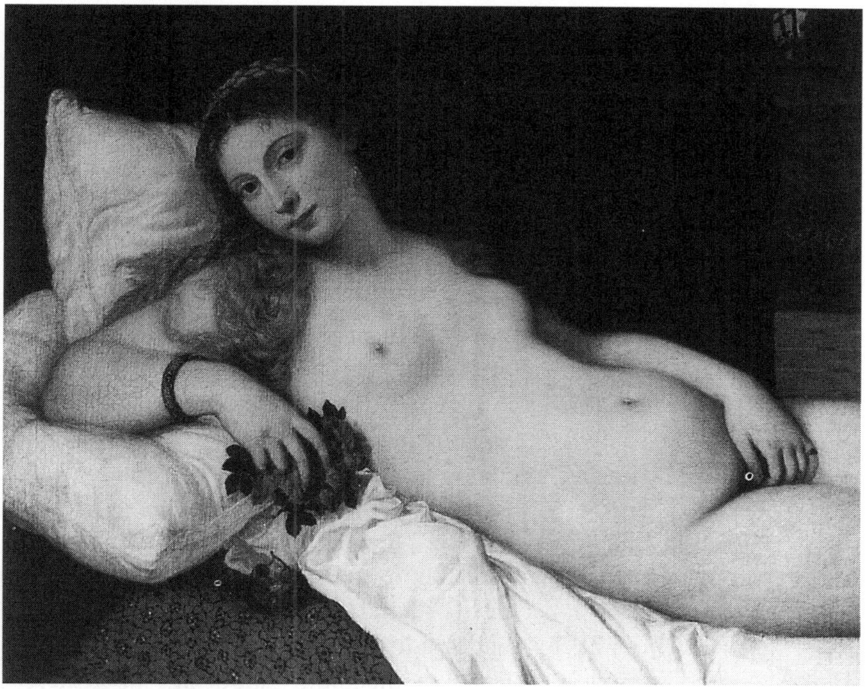

Figure 23. Titian, *Venus of Urbino,* detail of figure. Photo: Scala/Art Resource.

references to generation are entirely consonant with the traditional marriage symbolism of Titian's setting and attributes – the roses, myrtle, *cassoni,* dog, and so on. The same matrimonial context also explains Venus's gesture and her glance. In addition to consent and publicity, enshrined at Trent as two fundamental requirements of Catholic marriage, society expected sexual consummation to seal the marital union and children to bless it.[45] While her eyes indicate love and consent, Venus's gesture anticipates this consummation and fulfillment.

The *Venus of Urbino* is then a marriage picture, unless its every clue, every indicator of meaning, is purposefully misleading. But whose marriage? Titian's painting was apparently complete when Guidobaldo della Rovere wrote to his agent in Venice about obtaining it in 1538, although the correspondence does not make clear whether the duke himself had commissioned it. Although most historians have been inclined to doubt it, I consider that he did so.

The first known mention of the *Venus* appears in Della Rovere's letter of March 9, 1538, mentioning the "donna nuda" together with a portrait of himself ("il ritratto mio"), which was surely commissioned by him.[46] The reference to the portrait together with the *Venus* may in itself suggest that the latter work was likewise his commission. In his second letter regarding the *Venus,* dated May 1 of the same year, Duke Guidobaldo repeats his desire to own the picture and voices concern that another buyer, with cash in hand, may get it before he can find the money to fulfill his promise to Titian.

To be sure, less eccentric compositions, both sacred and profane, might be painted on speculation, kept in the shop for eventual buyers or to be offered to distinguished patrons, as Titian offered a *Venus* to Charles V and a *Magdalen* to King Philip.[47] Indeed, like Giovanni Bellini before him, Titian and his shop frequently replicated and varied successful compositions. But the *Venus of Urbino* was unique.[48] Surely it had been ordered by somebody, and that individual was most likely Guidobaldo della Rovere. To be sure, della Rovere's terseness leaves some uncertainty about this – but there is no uncertainty about his concern to get the painting, and his concern was in fact warranted by Titian's well-known readiness to satisfy any customer with cash in hand. Some eighteen years earlier, for example, the painter had entertained an offer from Alfonso d'Este for the *Saint Sebastian* completed in 1520 as a panel of the polyptych commissioned by Bishop Altobello Averoldi, papal legate to Venice, for SS. Nazzaro e Celso in Brescia.[49] That the *Sebastian* eventually went to its intended destination had more to do with Alfonso's apprehension about offending the legate than with Titian's probity in such matters. Even were Guidobaldo della Rovere the commissioner of the *Venus,* as I suggest, he would have had good reason for his anxiety that Titian might sell it to someone else, able and willing to pay on the spot. The duke's letter, therefore, does not preclude his having ordered the painting and indeed may imply the opposite. At the least, it demonstrates that della Rovere was familiar with the work and wanted very much to have it. Given the uniqueness of the composition, his interest in the *Venus* would make more sense were he in fact the commissioner. Guidobaldo was only twenty-four in the spring of 1538, when his portrait and the *Venus* were already completed – some six months before he succeeded his father on October 22 and presumably at least a year or two after the initial commission or commissions. Whatever combination of high-mindedness or crass self-importance may have motivated this precocious patronage of Titian we shall never know, but Guidobaldo's eagerness to have these paintings (which, we remember, he could not afford) suggests a deeper interest in the arts than historians usually perceive in him. At any rate, the duke was "sufficiently cultivated" to befriend such distinguished men of letters as the two Tasso and Annibal Caro.[50]

Some years ago, Theodore Reff suggested that the *Venus of Urbino* commemorated Guidobaldo's wedding to Giulia Varano in 1534.[51] Most scholars have dismissed the argument as untenable because Guidobaldo's bride was only ten years old when their marriage took place (the groom was twenty) – and this, moreover, was four years before Titian consigned the picture. It is worth recalling, however, that we do not know when the painting was commissioned and that Titian was in any case often notoriously slow to complete a work – perhaps especially so when he had not been paid. Many noble brides were espoused at comparably tender ages, usually with the understanding that their marriages would be consummated only after they had reached menarche. Sometimes provisions were made for the young bride to share her husband's roof but not his bed until she reached womanhood. Guidobaldo and Giulia may have been formally married in 1534, some two years after their "engagement," but it is almost inconceivable – both biologically and socially – that their union was consummated at that time. Such a marriage, involving an underage bride and a groom compelled to delay his sexual possession of her – and hers of him – could well explain the quirks of Titian's composition. The *Venus of Urbino* may have been conceived in anticipation of the hoped-for consummation of Giulia Varano's marriage to Guidobaldo della Rovere by representing the sexually and emotionally mature bride as she welcomes her husband to her bedchamber. And by 1538, Varano at fourteen would have been an adult by contemporary standards. (Indeed, according to recent studies, fourteen was the average age at menarche in the sixteenth century.)[52] Perhaps Guidobaldo hoped that the beauty of the goddess would enhance the beauty of the children his young wife would bear him, as promised by numerous physicians (including Scipione Mercuri, whose *Comare* was published in Venice in 1596 – replete with many invocations of Venus).[53] Or perhaps Guidobaldo saw the painting as a visual wish fulfillment in reference to his bride, hoping that Giulia herself, a child when she first came to Urbino, would be inspired by the beauty – and the sensuality – of the image. The Dominican friar Giovanni Dominici had counseled earlier generations to decorate their homes with sacred images precisely to influence the behavior of their children.[54] Guidobaldo and Giulia herself might have seen the *Venus* as the secular equivalent of such pictures, with a comparable power to influence the beholder. At the same time, as in other Renaissance marital imagery, niceties are preserved, decorum honored, by means of the classical idiom. Perhaps this disjunction between the actual identity of the Renaissance bride and her ancient surrogate, the goddess of love, made female sexuality safe(r) by distancing it, by shrouding it in classical fantasy. To deny Titian's woman (or Giorgione's or Lotto's, for that matter) her divinity is also to deny her sexual power: If she were merely a courtesan, her sexuality would be delimited by sixteenth-century Italian standards because its extramarital purpose is fornication, not gestation.

This explains various differences between the "Venus and the Musician" series and the uxorial *Venus of Urbino*. The musical Venus's head is more in profile, her body now more frontal, turned toward the beholder as though offered to him – a "no-strings" offering, without the binding glance. No longer *pudica* in any sense, she does not call attention to her pudenda, as the Urbino Venus does; and when the musical Venus holds anything in her other hand, we see that a phallic flute (the *flauto d'amore*) has replaced the bridal bouquet of roses. It's as though Titian has secularized his goddess in these later works, removing Venus from the domestic and marital sphere to place her in another world, or rather another role, where sexuality and love are not tied to procreation and hence to matrimony. Although in bed, these women are explicitly removed from the domestic realm; and that in itself makes these musical nudes extramarital.

For the *Venus of Urbino,* on the contrary, Titian created his only domestic interior. The wall hangings, the masonry and column of the window (or loggia), the *cassoni,* and the square patterns of the

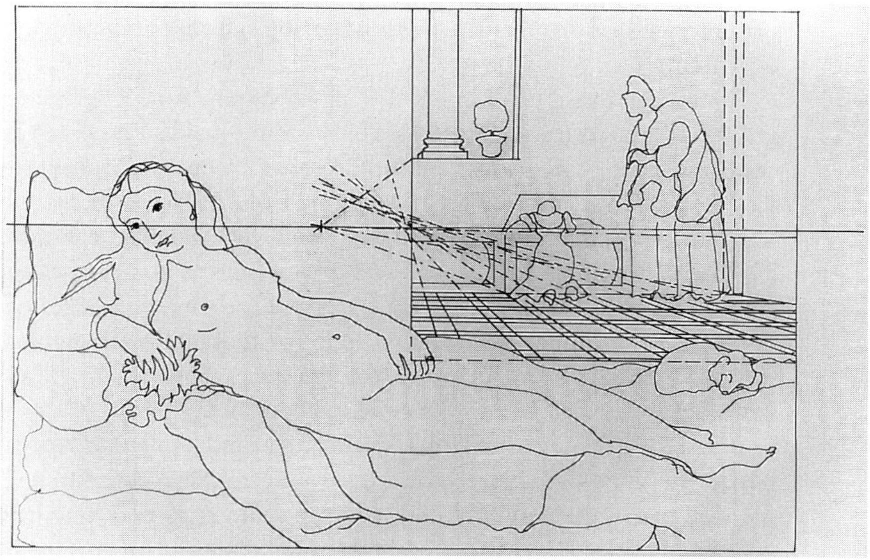

Figure 24. Titian, *Venus of Urbino,* diagram of perspective by Susanne L. Philipson.

pavement all serve as modules to assert the measurability of this space, convincing us of the perspectival illusion.[55] While insisting on the verisimilitude of his setting, however, Titian asserts not spatial unity but rather a disjunction between foreground and background, even though we are invited to recognize the contextual relation between the two: a bed in the foreground, bedroom furnishings in the background. But the vertical wall with its green curtain severs these spaces with surgical precision, and their apparent continuity is contradicted by the disjunction of scale. The standing maid measures slightly less than one-third the figure of Venus; the space represented here cannot provide the distance necessary to validate such disparity. Titian reiterates this disjunction by vanquishing the vanishing point of his own perspectival construction with Venus's eyes (Fig. 24). Following his spatial directives, we come to a point on the wall between the sill and the closed *cassone,* and somewhere above Venus's navel – that is, we come to nowhere. The force of this spatial logic loses to the power of Venus's gaze, which is further honored by every other trick in Titian's Venetian book – by the manipulation of color and light, the direction of folds in the various fabrics, and the elimination of any other glance (even the dog's) from competing for our attention.

Titian's lighting underscores the spatial disjunction. The background is lighted from the left, as the standing maid's cast shadow confirms. In the foreground, although Venus's feet cast shadows to the right, her red cushions are illuminated from the opposite direction. Their cast shadows create strong, almost parallel diagonals that lead the viewer's gaze to Venus's, where it wishes to go in any case. And these same diagonals join in space with others – the edges of the pillows and sheets – to form a series of triangles or triangular sections, echoing the patterns of the drapery against the wall, all framing Venus with their coloristic geometry.

The two geometric schemes, rectangular and triangular, meet where the edge of the foreground wall bisects the composition – the wall marks the center almost exactly – where, as everyone has long since noticed, Venus conceals her own triangular form. This is not compositional vulgarity but rather a means of honoring the female life force: Venus's body, or more precisely that part of her body associated with procreation in the Renaissance mind, is made both the pictorial center and the connection between Venus herself – that is, her individual personality – and her societal, familial role, encapsulated in the domestic background. In the *Sacred and Profane Love,* the same woman was depicted twice, in one narrative moment but in different states of being, in order to represent different aspects of her identity and status. In the *Venus of Urbino,* one woman is provided with two realms that are related not by the usual means of perspective or illumination but by her body itself. Spatial unity is illusory, then, as is its frequent concomitant in Renaissance art, temporal unity. Here one woman seems to have been captured in one passing moment, and Titian underscored the transitoriness of his scene with such details as the roses escaping from Venus's bouquet, the maid's rolling her sleeve, and so on. But temporal precision is deceptive in this seemingly unified setting. By her actions and demeanor, Venus presents not one moment but rather embodies the entirety of her relationship to her beloved. The *Venus of Urbino* may be understood as a metaphor, Titian's image of the woman as wife, transcending narrative time in order to express eternal truths – in this case, the verities of the wifely role as perceived by Renaissance people. Yet generative sex, although given pride of place, takes a secondary role to Venus's personality, which includes but is not subsumed by her sexuality. That the Venus of Urbino looks so forcefully at the beholder is assertive but not brazen. In short, the eyes have it: Venus's eyes, which irresistibly hold our own, assert her character, her intellect, and her power to choose.

NOTES

1. Sholes, "Uncoding Mama," p. 127. See also Caulfield, "Sexuality in Human Evolution"; Ciavolella, "Métamorphoses sexuelles"; Keller, " 'Gender/Science System' "; Laqueur, "Orgasm, Generation"; and esp. Rubin, "Traffic in Women."
2. I have discussed the painting at length in "Titian's *Sacred and Profane Love* and Marriage" and at greater length, with transcriptions of relevant documents, in "Titian's *Sacred and Profane Love:* Individuality and Sexuality in a Renaissance Marriage Picture." In the present essay, up to note 9, I reiterate information from these publications which is germane to the *Venus of Urbino.*
3. On the condition and recent restoration of the painting, see appendix II to Goffen, "Titian's *Sacred and Profane Love:* Individuality and Sexuality." For the white gown, which may be identified with the gown listed in the record of the restitution of Bagarotto's dowry, see Venice, Archivio di Stato, Consiglio de' X, Misc. Codici, May 16, 1514, published in Goffen, "Titian's *Sacred and Profane Love* and Marriage," pp. 113, 118.
4. See Goffen, "Titian's *Sacred and Profane Love* and Marriage," p. 113.
5. For the *Flora,* see Romani, "Flore," and for the *Miracle of the Speaking Infant* in the Scuola di Sant'Antonio, see Goffen, "Adultery, Madness, and Marital Misery."
6. The Ancients provided many illustrations of such idealized portraiture, and in Titian's day, Isabella d'Este provided the most egregious example. For the master's fictive portrait of her, c. 1534–6, now in Vienna at the Kunsthistorisches Museum, see Wethey 2: 95–6, cat. no. 27; and Ferino, "Portrait of Isabella."
7. Sodoma (Giovanni Antonio Bazzi) used the same attribute for his *Allegory of Celestial Love,* c. 1504, Siena, Monte dei Paschi di Siena, Raccolta Chigi Saraceni; see Goffen, "Titian's *Sacred and Profane Love* and Marriage," pp. 114–15; and Bartalini, in *Domenico Beccafumi,* pp. 242–3.
8. On this "home truth," see, inter alia, Kelso, *Doctrine,* pp. 273, 276, and passim.

9. See Goffen, "Titian's *Sacred and Profane Love* and Marriage," p. 119, with additional bibliography; and for a somewhat different interpretation, Béguin, "Vénus et Cupidon."
10. See note 42.
11. See inter alia Klapisch-Zuber, "Griselda Complex"; and Lydecker, "Domestic Setting," pp. 153–6.
12. Modern usage of this term is misleading; by *cassone,* Renaissance people sometimes intended a large chest to hold flour or grain, although in the sixteenth century, Aretino, among others, also used the word to mean a chest for clothing. See Battaglia, *Grande dizionario,* pp. 851–2; and Lydecker, "Domestic Setting," p. 54, who substitutes greatchest. Household inventories may distinguish *cassoni, forzieri,* and *goffani* (*cofani*); see Thornton, *Italian Renaissance Interior,* p. 192. On *cassoni* in general, see Schubring, *Cassoni;* Callmann, *Apollonio di Giovanni;* Watson, "*Virtù* and *Voluptas*"; and the forthcoming volume by Cristelle Baskins, *Adversity's Heroines: Narrative and Gender in Italian Domestic Painting.*
13. The critical issue is thus not the choice of word but the fact that "marriage chests" almost inevitably came in pairs, e.g., the two painted for Isabella de'Este's wedding in 1490, the two in the bedchamber of Pierfrancesco Borgherini in 1515, and the two commissioned by the father of a Ferrarese bride in 1502; for these and other examples, see Thornton, *Renaissance Interior,* pp. 195, 201, 204. As he explains and as this last example demonstrates, not all *cassoni* were purchased by the husband – but they seem always to have come in twos. Note also the pairs of greatchests provided by two fifteenth-century Florentine brides in Lydecker, "Domestic Setting," pp. 55, 157, although he also notes that "the tradition of having them in pairs seems to have vanished" during the Cinquecento.
14. The inventories are transcribed in Santore, "Julia Lombardo," pp. 62–79. Santore translates the terms for various types of chests as *cassoni,* a word that is not used in the documents themselves.
15. Although Titian's *cassoni* are carved, in keeping with contemporary taste, not painted like fifteenth-century greatchests, *cassoni* themselves were going out of fashion in the sixteenth century, at least in Florence; see Lydecker, "Domestic Setting," pp. 55, 158–9. For Titian's *cassoni* in relation to the meaning of the *Venus,* see also Arasse, "Le nu couché."
16. De Tervarent, *Attributs et symboles,* pp. 94–5. For the dog that likewise knows his master in the Prado *Danae,* see Nash, *Veiled Images,* p. 28.
17. The painting and its pendant, the portrait of Eleonora's husband Francesco Maria della Rovere, both now in the Uffizi, were restored in 1990 by E. Masini; see Cecchi, "Portrait of Eleonora Gonzaga della Rovere," and Valcanover, "Portrait d'Eleonora Gonzaga." For Titian's relationship with these patrons and their son, Guidobaldo II, see Varese,

"Tiziano e i Della Rovere"; Bo et al., *Tiziano per i duchi di Urbino,* passim, esp. Bernini, "Tiziano per i duchi di Urbino." According to Bernini (p. 20), Eleonora rejected the idea of posing for her portrait, which was based on the same model who posed for the *Venus of Urbino,* purchased by her son. On the Renaissance distinction between portrait and likeness – the former need not represent the latter – see note 6. Regarding the identity of the dog(s), see also Bernini Pezzini, "Eleonora Gonzaga," p. 41.

18. In the earlier version of this essay, published in the *Journal of Medieval and Renaissance Studies,* I suggested that Titian confirmed his reference to the duchy of Urbino by means of the bifore fenestration, a feature typical of Urbinate architecture. The rectangular bifora is indeed characteristic of Urbinate ecclesiastical architecture but was not used for palaces, as Dr. Sabine Eiche explains in a letter to me. Recognizing that Titian's column is in any case too large for a window, she suggests that the opening may represent a loggia.
19. Ranum, "Refuges of Intimacy," p. 252. This view has been espoused by others, perhaps starting with Wilhelm Heinse, who declared that "Titian did not wish to paint any Venus but rather only a courtesan"; *Ardinghello,* p. 332. Tietze followed suit, asserting that there was "no hint of any mythological connotation" in sixteenth-century mentions of the *Venus;* see his "Early Version of Titian's *Danae,*" pp. 206–7. Heinse's and Tietze's interpretation has been embroidered by more recent scholars, among them Ginzburg, in his classic essay included in the present volume and first published in Italian as "Tiziano, Ovidio e i codici della figurazione erotica del Cinquecento"; and Ost, "Tizians sogenannte 'Venus von Urbino.' " Cf. Panofsky, *Problems in Titian,* pp. 109–71. For bibliography prior to 1978 and for technical information, see Agostini, "Venere d'Urbino." For a historiography of more recent bibliography, see Goffen, "Renaissance Dreams," pp. 695–701.
20. For the painting in London, the National Gallery, see Lightbown, *Botticelli* 2: 55–6, cat. no. B41.
21. Ibid.
22. See Goffen as cited in note 2.
23. Hope, *Titian,* p. 82. Elsewhere, Hope calls these kinds of paintings "mere pin-ups," adding for good measure that "the girls were seen as little more than sex objects"; "Problems of Interpretation," p. 119.
24. On Titian and Manet, see the essays by T. J. Clark and by David Rosand in this volume.
25. *Titian,* p. 82.
26. Letter of Francesco Maria della Rovere to his agent Leonardi in Venice, May 2, 1536: "quel retratto di quella Donna che ha la veste azurra";

published by Gronau, *Documenti,* p. 92, no. 28. See also Zecchini, "La Bella," and Goffen, *Titian's Women,* chap. 2.

27. On the use of the same model, see Wethey, *Titian* 2:23, 106.
28. Cropper, "Beauty of Woman."
29. The letters were published by Gronau, "Kunstbestrebunden," p. 19 and docs. 31 and 33; and rpt. in idem, *Documenti,* pp. 93–4, docs. 31 and 35.
30. Vasari-Milanesi 7: 443. For an analysis of Vasari's text, see Pardo's essay in this volume. The papal legate Giovanni della Casa had seen the *Venus* in 1544; Campana, "Giovanni della Casa," p. 382. On the palace itself, see Valazzi, ed., *Corte di Pesaro,* passim, esp. Eiche, "Corte di Pesaro."
31. For the reconstruction and a discussion of epithalamic imagery, see Anderson, "Giorgione, Titian and the Sleeping Venus." See also Howard, "Dresden *Venus* and Its Kin"; and most recently Pleynet, *Giorgione et les deux Vénus.*
32. Michiel, *Notizie,* ed. Morelli, p. 66; *Der Anonimo Morelliano,* vol. 1, *Text und Übersetzung,* ed. Frimmel, p. 88.
33. For the story of how she provoked one ardent viewer, see Pliny, *Historia Naturalis,* book 36, chap. 21.
34. Gentile's statue was the subject of a Latin epigram; see Ziliotto, *Raffaele Zovenzoni,* p. 109.
35. See Goffen, "Bellini's *Nude with Mirror.*"
36. See Manfrini, "La Maddalena." For the location of the *Venus,* see note 30.
37. Brown, "Venus with a Mirror"; and Valcanover, "*Vénus à sa toilette.*"
38. For the Uffizi *Venus,* see Squellati, "Venere con Amorino." For *Venus and the Lute Player,* early 1560s, see Zeri and Gardner, *Italian Paintings,* pp. 77–9. Titian painted numerous variants of the theme, e.g., *Venus with an Organist,* Madrid, Museo del Prado (inv. no. 420), dated c. 1550; see Urrea, "Venus with an Organist and Dog"; and Giorgi, *Tiziano: Venere, Amore e il Musicista.*
39. I first posited this interpretation in "Renaissance Dreams," p. 699, citing Lemay, "Anthonius Guainerius," pp. 331–2 and passim. I suggested that Guainerius's early-fifteenth-century "Treatise on the Womb" might be an anomaly with only fortuitous bearing on Giorgione's and Titian's imagery. Now I have found, on the contrary, that whatever these artists may have intended, physicians and theologians commonly related female masturbation *in the context of the marriage act* to gestation.
40. Fourteen of seventeen Renaissance theologians studied by Jean-Louis Flandrin allowed female masturbation to achieve orgasm and thus, as they believed, to encourage gestation. See Flandrin, "Sex in Married Life," pp. 114–29, esp. p. 119. As Flandrin notes, this "behavioural reality" was related to an understanding and eventual acceptance of sexual pleasure

and to the conception of marital love. See also Noonan, *Contraception,* p. 322, on the declaration of the Council of Trent regarding love in marriage (Session 24, November 11, 1563). Affirming the indissolubility of marriage, the council quoted St. Paul's injunction: "Husbands, love your wives as Christ loved the Church."

41. Galen, *On the Usefulness of the Parts of the Body,* vol. 2; and Bullough, "Medieval Medical and Scientific Views of Women," pp. 493–7, on Galen's recommendations (followed by Trotula and Avicenna, inter alia). Adelman, *Marcello Malpighi,* vol. 2, part 2, *Main Currents of Embryological Thought,* esp. pp. 744–58, dealing with embryology from Galen (published in Greek by Aldus in 1525; Latin translations began to appear in 1541) to Fabricius, *De Formatione ovi et pulli* (published in 1621). See also Laqueur, "Orgasm, Generation." Similarly, on the necessity of the female "emission," see Mondino, *Anothomia Mundini;* Massa, *Epistolarum Medicinalium,* vol. 2, fols. 136r–v, Epistola 19 (dated 1555), "Consilium . . . de morbo Gallico," on coitus; also Falloppii, *Omnia, quae adhuc extant opera;* Mercuri, *La comare,* p. 6: The womb's anatomy is related to the female sexual response; "si gonfia anco alle donne ne gli appetiti di Venere." Finally, Paré, *Oeuvres,* on sexual pleasure, simultaneous emission, and gestation, e.g., pp. 454, 586–7.
42. Venus is invoked, for example, by Guainarius (cited in note 39) and by Mercuri (cited in note 41).
43. For the equation of male with right and warmth as opposed to female-left-cold, see inter alia: Galen, *On the Usefulness of the Parts of the Body,* pp. 626, 628; and Mercuri, *Comare,* p. 36. Mercuri (p. 1) had already explained that these unfortunate female characteristics accounted for the difficulties of parturition: "essendo la donna di molta humidità ripiena, e di pochissimo calore, come vuole Hippocrate, e Artistotele in mille luochi; è per ciò anco più fredda de gli huomini." See also Benedek, "Beliefs about Human Sexual Function," pp. 103–5 (citing Galen, book 14).
44. Mercuri, *Comare,* p. 37, reiterates this Pythagorean theory: If more semen comes from the right testicle and is emplanted ("formentato") on the right side of the uterus, "certamente sara [il bambino] maschio . . . ma all'incontro se il seme humano procederà più dal testicolo sinistro . . . e sarà ricevuto nella parte sinistra dell'Utero, all'hora sarà femina per la fredezza, e debolezza delle parti cosi mandanti, come recipienti." See also Horowitz, " 'Science' of Embryology," pp. 88–9, on the persistence of the theory.
45. See Goffen, "Titian's *Sacred and Profane Love* and Marriage," p. 117, with bibliography in the notes.
46. This and the following letter are cited in note 29.
47. Titian announced the gift of "una figura di Venere" for Charles V in a

letter to the emperor dated December 8, 1545, published in Ferrarino, *Tiziano e la corte di Spagna,* p. 25, no. 31; cf. p. 23, no. 27, a letter from Diego Hurtado de Mendoza to Charles, October 5, 1545, which may refer to the same picture, here identified only as a "quadro de fantasia." For the *Magdalen,* see Goffen, "Titian, His Donors and Sacred Subjects," p. 91, citing the artist's letter to King Philip of April 2, 1561.

48. Titian's Naples *Danae* originally repeated the background motifs of the *Venus of Urbino,* as revealed in X-radiographs (Fig. 12). I suggest that he changed the background in the *Danae,* overpainting the servants and *cassoni,* precisely because these references to marriage were no longer relevant.
49. See Goffen, "Titian, His Donors and Sacred Subjects," pp. 86–7.
50. Cecini, "Cultura e letteratura," p. 334. The duke's second wife, Vittoria Farnese, especially encouraged the friendship with Caro (1507–66).
51. Reff, "Meaning of Titian's 'Venus of Urbino.' " Despite his passion for a daughter of Gian Giordano Orsini, by December 26, 1532, Guidobaldo had acceded to his father's wish that he marry Varano; the marriage was celebrated two years later, on October 12, 1534. Francesco Maria died four years later, and Guidobaldo succeeded to the title on October 22. Giulia herself died on February 18, 1547, and Guidobaldo remarried less than a year later, taking Vittoria Farnese, daughter of Duke Pier Luigi of Parma, as his bride on January 30, 1548. See Petraglia, "Regesto," pp. 9–16, esp. pp. 12–13.
52. Amundsen and Diers, "Age of Menarche," pp. 363–9.
53. Although the placement of the painting before 1548 is not documented, it was probably always displayed in the *guardaroba.* Paintings and other precious objects were customarily kept there, as Dr. Sabine Eiche kindly informs me (written communication). Della Casa saw the *Venus* in 1544 and Vasari four years later, specifying the *guardaroba;* they are cited in note 30. On the power of images to influence the appearance of the unborn, Mercuri, *Comare,* p. 52, cites Hippocrates and Empedocles and accordingly recommends the display of appropriate statues or paintings: "tenere in camera pittura, ritratti, ò statue de' suoi parenti, ò d'altre persone illustri, ma fatte da mano eccellente, e belle; overo nell'atto venereo ricordare alla donna l'effigie di cui si desidera la similitudine." See also p. 78, with a reference to Avicenna.
54. Dominici, *Regola del governo di cura familiare, parte quarta,* pp. 34–5.
55. It is not clear whether the opening in the wall is a window, as generally assumed, or a loggia; see Dr. Sabine Eiche's comments as cited in note 18.

4 DANIEL ARASSE

THE *VENUS OF URBINO,* OR THE ARCHETYPE OF A GLANCE

Titian's *Venus of Urbino* represents the first great fetish of the nude female body offered to a (male) glance in Western painting (Figs. 1, 15). It is not, strictly speaking, the prototype of the reclining nude woman, which, in various guises, haunts museums and private collections; the *Sleeping Venus* of Giorgione better fills this role, despite its own antecedents (but we may ask whether a prototype *can* exist at this level). Rather, the *Venus of Urbino* constructs the European archetype of the "nude woman" in painting, the *donna ignuda,* as the panel was called before Giorgio Vasari, in 1568, baptized this naked body with the name of "Venus."[1] Today, more than three centuries later, it is difficult to ignore the fact that, of all the reclining nude women that tradition offered him, Manet invoked Titian's *Venus* in order to conceive his own *Olympia.* Thus, at the very beginning of modern painting, Manet reanimated or reaffirmed the effectiveness of a configuration that had become

This chapter provisionally concludes a reflection first sketched in 1976 at the international congress on *Tiziano e Venezia;* taken up again in two subsequent publications (*Tiziano, Venere d'Urbino* and "Le nu couché dans la peinture de la Renaissance"); and emended as a result of my participation in a seminar held in November 1991 at The Johns Hopkins University in Baltimore, at the invitation of Professor Michael Fried. In particular I should like to thank Professors Fried, Elizabeth Cropper, and Charles Dempsey for their very fruitful observations offered on that occasion, and also Professors Rona Goffen and David Rosand for the many conversations that we have had about the Venetian nude woman, the *donna ignuda.* (Translated from the French by the editor.)

banal and prostituted by Alexandre Cabanel (1823–89) and other masters of the Academy.

Today, to analyze the *Venus of Urbino* yet again, to attempt to liberate what Titian's original idea and invention might have been, is therefore inevitably to become an archaeologist of this (male) glance, to question the position that this painting assigns to its viewer. Because the canvas is closely tied to the actuality of Venetian painting in 1538,[2] this analysis proceeds by returning to the history of *this* painting, that is, to the historical situation of the female nude in Venice when Titian undertook his work. The historical circumstances that surround the gestation of the painting are so well known that one no longer takes note of them. Yet this painting occupies a unique place in Titian's oeuvre, as it does in the history of the nude woman in European art; only these original historical circumstances offer the possibility of outlining the painting's initial originality – before perception of it became clouded and overdetermined by the diverse artistic and critical interpretations constructed about it.

One tends to forget, for example, that of all those paintings of reclining nude woman that have contributed so much to Titian's glory, the *Venus of Urbino* was the first that he painted, when he was almost fifty years of age.[3] Yet the isolated reclining female nude had already existed for some time in Venice. To be sure, one thinks of the *Sleeping Venus* painted by Giorgione (and completed by Titian) around 1507–10, and also of certain other female nudes realized before 1538 (Fig. 3). By the time Titian tackled the theme, the type of the nude woman or *donna ignuda* was well defined: About 1520, with his *Reclining Nude in Landscape,* Palma Vecchio had awakened the nude woman, and already she was beholding her beholder (Fig. 10).

The *Venus of Urbino* is not only the first isolated reclining female nude by Titian (as opposed to those represented in narrative *poesie*),[4] it is also the only example that he painted of this type: a reclining female nude presented outside of any action, outside of any narrative, and engaged with her viewer in a direct exchange of glance.[5] In the series of paintings of Danae, beginning in 1545–6 with the Farnese *Danae* (Fig. 6), or in the Venus series, beginning in 1548 with *Venus with the Organist* in the Prado (Fig. 13), the nude is (more or less) engaged in a mythological situation or narrative, and the relation of glances in which the nude is implicated is played out within the interior of the painting. Now, far from being negligible, this difference transforms the relation of the scene and the viewer: Whereas the viewer is seen envisaged, and questioned by the *Venus of Urbino,* in the later works he is ignored or taken to be absent. One could say, to repeat the terms of the American art historian Michael Fried, that the "absorption" of the reclining female nude is radically altered, with Titian, into her initial "theatricality."[6] The *Venus of Urbino* thus appears as a relatively isolated invention in the context of the painter's oeuvre, as a *prototype* profoundly transformed in the series of paintings to which it gives birth.

Returning to Giorgione's *Sleeping Venus* as the model for his own female nude – twenty-five years later, we must remember – Titian reconceived the figure and its presentation. Not only does Venus's hair change in color and coiffure, but the gesture of the arms is also different: The right arm repeats the position adopted by Palma Vecchio, among others, and the left hand preserves the self-caressing action of Giorgione's model as she conceals her pudenda. Once again, this last detail is significant, as Titian is the only Venetian to maintain the gesture. It had originally been Giorgione's idea to give his reclining and sleeping nude the gesture of the *Venus pudica,* which is normally a standing figure. But when Titian gave this gesture to an awakened figure, its context changed. Thus the gesture can acquire a precise sexual meaning, recently underscored by Rona Goffen, which is far removed from its traditional connotations of modesty (Fig. 15).[7] Aside from these details, Titian's most obvious innovation in reference to Giorgione's prototype remains the fact that Venus is now presented in a sixteenth-century interior setting. The setting's contemporaneity is reinforced by the presence of two figures in the background, immediately identifiable as two servants, and of two *cassoni* or greatchests that define the room where they are found as a bridal chamber.[8]

These details serve as the basis of my analysis. It is not concerned with the theme of the painting. David Rosand and Rona Goffen have answered this long-debated question. The painting's general context, both iconographic and formal, relates it historically to the genre of "marriage picture," without necessarily requiring us to discover exactly which marriage occasioned its commission: By

1538, the image type of marriage picture had been freed from the particular conditions of commission.[9] It is clear, moreover, that the importance of the *Venus of Urbino* in the history of the depiction of the female nude is related less to its iconography than to its visualization. In early-sixteenth-century Venice, as Rosand has convincingly explained, the nude "exists as a foundational structure, a generic sign latent with a range of significance – from *una Venere mondana* [a worldly Venus], goddess of base passion, to the celestial deity of divine love."[10] I would like to consider how this "foundational structure" functions in the *Venus of Urbino*. My approach offers a means of solving three fundamental problems presented by the painting: first, understanding why, more than any other Venus by Titian, *this one* has been the cause of virulent iconographical debate; second, understanding how the painting has been able to provoke so many contradictory reactions that its viewers seem to run through the entire "range of significance" or spectrum of possible explanations that may be applied to the nude woman in general;[11] and finally, why, among the numerous reclining female nudes that crowd European painting, Manet chose this one, 325 years later, to create *Olympia*.

A preliminary observation: Not only did Titian never return to the structure that establishes the "theatricality" of the *Venus of Urbino,* but, as X-radiographs demonstrate, the "absorption" of the Farnese *Danae* (Titian's second reclining female nude) is accompanied by the purposeful exclusion of the spatial structure of the prototype, that is, the presentation of the nude in the interior of a contemporary palace. In the *Danae,* the frightened Cupid in effect superimposes himself on the motif of the kneeling servant in front of the chest (details visible in the X-radiographs, Fig. 12). At the same time, the room is replaced by a vague representation of the exterior. Whatever circumstances may have prompted Titian to reprise and alter the right half of his composition in this way, from this point on in his oeuvre, he excludes the double motif of the bed chamber and the marriage chests from the settings for his nude women.[12] The *Venus of Urbino* is thus Titian's only canvas in which the nude woman is presented, with her servants, in a palace interior. It is nonetheless necessary to ask again what exactly Titian represented in the *Venus of Urbino* because, looking closely at the composition, one sees that its spatial setting is not clearly defined.

The setting is approximate, so to speak, and its very inexactitude impedes our understanding of what motivated Titian's structural decisions in 1538.

In considering the painting on the "pre-iconographic" level, as the art historian Erwin Panofsky has explained, "objects . . . can be identified . . . on the basis of our practical experience."[13] That is to say, we can identify the setting as a bedroom at first glance on the basis of general knowledge of Renaissance interiors (leaving for a later moment the interpretation of the meaning of this setting). But whatever Panofsky may say about this first, pre-iconographic level of interpretation, the fact is that Titian's space is not so easily understood. The elements that establish the vertical and horizontal articulation between the bed and the chamber are in fact indeterminate, "indescribable." In his late work on Titian, Panofsky describes the vertical caesura of the painting as "the edge of the curtain."[14] But this pre-iconographic description is manifestly imprecise: Titian would never have painted curtain drapery in such a rectilinear fashion. Moreover, there are no indications of folds or pleats in that dark area behind the green fabric: Nothing allows us to identify that dark surface as a textile. Rather, we must see here, behind the upper part of the nude body, a "presentation screen" comparable to that in the Magnani *Virgin and Child with Saints Catherine, Dominic, and a Donor,* for example, painted by Titian about 1513–14.[15]

The narrow horizontal band that ends the pavement is likewise indeterminate. Panofsky recognized here the "edge of the tiled floor."[16] But this identification is as arbitrary as that of the dark "curtain edge." How can one explain the interruption of this tiled floor in the interior of the setting? Would one or more steps divide the chamber in two? This is unlikely. Titian has not troubled himself with painting (or "describing"), with justifying literally (by name) this double interior edge in the scene, where the two parts of the image meet. In effect, these two elements constitute borders, but they are the borders of areas that construct the scene in its entirety; and, as we shall see, their function is to be considered apart from all pre-iconographic identification.

Much is known about Venetian Renaissance palace design and furnishings, based on surviving examples, on representations of interiors, and on written accounts.[17] And what we know of Venetian palaces makes it most unlikely that Titian's *Venus of Urbino* represents a unified, coherent interior. That is, Titian's setting does *not* imply the continuity (or continuous depth) of the fictive space that begins with the place occupied by the bed in the foreground and extends to the chamber wall in the background. Given the customary height of actual sixteenth-century beds, in order for the viewer to interpret Venus's bed and the chamber as being at the heart of the same interior, it is necessary to posit one of two unlikely explanations. Either there is a considerable difference in level between the two areas in the center of the same chamber, or Venus's bed is made of two great cushions placed against the floor – a most improbable situation in this imaginary Venetian palace where servants carry out their duties.

These two spaces are not *continuous:* Rather, they are *contiguous.* Titian's composition is based on the juxtaposition of the two – their forced contiguity within the picture. Their articulation is arbitrary, fundamentally artificial. The best illustration of this is undoubtedly provided by the manner in which Lambert Sustris banalized the arrangement in his painting dated about 1540 (Fig. 25). Sustris's *Venus* represents a self-evident reference to the *Venus of Urbino.* (The window, the myrtle, the coffers, and the kneeling servant suffice to prove this point.) But Sustris has normalized the presentation of the interior space. For example, in painting the rear angle of the bed and the wall edge that projects laterally, Sustris establishes an indisputable continuity between foreground and background. Moreover, in making the curtain overlap the vertical articulation, he departs (awkwardly) from the arbitrary character of this detail in Titian. And the point of view adopted by Sustris clearly raises the bed in relation to the room while distancing the room. In thus normalizing his composition, Sustris shows how the composition of the *Venus of Urbino* is based instead on the juxtaposition of two distinct spaces. Titian's structural choice leaves its mark both on the "pre-iconographic" indeterminateness of the elements (we cannot identify them so easily as we thought at first glance), which serve to relate the two zones, and on the relative geometric rigidity of the setting. Only the curves of Venus's left thigh and of the spinal column of the sleeping dog exceed the limits of their site and inscribe themselves on the surface (on the geometric pavement), thus making the transition from one zone to the other more fluid.

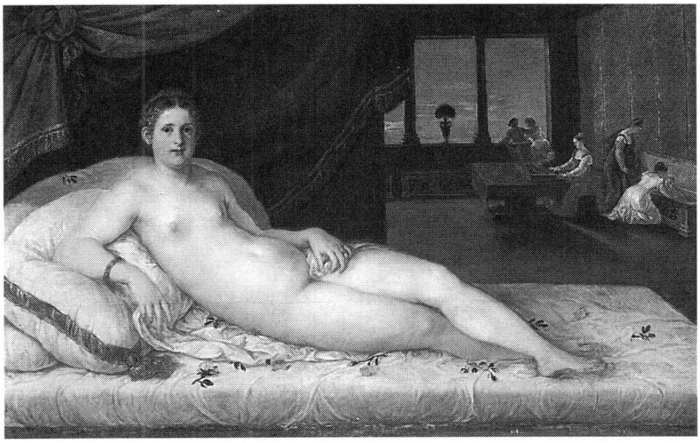

Figure 25. Lambert Sustris, *Venus*. Amsterdam, Rijksmuseum. Photo: Rijksmuseum, Amsterdam.

Despite these spatial differences, the two spaces are interconnected. Each space is inconceivable in isolation. They are bound by a precise dialectic that attributes both contrasting and complementary values to each zone. A space of repose, containing the bed, is dominated by the horizontal; the chamber in the background is scanned by multiple verticals that echo and give rhythm to the actions of the figures. In the foreground, curves triumph (for example, contours of the woman's body and of the dog, folds of drapery on the bed, the tassel of the green fabric screen). In the background area with the greatchests, the perspectival patterns of the ground, the tapestries, and the window multiply the straight lines. To the nudity of Venus's body is clearly opposed the theme of clothing, carried and prepared by the servants. As a corollary of this opposition, however, some of the particular circumstances of each area are recalled within the other. For example, the mattress rests on a straight line that Titian has taken care to make visible, whereas the longitudinal wall of the greatchests is curved, convex; the servant who holds one chest's cover bares her right arm as she raises it, and this gesture partially reveals the nudity of flesh entirely revealed in the foreground. This servant's gown brings a touch of red to the background, placing there a color recalled in the foreground by the mattress, made visible by the calculated disorder of the sheets.[18]

It is undeniable, therefore, that the structure of the *Venus of Urbino* depends on the placement of these two areas or sites in (artificial and dialectic) relation to each other. The perspective that designs the pavement of the chamber and unifies the canvas *conceptually* makes possible the elucidation of the principle of unity that inspires this disposition.

Titian rarely utilizes this kind of visible geometric perspective to construct a picture space.[19] It is exceptional in his work that the perspectival elaboration be so manifest.[20] In any case, one thing is certain: The *Venus of Urbino* is Titian's only painting of a nude woman in which geometric perspective is such a powerful element. Sustris eliminates it in his own painting. These facts invite a closer consideration of the construction of the *Venus of Urbino* and its effect. Precisely in assigning a theoretical place to the glance of the viewer – a glance that is far from indifferent – the perspective construction associates the two zones of the painting in a precise and unexpected way.

Titian's perspective places the horizon line of the composition (and therefore the theoretical gaze of the viewer) at the height of the head of the servant kneeling before the greatchest, which is also the height of Venus's left eye. The principal vanishing point is placed directly above Venus's (hidden) sex. This arrangement is very simple but too obvious not to have been calculated, and it leads to two consequences. First, the horizon line establishes an internal bond, latent but undeniable, between the position of the principal figure and the construction of the room located in the "background." Second, the viewer finds himself situated closest to Venus (this is the impression given by the body's emergence in the foreground), theoretically as though kneeling before her. This kneeling posture is suggested both by placing the bed against the floor in such a way that it seems to continue the plan of the ornamental tiling and by locating the (theoretical) glance of the beholder at the level of the nude's left eye. By dismantling the perspective composition, this analysis explains evidence that is concealed in the painting, thus clarifying Titian's conception: Standing *before the painting,* we are supposed to take the position that is assumed by the servant kneeling before the greatchest *within the painting.* In its very arbitrariness, the disposition of the painting is a tactical device, producing unperceived effects that are all the more effective because of their imperceptibility.

At this point, however, our interpretation must be nuanced. What we have just explained about Titian's composition refers to the *theoretical* position of the viewer, implied by the internal arrangement of the picture. Our *actual* position is evidently different, and Titian's invention takes this difference into account.[21]

The greatchests are iconographically important because they relate this nude woman to the theme of matrimony. At the same time, as we have already noted, with their convex form in a space defined by straight lines, these chests repeat the echo of the curve motif dominating the foreground. But their role does not end here. The first entirely nude, isolated, reclining women in European painting were those painted on the interior of the covers of marriage chests (Fig. 8). Kenneth Clark went so far as to see in these intimate, hidden nudes the "real predecessors" of Giorgione's *Sleeping Venus*.[22] But were that the case, Giorgione would have produced an Arcadian Venus, presented outside of any social context. A quarter of a century later, when Titian returned to Giorgione to fulfill the commission of painting a nude woman, he socialized his model and underlined "less her classical pedigree than her contemporary social function."[23] In other words, the *Venus of Urbino* is an urbanized Venus. With an awareness of tradition that one often finds in his work, Titian returns to the social origins of the nude woman: He seeks her where she was already to be found, presented in isolation and removed from any action, the pure object of intimate contemplation. That is to say, Titian finds her in the interior of marriage chests – and he makes her the very foreground of his composition.

From this point of view, the arbitrary and artificial character of the edges that isolate the chamber of the background make it almost a painting within the painting. But far from being conceived as a "genre scene" that is almost detachable from the principal figure, it must be understood in relation to the entire structure of the painting. In Freudian terms, it can be seen as a " 'dream within the dream,' " that is, "what the dream-wish seeks to put in the place of an obliterated reality" because "what has been 'dreamt' in the dream is a representation of the reality, the true recollection, while the continuation of the dream, on the contrary, merely represents what the dreamer wishes."[24] It can be seen also as a "painting within a painting" that, as André Chastel suggested, produces "a scenario of the production" of the painting where it is found.[25] This is not a scenario to be interpreted anecdotally (the servants taking or replacing their mistress's garments in the greatchest) but rather theoretically and conceptually. That is, the "scene" of the background indicates at once the historical origin of the figure of the isolated, reclining nude woman and that of the idea that is given birth in the painting itself.[26]

Two elements confirm this evolution of Titian's invention. First of all, there are the various responses that the painting itself provokes and their ambivalence – reactions that sometimes make the purity of a celestial Venus recognizable in this figure, sometimes the sex appeal of a contemporary courtesan. This ambivalence is produced by the structure of the painting, where Titian has literally "prostituted" the body of the female nude: He has placed the nude in the foreground of this scene created by the "theatricality" of the painting. Now because the conceptual unity of this theatricality is not based on the iconographic theme but rather on the duality of the spaces, the juxtaposition of these zones allows an "open" reading by the (male) beholder. His interpretation can oscillate between two extremes. He may see the painting in relation to contemporary culture, and then it will be the splendor of the nude Venus, the pure "celestial Venus," that is offered to the beholder's gaze. Or it may be the nude display of a bodily intimacy normally concealed in the real world, and then the viewer may come to find obscenity in this figure offered in the foreground of the painting. Between these two extremes, the painting allows multiple interpretations that depend finally on the disposition of the beholder.[27]

The second element is in contradistinction to the first. If the articulation between the two zones of the work cannot be conceived in terms of representational space, if this articulation is not describable in pre-iconographic terms, it is precisely because it marks, within the painting, the operation that has constructed the painting. It is not possible to name referentially that which articulates the two zones of the painting because it is this articulation itself that establishes the painting, that is, its condition of possibility. In a way, if the representation becomes opaque here, if, with this double edge placed paradoxically at the center of the image, the representation loses its transitive transparency as a sign, it is because this (pictorial) sign presents itself reflexively. That is, it presents itself as representing (an edge, a limit, an internal articulation).[28]

The interpretation cannot end here, however. That would be to ignore a major fact about the work, mentioned earlier, that is decisive for the effect that the *Venus of Urbino* has on the viewer. As we have seen, the body of Venus is not located in the same (fictive) space as the room with its marriage chests. The spaces of the bed and of the chests constitute two sites, contiguous but not continuous, two heterogeneous zones that owe their unity only to the organization of the canvas that they construct. Indeed, it is necessary to be fully aware that the body of Venus and the bed of her presentation are simply *in front of* the represented chamber – before this chamber and separate from it – in a place of indeterminate spatial coordinates that is nonetheless situated between two precisely defined spaces: the fictive space of the chamber in the painting (where the perspective assigns us our theoretical position in front of the canvas) and the space of the actual chamber where we find ourselves with the painting and from which we envisage it. Situated between these two spaces, the place where Venus is painted is an unlocatable "in between" ("entre deux"), the in between where the body of painting is made incarnate.[29]

This singular spatial situation invites the exceptional (and troubling) effect of an unexpected appearance of immediacy and of an absent presence.[30] This body is there, at the closest point, almost as though it could be touched (like the servant with the arms plunged into the greatchest); but the body remains all the more untouchable because, in order to see it, the viewer must step back and get some distance to envision this life-size figure (the painting measures 119 cm high by 165 cm long). This manner of presentation is unique to the *Venus of Urbino* in Titian's oeuvre, and it makes of the nude woman's body, in its very immediacy, a (pure) object of the glance, a (pure) body of painting, untouchable despite its proximity, offered only to the visual or scopic impulse.[31] That is to say, the beholder sees Venus but cannot touch her.

This dialectic between seeing and touching could well be essential to the picture (to its effect and to its place in the history of painting). It is not only the perspective and the immediacy of the figure that call us close to the painting – although at the same time, in order to see it better, we have to step back. In addition, within the painting itself, this relation between seeing and touching is remarkably pronounced in the figure of Venus. As we have seen, Titian is in effect the only artist to preserve the gesture that Giorgione had given to the left hand of his *Sleeping Venus* even while awakening the figure. At the same time, this gesture acquires a radically different value and meaning. With Giorgione, the figure's sleep could make one suppose that her gesture was involuntary – that it might be a modest gesture (that of the *Venus pudica*) or one that unconsciously manifests the erotic nature of the dream that inhabits this body. Thus, the nature of her gesture remains uncertain. Titian's *Venus,* on the contrary, is awake; she does not dream; she knows she is seen; she knows that she touches herself; she sees us, and she touches herself.

We can only contemplate this figure, who is so aware of her own body under our gaze. The gesture with which she touches herself, in the center of her body and of the painting, is directly under the point where the perspective fixes our eye. Her gesture and her touching confirm that our relationship to this body can only be visual, made possible by means of the glance.[32] At the same time, this painted body places us unfailingly under its own powerful gaze. Whatever the position from which she may be seen, the nude woman holds her gaze toward her beholder.[33]

As Mary Pardo has recognized, "the perspectival inset in the *Urbino Venus* is emblematic of the Albertian deplacement from touch to vision."[34] Pardo is also correct when she relates the conception of the glance in the *Venus of Urbino* to the reality of amorous writings in Venice, such as those formulated by Sperone Speroni in 1537, assuming the voice of the poet-courtesan Tullia of Aragon.[35] In placing us thus under the power of her own gaze, the *Venus of Urbino* exerts fully its "subjective effect"; it constitutes its beholder as a "pathetic Ego," Ego enjoying sight without the ability to touch, Ego not touching precisely in order to see.[36]

Without discussing further this fundamental, complex theme, however, it is important to underline how this dialectic of seeing and touching lies at the heart of Titian's pictorial art, and especially of his future development. As we know, and as Marco Boschini described so magnificently in his much-quoted passage on Titian's technique, Titian will touch his canvases more and more in order to paint them – and in a revealing way for us, the Tuscan Vasari will admire how "one cannot see them close up but they become perfect when seen from afar."[37] This is not the case with the *Venus of Urbino,* a masterpiece of Titian's first manner, executed "with great finesse and extraordinary care."[38] But the future dialectic (which was to become so ponderous in the debates on colorism) of "touching in order to paint, withdrawing in order to see" is already posed here. It is not yet founded on that *maniera* of touch that will be seen in the Farnese *Danae;* rather, it is enunciated here in the rapport that the *Venus of Urbino* establishes with its viewer, under the form of an extraordinarily limpid design, of an *idea of painting:* painting Venetian style.

Felt even in the relative, almost theoretical rigidity of the disposition of the composition, this character of design surely helps explain why the papal nuncio Giovanni della Casa, upon seeing it, called the *Venus* a "Theatine nun" compared with the Farnese *Danae* of 1545.[39] Finally, perhaps it also helps to explain why Manet returns to the *Venus of Urbino* to paint his *Olympia* if, as Michael Fried thinks, Manet "constructs his painting around the constitutive presence of the spectator so that, paradox of paradoxes, this ideal spectator ends by taking the place of the actual spectator."[40]

NOTES

1. As Mary Pardo underscores in her beautiful study "Artifice as Seduction," p. 60. (I thank Professor Elizabeth Cropper of The Johns Hopkins University for having brought my attention to Pardo's essay.) In the letter that Guidobaldo II della Rovere addresses to his agent in Venice, he speaks only of a "nude woman" (*donna ignuda*). Nonetheless, it is appropriate not to give too much value to this phrase: In 1538, the term was generic and can refer equally well to an anonymous nude as to a known mythological figure, such as Danae in the famous letter from the papal nuncio Giovanni della Casa to Cardinal Alessandro Farnese of September 20, 1544 (published, among others, by Hope, "Neglected Document," p. 189, and quoted in note 39). On this point, see also Goffen, "Renaissance Dreams," pp. 695–6; and Goffen and Rosand in the present volume.
2. On this point, see Pardo's observations in "Artifice as Seduction," pp. 58–9.
3. Titian's first two isolated female nudes are presented as standing figures: the *Venus Anadyomene,* or *Venus Emerging From the Sea* (c. 1520; Edin-

burgh, National Gallery of Scotland); and the *Lucretia* (c. 1523; Hampton Court, Collection of Her Majesty the Queen of England). Titian contributed only finishing touches to Giorgione's *Sleeping Venus,* and the nymph sleeping in the lower right corner of the *Bacchanal of the Andrians* (Madrid, Museo del Prado) is not an isolated figure. According to Harold E. Wethey, one must presuppose the existence of a "lost original by Titian" for the *Sleeping Venus with Roses* in Darmstadt, the Gemälde Galerie, and its various known variants. But in that case, Titian would have repeated Giorgione's pose literally, contenting himself with showing the figure reclining in an indeterminate place, perhaps a loggia separating the figure from the landscape, where Giorgione had submerged it. It seems to me that the intervention in regard to the model is too timid to be attributed to Titian.

4. For the meaning of *poesie,* see the Introduction, note 1.
5. For the Italian artist's conception of *(i)storia* or narrative, see Alberti, *On Painting,* pp. 95, 99, and esp. pp. 103–7.
6. These conceptions are borrowed from Fried, *Absorption and Theatricality.*
7. See Goffen, "Renaissance Dreams," pp. 698–701, and her essay in this volume, pp. 73–8.
8. Goffen, "Renaissance Dreams," pp. 700–1, nn. 29–30, and in this volume, pp. 66–8.
9. See the essays by Goffen and Rosand in this volume.
10. See the essay by Rosand, p. 52.
11. The quoted phrase is from Rosand's essay, p. 52.
12. For the X-radiograph of the Farnese *Danae* (Fig. 12), see Mucchi, "Radiografie," pp. 297–304, esp. 301; and Rosand's essay in this volume. On the (eventual) moral significance of this frightened Cupid, see Kahr, "Danaë: Virtuous, Voluptuous, Venal Woman," p. 47.
13. See Panofsky, *Studies in Iconology,* p. 9, for the meaning of "pre-iconographic" description.
14. Panofsky, *Problems in Titian,* p. 21. For the curtain, see our Preface.
15. For the painting in Mamiano (Parma), the Magnani-Rocca Foundation, see Valcanover's catalog entry in *Titian, Prince of Painters,* pp. 162–4, cat. 9.
16. Panofsky, *Problems in Titian,* p. 22.
17. On these subjects, see Goy, *Venetian Vernacular Architecture;* and Thornton, *Italian Renaissance Interior.*
18. This placement of the zones in relation to each other, with various echoes of their constituents, seems also to govern the distribution of plant motifs. In the background, outside, nature itself draws a tree with an irregular form; on the window, the potted myrtle plant is perfectly cut; on the coffers and the tapestries, the plant theme is treated as a decorative motif. In the foreground, the plant motif is found again in the bouquet of cut

roses (Venus's flower) clasped in the figure's right hand; one flower has become detached from the bouquet and is placed at the juncture of the drapery and the mattress, this last being covered with a fabric with a decorative motif of a dense accumulation of red flowers.

19. One finds a comparably emphasized perspective in the *Annunciation* painted in 1520 for the Malchiostro Chapel of the Cathedral of Treviso. But this very perspective contributes strongly to the dramatic effect and to the theological meaning of the composition.
20. This perspective is manifest, but it is also approximate. It is not the geometric rigor of perspective that interests Titian but its visual effect. The orthogonals converge at different points (Fig. 24); the background wall is too close to the coffers, the standing servant masking the incoherence that would be evident if the angle of the wall were visible. Establishing the apparent regularity of the perspective grid, the "distance point" is situated almost at the edge of the painting, a position responding less to a desire for "legitimate construction" than to traditional studio practice.
21. On the attention that Titian pays to the position of the beholder, taking into account the internal disposition of the composition, see in another context Rosand, *Painting in Cinquecento Venice,* pp. 51–69.
22. Clark, *The Nude,* p. 173.
23. See the chapter by Rosand in this volume, pp. 43–4.
24. See Freud, *Interpretation of Dreams,* p. 338.
25. Chastel, "Le tableau dans le tableau," p. 75.
26. On the autonomy of the representation as created by the edge and/or the frame in classical painting, and on the way in which the *Venus of Urbino* is related to this general problematic, see my essay "L'Opération du bord."
27. On this point, see my previous observations in "La signification figurative chez Titien," p. 154 and passim.
28. For these terms, see Récanati, *La Transparence et l'énonciation,* pp. 20f., 31f. For their efficacy in the domain of visual analysis, see, among other works by Marin, "Mimésis et description," pp. 25–36.
29. On this concept of the "in between of the incarnation," "entre deux de l'Incarnation" (in the context of the Annunciation), see Marin, "Annonciations toscanes," pp. 125–63, esp. pp. 143ff. One thinks of the passage of the *Dialoghi* where Sperone Speroni admires "how the sky is the paradise of the soul, thus it seems that in his colors God has replaced paradise in our bodies, not painted, but made holy and glorified by his hands." The text is cited by Crowe and Cavalcaselle, *Titian, His Life and Times* 2:40. One also recalls Bataille's commentary on Manet's *Olympia:* "Manet departed from realism by virtue of the power he had . . . of not locating his subject *anywhere*" (Bataille's italics). See Bataille, *Manet,* p. 67.
30. The effect establishes the *aura* of the figure, "unique apparition of a

distance, as close as it can be," as Benjamin defines it in "L'oeuvre d'art," p. 145.

31. *Scopic* is a Freudian term referring to the pleasure of vision, as opposed to voyeurism, which is considered to be inherently sadistic (editor's note).

32. To analyze this technique of the glance and of this calling scopophilia ("visual pleasure") into play would be to continue probing Titian's exacting treatment of the theme of the opposition of the hidden and the revealed, and how he profoundly reelaborates Giorgione's eroticism. Thus, for example, in the Dresden *Sleeping Venus,* the raised right arm exposes to the gaze a shaved underarm. The same arm is lowered in Titian, and the hair, now blond, has insinuated itself and veiled the secret fold of the invisible underarm. Nonetheless, the hair succeeds in representing, under deplaced form, that which the *Sleeping Venus* had effaced: the mark of the body's "immodest" hair. In the *Venus of Urbino,* the blond hair thus becomes the sign of that which is hidden and plays the role of authorized representation of such immodest hair, thereby illustrating the traditional erotic process of dissimulation to make visible what would normally be unseen. This interpretation is confirmed by the fact that a similar tactic transforms the pudenda: Although Giorgione left the pudenda visible, Titian creates a deep shadow, anatomically unjustified, covering and suggesting that which the hand shows while yet concealing it.

33. For the unexpected reactions that this situation can invite, see the chapter by Rosand in this volume. To these examples, one may add that of Stendhal (1783–1842) in the *Souvenir d'égotisme,* rpt. in his *Oeuvres intimes* 2:444–5.

34. Pardo, "Artifice as Seduction in Titian," p. 81.

35. Ibid., p. 57: "By insisting on the male lover's passivity, Tullia inverts the Aristotelian tenet that loving is higher (because more active) than being loved."

36. Marin, "Le Trompe-l'oeil," p. 83. Marin (like Arasse in his French text) uses the psychoanalytic term *jouissance,* in reference to the Ego's experience of the *jouissance* of sight. French distinguishes between *plaisir* and *jouissance* in a way that English does not, and so the term *jouissance* is generally retained in English. Crudely put, *jouissance* is the culmination but also the destruction of *plaisir* (editor's note).

37. Vasari-Milanesi, *Vite* 7:452. For Boschini's description of Titian's technique, see *La carta del navagar pitoresco,* pp. 711–12. Boschini quoted Titian's former associate, the painter Jacopo Palma il Giovane (Palma the Younger), on the master's habit of working on a painting for a period of time, then turning it to the wall for perhaps an even longer time, then returning to it, and so on. At each stage, Titian applied paint with a remarkable variety of brushstrokes, sometimes loading the brush with

pigment and sometimes painting very thinly with pigment or with glazes. The result in the late works is often a tapestry-like effect of interwoven patches of color and light (editor's note).

38. Vasari-Milanesi, *Vite* 7:452.
39. Cited by Hope, "Neglected Document," among others: "a nude that will make the devil descend on Cardinal San Silvestro; and that [picture] which your most reverend lordship saw in Pesaro in the chamber of the lord duke of Urbino is a Theatine nun next to this one" (editor's translation).
40. From the preface of the French edition of Fried, *Absorption and Theatricality: La Place du spectateur,* p. v. Professor Fried kindly provided his own translation of the passage, which does not appear in the English edition of his book.

5 MARY PARDO

VEILING THE *VENUS OF URBINO*

> Yet, in truth, among the disguises of fiction rhetoric has no part, for whatever is composed under a veil, and thus exquisitely devised, is poetry and poetry alone.
>
> Boccaccio, *Genealogia deorum,* XIV, 7[1]

When I last saw the *Venus of Urbino,* it was resting, feet down, on its narrow end, at a provisional location in the Uffizi[2] (Fig. 1). Until a photoflood lamp was switched on nearby, the gloom of a summer storm kept Titian's golden *donna nuda* more heavily veiled than if she had been wearing a nightshirt. This strange encounter had positive consequences. For one thing, it confirmed a long-held faith in the masterpiece's ability to hang on to its aura, even when rotated by 90 degrees and exposed to a cruelly unflaterring light. And it emboldened me to scan that ancient surface, if not against the grain, at least as if from the wrong side.

At close range, the figure betrayed an uneven patchiness in the flesh tints, and her ornaments (the filigree and jewels of her bracelet, the gemstone in her ring) seemed forever robbed of their luster. Almost imperceptible were the raised profiles of the golden fringe crossing the green expanse of the curtain and hanging down to the juncture between the woman's head and the pillow. The pattern on the dark "screen" behind the curtain – which in the Theodor Verkruijs etching commissioned before 1723 reads as a variation on the damasked hangings of the adjacent room – showed up as a few random, floating strokes of an ocher tint.[3] And yet, for all its murky passages and wear, the *Venus* presented a notably cohesive surface appearance. In a kind of dialogue, Titian's paint film could be seen to incorporate the assertive grid of the canvas weave, sometimes caressing it into the grain of a depicted object, sometimes "rubbing it the wrong way," as in the painterly counter-patterning of the bedsheets. This literal texture not only bound the figure – with its minimal modeling – to the rest of the image but, more particularly, rendered inescapable that image's insistently textile and textural appeal.

Our earliest literary "snapshot" of the *Venus of Urbino,* in Vasari's *Lives* of 1568, specifies "a very young recumbent Venus (*una Venere giovanetta a giacere*), with flowers and certain finely-woven fabrics about her, very beautiful and well finished."[4] The syntax appropriately blurs the line between the *panni* and the flowers. And flowers there are, both in the figure's right hand (wilting, as if from her body's heat) and on the flowered red mattress cover on which the sheet is partially spread. A blossoming stem has dropped to the mattress, linking (like the pale yellow of the "real" and "dyed" stamens) the woven and the organic references to a rose bower from which the *giovanetta* awakens.[5]

Vasari's praise of the *panni* betrays an almost subliminal awareness that the figure's immediate surroundings are not the only thing about the painting that is a matter of fine fabrics. His remarks also apply to the background setting, with the variously clothed female attendants engaged in handling clothes taken from a *cassone* housed in a room that is itself clothed in silk hangings. It is true that the anecdotal scene in the background does not solicit the same scrutiny of surfaces as the foreground, where the gleaming sheets, the pillowcases with emboidered borders, the jerseylike mattress cover, the fringed curtain, and the sleeping dog's fur (an enchanting spotted fabric in its own right) have a palpability that invites comparison with the figure's more vaporous modeling.[6] Nevertheless, the surface continuity between the close-up space of the nude "unwrapped" on the bed clothes and the telescoping, tapestried perspective of the adjoining room implies a mysterious coincidence (as with the obverse and reverse of a medal) between the baring to sight of the *Venere giovanetta* on the near side of the curtain divide, and the opening onto a dawn sky of the measured interior on the far side.[7]

How does this painting's magnetism arise? Why is one enthralled in its presence? If one is not to give the skeptical answer – that it is no more than a historical *frisson,* its "relevance" secured for our century by Manet's great modernist revision – one must seek a historical justification. What is it in the *Venus* that invites reflection beyond (but still about) the figure's carnal appeal? I have just suggested (and in this I follow David Rosand) that Titian's acknowledgment of painting's inescapable physicality, both as a material and as a metaphorical – embodying – process, seems part of an answer.[8] I believe it is also possible to offer a historical hypothesis concerning the evident role of the canvas support as a protagonist in the finished work.

In the pages that follow, we will take a detour through the early Quattrocento in search of a theoretical foreshadowing of Titian's concern with surfaces in the *Venus of Urbino.*[9] It is a rather quixotic undertaking, but I am persuaded that it should be attempted, if only to probe the limits of what may be claimed for Titian's (or indeed any painterly painter's) artifice. In a previous essay, I suggested that both as a display of the painter's art and as an object of erotic stimulation, the *Venus of Urbino* acknowledges habits of imaginative projection first explored in the Petrarchan lyric tradition and amply popularized in the Cinquecento's polite literature on love, beauty, and the arts.[10] Such a claim is easier to make about the image and its style; Titian's pictorial handling does not match up so readily with Renaissance treatments of literary process. I could not ground in period sources my conclusion that the carnality of the *Venus*'s figure is inseparable from the assertiveness with which the canvas support magnifies the passage of light across the reclining beauty's illusionistic skin. The painting's erotic "message" appeared to reside in an intimate dialogue of real and depicted surfaces, but I could offer no prototypes or foreshadowings to Titian's approach.

In this essay I attempt partially to ground the "poetics" of the *Venus of Urbino*'s facture through an examination of Leon Battista Alberti's treatment of painting as an art of surfaces, both two- and three-dimensional. Alberti's text provides a Renaissance model (however technically outmoded) for approaching the metaphorical implications of painting on a canvas support. However, before taking up *Della pittura,* I must first comment on Daniel Arasse's earlier analysis of the *Venus of Urbino* because it too identifies the Albertian text as a critical matrix from which to approach Venetian Cinquecento painting.

Arasse suggests that the pleasurable unease provoked by the *Venus of Urbino* comes from the way in which by putting an intimate nudity on display in the foreground, the composition audaciously short-circuits the decorum that governed the Renaissance uses of private space.[11] Taking his cue from the activity at the *cassone* in the background, he claims that in the realm of domestic representation, a reclining nude woman does not normally belong on the bed, but rather inside the *cassone* lid – the habitual location for such images in fifteenth-century Florentine marriage chests (Fig. 8). Titian's invention effectively lays claim to a new type of private/public space, that of the art collector, in which the display of sovereign artifice justifies the fetishizing contemplation of a normally "censured" nakedness.

For Arasse, the viewer who accepts the logic of Titian's perspectival construction and imagines himself peering closely at the *Venere* not many feet above floor level effectively duplicates the posture of the kneeling maid in the background, the one figure in the painting who is able to see the inside of the *cassone* lid.[12] This *cassone* (and hence the image plucked out of it) denotes the sphere of intimacy associated with the individual user whose personal possession it is. It is distinguished from the sphere of privacy denoted by the chamber that houses the *cassoni,* which is more properly familial, and mediates transactions with the public sphere. The public sphere, for its part, would be embodied in the exterior landscape beyond the balcony.

While rightly focusing attention on the structure of Titian's illusions, Arasse's interpretation of the *Venus*'s telescoping spaces may raise as many problems as it answers (nor are we given evidence that *cassone* lids in Cinquecento Venice harbored painted nudes).[13] But his conclusion about the painting's meaning does not depend, in the final analysis, on the verifiability of the *cassone* reference.[14] Rather, the *Venus* is unsettling because – whatever their source – its setting and its deployment of the figure do seem to implicate the viewer in an intimate exchange. For Arasse, the self-consciousness of Titian's design qualifies the *Venus* as an allegory of the power of painting to render desire visible. It is this power, manifested in the image's capacity to join the spectator's to the painter's erotic fantasy – and already figured in Giorgione's prior image of the *Sleeping Venus* (Fig. 3) – that Arasse refers back to Alberti's century-old treatise. In the *De pictura* of 1435, Alberti claimed that the inventor of painting, "according to the poets," was Narcissus: Painters, like Narcissus, seek to embrace an image of beauty on a reflective surface and leave behind a material token of their effort (the flower of painting). In Arasse's reading, the *Venus*'s intent beholder recognizes on the surface of the painting the mirrored image of (his) desire.[15] To be sure, Alberti's troubling insight (after all, Narcissus dies) would likely not have prepared him for paintings like Titian's; but it does link the art of painting to psychological mechanisms that continued to be invoked in Cinquecento discussions of amorous – and artistic – seduction.

It is worth noting that Alberti's brilliant "rhetoric" for painters had no direct successors or rivals until about 1550; for the first half of the sixteenth century it was virtually the only work available on the theory and practice of pictorial illusion. *De pictura* became the object of renewed interest during the decade that followed the completion of the *Venus of Urbino* in 1538. The Latin *editio princeps* appeared in Basel in 1540, and in 1547 a Tuscan vernacular version was published in Venice by Ludovico Domenichi; soon afterward, the Venetian Paolo Pino closely modeled his *Dialogo di pittura* of 1548 on Alberti's text even as he brought it up to date.[16] I will cite Alberti in Domenichi's translation because its *volgare* is closer than Alberti's own Italian version to the sorts of usage familiar to Titian (who was already intimate, in 1538, with the art critically fluent Pietro Aretino). Although I am not claiming that *De pictura* was being read in the 1530s (although it could have been), I believe it was continuously relevant to students of painting up to the end of the century.[17]

Arasse grounds Titian's public presentation of desire by citing a passage from the beginning of Book II of *De pictura;* I begin with the textile analogies that illuminate Alberti's expository strategy in the first paragraphs of Book I. Briefly, I am treating this aspect of Alberti's text as a marker for the transferral of concepts and images from poetics and rhetoric to the youthful field of Renaissance art criticism and theory. In this instance, I suggest that a certain conception of rhetorical ornament lies behind Alberti's choice of illustrative analogies for the geometry of vision and its objects; it is also the supplemental justification for the tracing device he urges on the painter as an aid in the process of composition. I view Titian's *Venus of Urbino,* with its textile and perspectival enrichments, as a contribution to the meditation on artifice initiated by Alberti a century earlier.

De pictura opens with a sensible disclaimer that is also a methodological statement:

> As I am to write on painting in these brief commentaries, and so that my arguments may be clearer, I will first take from the Mathematicians those things which will seem to me necessary to the subject. . . . But in my every argument, I want this, above all, to be considered, that I do not discuss these things as a Mathematician, but as a painter. Because they, with their mind alone, after removing all matter, measure the shapes and forms of things. But we, wishing the thing to be placed before the eyes, will make use in our writing of a – so to speak – coarser Minerva [*una più grassa Minerva*].[18]

As the sense of the passage indicates, Alberti's "heavier Minerva" is the kind of literalizing exemplification by which one may, for instance, narrow the gap between the abstraction of optico-mathematical principles and the material embodying of pictorial structure. As such, it differs from the classical attestations familiar to Alberti, where the phrase does not have pedagogical aims but rather means something like "down-to-earth, commonsense perceptions/observations" and may be contrasted with speculative argument.[19] Alberti mobilizes his *più grassa Minerva* within a few sentences of his brief exordium; after giving concise definitions of point and line, he introduces the all-important concept of "surface": "If many lines, like threads on a cloth, are joined closely together, they will produce a surface. For the surface is the extreme part of the body, which is known not through its depth, but only its height and breadth."[20] Among the properties of the surface, the contour is the "border" or "hem" (*ora o . . . lembo*), whereas the expanse of surface proper moves textile into quasi-anthropomorphic analogy, as it "is in a manner of speaking like a kind of skin (*una certa pelle*) stretched over the entire back (*dorso*) of the surface." The coincidence of skin and cloth in Alberti's figurative treatment of the surface implies that the pictorial object to be analyzed is like a body.

These brief but vivid illustrations have a double purpose. They make tangible the process of subjecting the outward forms of things to a "mathematical" analysis, but they also "pre-assimilate" the forms thus analyzed to the flat surface on which they will be depicted. Alberti no doubt had in mind paintings on walls or wooden panels, but his textile model for the surface – a kind of garment with a linear "hem" – had the advantage of being pliable and therefore of demonstrating a kind of representational topology in which things could be readily visualized as passing from three to two dimensions and back. At one level, the coarser Minerva at work here seems to be literally the artisan-goddess who invented the craft of weaving.

Alberti's third textile link in Book I is from the surface of things to the organ of perception. When he turns his argument to the visual rays, he immediately transmutes them into the stuff of which embroideries are made: "Let us imagine that the rays, in the form of extremely slender threads, are tautly bound at the summit in a kind of bundle, and these are received together within the eye, where the visual sense resides; and there they are like a trunk of rays."[21] The extrinsic or "measuring" rays issuing from this "trunk" attach themselves to the contour of a surface "like teeth" and form a pyramidal "cage" around the intrinsic or color-absorbent rays. These rays are like the chameleon, and are "stained" (*si macchiano*) with whatever color they happen to find on the surfaces at the base of the pyramid. Alberti's rays are animated entities: They wound, they bite, they grow tired (when they weaken after traveling great distances). Their description shifts attention away from the textile imagery, almost as if in anticipation of the human yardstick figure that facilitates the subsequent laying out of the perspectival *taglio,* the "cut" or intersection of the visual pyramid that opens up the painter's illusionistic window.

However, the woven cloth introduced at the beginning of Book I is not forgotten; it is allowed a triumphant return at the beginning of Book II, Alberti's much-discussed essay on visual *elocutio.* The *superficie*/cloth reappears metamorphosed into a compositional aid on whose value Alberti waxes defensive:

> Now set to work on circumscription, for which, if it is to be well understood, I judge nothing better suited than that veil

> (*velo*), which among my friends I am in the habit of calling the intersection (*taglio*) . . . which I place between the body to be represented and the eye, so that the visual pyramid may pass through the translucency of the veil. . . . And first of all, it always represents the same surfaces in a fixed place. . . . Nor will I listen to those who claim it is not useful for painters to grow accustomed to such things, which – though they give much help in painting – nevertheless are such that, without them, the artist can do nothing on his own.[22]

By calling *taglio* this woven, gridded mesh, through which one's view of an object can be stablized for accurate translation onto another surface, Alberti makes explicit the hidden conceptual link between the simple *superficie*/woven cloth with which he opened Book I and the perspectivally marked picture surface (the "window," or intersection/*taglio*) with which he concluded it.

Circumscription or contour drawing is the first procedure in the triad (circumscription, composition, and the reception of lights) identified by Alberti as "the parts of painting." By inserting the *velo* at this point in his exposition of circumscription, he subtly reminds us that *circonscrittione* is but the rhetorically activated version of the *orlo* or *lembo,* the figurative outer boundary of a surface in his geometric primer. Likewise, he underscores the fact that the central process of *compositione* begins with the rhetorical mobilization of surfaces:

> The first parts of the work are therefore the surfaces, because the members are made from these, and from the members the bodies, and from the bodies the *historia,* from which is drawn the final and perfect work of the painter. From the composition of surfaces arises that elegant refinement (*elegante leggiadria*), and grace (*gratia*) in bodies that is called beauty.[23]

If Alberti's ostensible motive for introducing the veil is the need for an accurate rendering and transposition of visible forms, his argument quickly shades into the demand for a beautiful image.

Alberti gives a lengthy account of the *velo,* which – like the textile similes in Book I – performs multiple functions, but on a higher level: In one sense, he just describes an ordinary tracing device (evidently received with some scorn by professional painters); but like a mirror, it is also an "objective" instrument for verifying the geometrical accuracy of the visual process and the "fit" between vision and representation. Not as transparent as a glass pane, not as opaque as the material support for the painted "view," but porous, flexible, fragile, it also contributes its own metaphorical associations to Alberti's vision of painting. The most evident derives from the system of classical rhetoric. Elocution is the "garment of style" (the verbal figures and tropes, the syntactical patterning) with which language is clothed in sensuous immediacy before it can claim artistic status. The *velo,* then, is a kind of provisional figured garment in that it primarily assists the construction of spatially assertive forms, with their complex interplay of undulant contour (hems or borders, implicitly decorative) and volumetric projection.

In *De pictura* – where the articulated figure corresponds to the elegantly balanced periodic sentence (Cicero calls it *circumscriptio*) that is the cornerstone of literary composition – the *velo,* as the chief tool of *circonscrittione,* is literally a device for the making of figural ornament.[24] But it is also a device for masking and regulating appearances: It is "made from very fine threads and woven very thinly, dyed whatever color I wish and divided by thicker threads into parallel portions. . . . [And] it is of the greatest assistance in finishing the painting, because you can see the thing itself in relief, rotund and circumscribed, and painted (*dipinta*) on this *veil*'s plane surface." In Book III, Alberti reveals the identity of the *velo*'s painter: "Those who paint have always sought to represent things as we see them depicted on the *velo* by nature herself." But when Nature paints, she is not a mere naturalist: "[From copying sculptures] we learn to render likeness as well as the actual lighting. In order to study this lighting, it is very helpful to dim your vision by lowering your lashes, so that the lighting will appear obscured, almost as if it were painted with the help of a *taglio.*"[25]

This "veiled tableau" tinted an arbitrary color, marked with a linear grid that allows one to segregate the object into evenly measured parts, is like a work of art in its own right.[26] At the level of the composition of surfaces, where the beauty of the painted image originates, the *velo* indeed furnishes the recipe ("dim the lighting") for the creation of those desirable tonal gradations that correct raw natural appearance. But the association of Alberti's veil with linear drawing points beyond the properly corrective aspects of naturalistic representation. Alberti says little about the graphic invention of the painting's "idea," but inasmuch as his tracing device serves the preparatory infrastructure of the *historia,* it operates close to its poetic matrix – that dim region where subject matter, written or imagined, becomes visible shapes and figures.

It is this "surplus" quality in Alberti's veil that leads me to surmise a rich literary ancestry for its significance in *De pictura*. The Ciceronian principles he adapted to painting had long been couched in textile analogies – as in Quintilian's introduction to rhetorical *compositio:* "There are then in the first place two kinds of style: the one closely welded and woven together (*vincta atque contexta*), while the other is of a looser texture (*soluta*)."[27] The "woven" is, in fact, the periodic style, on which Alberti's theory of painting was founded.[28] But the image of the veil was also a figure for the entire legacy of medieval poetics, with its attention to allegory and prophetic utterance, and its affinity for the marvelous and the ornate in painting.[29] If Alberti could not subscribe to a radically "poetic" model of painting in this sense of the term, his rhetoric of painting nonetheless could present itself as a corrective, working from within the tradition. I take this to be the figurative sense of the *velo* in *De pictura:* not just an aesthetic "modulator," but the emblem of Alberti's classicist revision (not rejection) of a precedent legacy of artifice.

Whether Alberti invented his viewing/tracing device, as he claimed, or merely adapted it from newly developed workshop tools used in transferring images to scale, he was responsible for its transmission to the subsequent literature of the arts.[30] A brief survey of the evidence allows us partially to bridge the gap between Alberti's time and Titian's and to evaluate the impact of the Albertian device. We begin in the second half of the fifteenth century, with Antonio Filarete: The architecture treatise he wrote for the Milanese court included a paraphrase of Alberti on painting. The account of composition cited a sturdier version of the veil, to be used "for learning to copy well from nature (*bene ritrarre del naturale*), and thus in relief."[31] Also at the Milanese court, in a manuscript on painting datable to the 1490s, Leonardo recommended a similar device for "Learning to pose a figure well."[32] His square frame or stretcher (*quadro over telaro*) held a net (*rette*) made of threads arranged in a grid (*riquadrato con fila*).

As the heading suggests, its chief purpose was to ensure a correct alignment of body parts in the pose of a *nudo* to be represented in a painting. To use Alberti's terminology, Leonardo's net was an aid in the *compositione* of members into bodies; he did not seem to value it for the contour–tracing of *circonscrittione,* which Alberti had linked so closely to the composition of limbs.

Like Filarte's *quadro* stretched with perpendicular intersecting wires or threads, Leonardo's net exhibited a much greater transparency than Alberti's. The aesthetically crucial obscuring of light contrasts achieved by the *velo* was not ignored in Leonardo's pictorial advice, however. Rather, he proposed an expedient that displaced the veil's role from that of screening the model to screening the source of light, thus affecting the very setting in which painter and model stand together. Leonardo's precept, from the same series of manuscript notes on painting that introduces the net, is celebrated for its evocation of the quintessential Leonardesque penumbra:

> If you have a courtyard which you could for your purpose cover with a linen awning, the light there will be good. Otherwise, when you wish to represent someone, do it in dull weather or towards evening. . . . Pay attention in the street towards evening, when the weather is bad, to how much grace and sweetness (*quando è cattivo tempo, quanta gratia e dolcezza*) can be seen in the faces of the men and women. Therefore, o painter, use a courtyard where the walls are colored black . . . and when it is sunny it should be covered with an awning. Alternatively, work on a painting towards evening when it is cloudy or misty, and this will be the perfect atmosphere (*aria*).[33]

The antithetical pairing of bad weather with sweetness and grace, making the one give birth to the other, plays poetically on the double sense of the word *aria,* which denotes air, atmosphere (and by extension weather, climate), as well as the "look," the animation, the style of a person.[34] Without overtly claiming kinship to the Albertian *velo,* Leonardo's formula for veiling and dimming the courtyard studio conveys a like effect of aesthetic filtering. With its help, real bodies are transmuted into perfected and magically heightened apparitions, their physical bulk subtly transformed into a crepuscular glow. As with Alberti, this tonal beautification of the figure is also its induction into an illusionistically "cloaked"

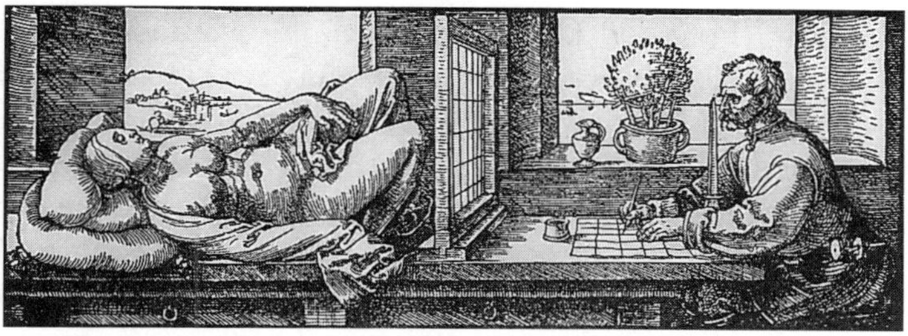

Figure 26. Albrecht Dürer, *Artist Representing Reclining Nude* (Perspective Study), woodcut, c. 1525, from *Unterweysung der Messung (Treatise on Measurement),* 2d ed. (Nuremberg, 1538). Photo: Foto Marburg/Art Resource.

two-dimensional world, all the more compelling to sight for having been rendered inaccessible to actual touch.[35]

Leonardo – who stopped in Venice in 1500, on the very eve of Venetian painting's renewal by talented immigrants from the mainland – was the chief agent of a modernized Albertian theory at the turn of the century.[36] To be sure, his discussion of the "life-study" net did not acknowledge the emblematic possibilities of *De pictura*'s *velo,* and he preferred to illustrate the perspectival intersection with a pane of glass (another Albertian example).[37] But he drew radical – and influential – conclusions from the *velo*'s lesson concerning the modulation of tones as a source of pictorial grace.

The net as intersection, serving as a component in an apparatus for making tangible the process of perspectival vision and representation, had a significant life after 1500 in the work of another illustrious painter-theorist. Albrecht Dürer, who sojourned in Venice in 1506 and perhaps as early as the mid-1490s, concluded the final chapter of his celebrated treatise on measurement (first edition, 1525; second edition, 1538) with a section on perspective construction. Its closing pages offered the craftsman who might feel overwhelmed by Dürer's geometrical demonstrations several illustrations showing the use of sighting and tracing devices, accompanied by detailed instructions for their manufacture and use.[38] One of these images, prepared after 1525 and placed at the close of the posthumous 1538 edition of the *Unterweysung der Messung,* presents the artist copying a reclining nude through "a frame with a lattice of strong black thread" (*ein ram mit einem gitter von starckem schwartzen zwirn*) (Fig. 26).

This remarkable visualization, appearing in print the very year of the *Venus of Urbino*'s completion, wordlessly – and programmatically – enacts the transmutation of erotic desire into representational display to which Arasse has called attention in Titian's painting (and in the Albertian Narcissus). As Dürer renders it, the process is mediated (or motivated) by the lattice, which in the context of the other devices introduced with it is a proper perspectival apparatus, not just an aid for image transfer and the manipulation of scale.[39] The accompanying text explicates what Joseph Leo Koerner calls a visual "regimen" whose strictness "renders the whole scene unintentionally comic."[40] Dürer calls the lattice tracing a more convenient approach than copying (*conterfeten*) the image through a glass pane "because it is less restricted (*es freier ist*)"; but then he dwells at great length on the importance and use of the vertical sighting device (rendered as a little obelisk before the artist's face). This sight keeps the draftsman's monocular inspection of the gridded model tethered to a single immutable point.

As Koerner puts it, in Dürer's rendering of the artist-nude model relation "Eros . . . is controlled by the machine of representation that institutes the self of the artist as . . . closed off, and therefore protected from the lure of the object." In this image (and by contrast with the more elaborate devices that precede it in Dürer's text) the *gitter* made of stout black threads is at the boundary – and confluence – of cognitive alertness and voluptuous self-forgetfulness, ascetic self-control and pleasurable anticipation.[41] It indeed suggests the way in which the Albertian intersection also doubles as a mirror of Narcissus – and this, in turn, allows us to understand the aim to seduce at the heart of Alberti's (and by extension Leonardo's) rhetorical "veiling" of light–dark contrasts in the interest of generating "grace."

Dürer's illustration of the lattice is not also an illustration of its accompanying text, but rather a commentary and amplification. If the text dwells on technical procedures, the illustration snares an elusive psychological relation as the consequence (or the motive?) of representational exactitude. Dürer had the opportunity to study Alberti's text, a copy of which was available in the former library of the astronomer Regiomontanus, catalogued by Pirckheimer in Nuremberg.[42] Certainly Dürer's contribution as a literate artist brought to fruition that combination of artisanal practicality and theoretical ingenuity to which Alberti had aspired when he claimed to address a nonscientific public with the aid of his *più grassa Minerva.*

I have given some attention to Leonardo's and Dürer's nets because they demonstrate that the Albertian *velo* bore offspring well into the Cinquecento, devices in which material expedients sustained theoretical reflection and more. But Alberti's contribution remained distinct from those of his successors. As might be expected of an art theorist who started out as a professional scholar, Alberti in 1435 was notably indifferent to the materiality of the painter's means. However, in addressing the basic mechanisms of representation and perception, he alone directly tied the physicality of the *velo* to the poetics of painting (not just its technical arsenal). In this way, he called attention to the depth of association available to artists aware of painting's materiality as a kind of pictorial content. How the very weave of the canvas surface became a partner in the "internal dialogue" of Venetian Cinquecento painting remains an open question. No doubt the great *teleri* with historical scenes commissioned by the Republic for the decoration of the Ducal Palace offered an unparalleled chance for ambitious painters to acquaint themselves with the resilience, the translucency, the architectonics of woven cloth. No doubt a long tradition of painted processional banners made it possible to think of pigmented cloth as a bearer of real, potent presence. I like to think that the metaphorical dimension of the Albertian legacy also played a part.

I certainly do not mean to suggest that Titian had in mind the literary precepts of Cicero, or even the poetry of Petrarch, when his brush stroked the surfaces of the *Venus of Urbino.* I do mean to suggest that Alberti bequeathed to Titian some excellent, poetically charged reasons for situating his velvet-contoured nude in a figured world that reiterates, over and over, its origin as an expanse of colored fabric. I would even go so far as to claim that the chief ornament in the *Venus*'s realm, the inhabited perspectival enclosure with its open window, pays homage to Alberti's conflation of the veil with the perspective "window," or *taglio* – a fusion that justifies one's fantasy, in the face of pictorial illusion's "transparency," that something lies under or behind it.

The *Venus of Urbino* owes a measure of its art historical reputation to the fact that it provided the template for Titian's subsequent series of mythological figures reclining on richly appointed beds, beginning with the great Naples *Danae* of 1545 (Fig. 6). But in a more general sense, the *Venus*'s tapestried world stands for a chief characteristic of Titian's oeuvre, which often relies on eye-catching expanses of illusionistically rendered fabric as a means of animating the space of representation. It is certainly in the redering of fabric and its ornaments (gilded braids, hems, buttons), and in jewelry pressing against skin, that the *Venus of Urbino*'s progeny directly recalls the charms of its less painterly parent. Virtually none of the later nudes shares its directness, the candor of the gaze, the left hand's intimate grasp.

However, among the *Venus of Urbino*'s bejeweled offspring, there is one – of different format – that approaches it in seductiveness by the way it acknowledges the viewer. It is the majestic seated *Venus with a Mirror,* in Washington, DC (Figs. 20–21), who turns away from us to look into a mirror from which, after all, she does look out at us, but only as a luminous rectangle from which all but the left shoulder, cheek, eye, and thatch of golden hair are withheld. In its very facture, confluence of desire and "speculation" are anticipated by Alberti's textile grid and his mirror of Narcissus.

The Washington *Venus* is partially nude: A fur-lined, wine-red velvet cloak is draped about her lower body and slides off her right shoulder. Her right hand, in a modified *pudica* gesture, crosses her torso and grasps an edge of the cloak, burying the fingers in the brown fur of the lining. But it is not exclusively her cloak. As the radiographic evidence shows, the figure was painted over a double portrait of a young couple, and Titian has allowed his Venus literally to borrow part of the man's fine garment, which was not painted over but retailored (Fig. 27).[43] The earlier painting does not die after all, but stays alive in a fur-lined cloth. To be sure, Titian expediently reused a preexistent patch of fine painting. But his practical choice need not preclude more imaginative readings of this particular figure of love – rising, as it were, from the obliteration of an amorous couple, taking with her the male companion's garment and preserving, through all these metamorphoses (that spawned as well a pair of Cupids and a doubled, but halved, image of the goddess), the oblique grain of the canvas support, which shapes the ridges of shimmering paint.

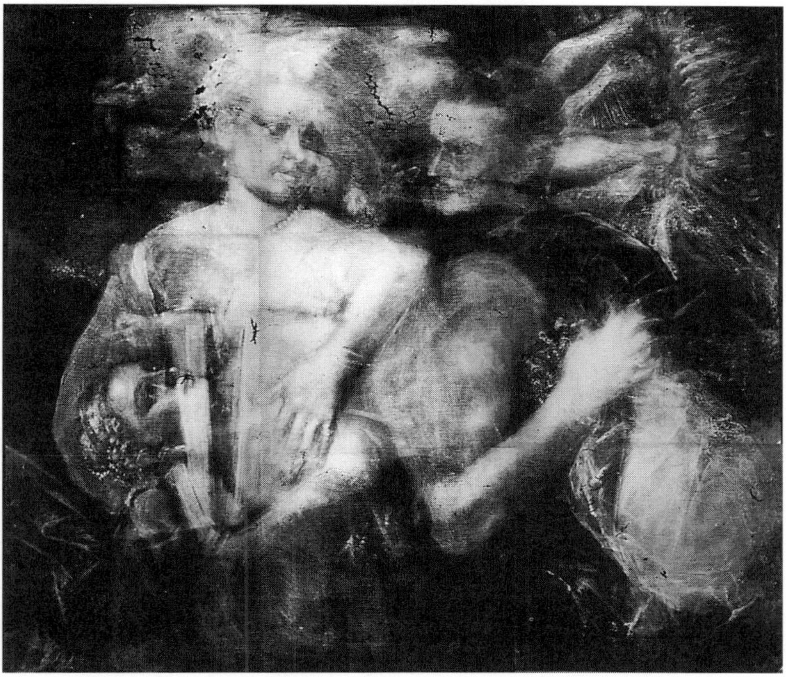

Figure 27. Titian, *Venus with the Mirror,* X-radiograph. Washington, DC, National Gallery of Art, Andrew W. Mellon Collection. Photo: National Gallery of Art, Washington, DC.

ACKNOWLEDGMENTS

I thank my colleagues Helen Hills and Andrea Bolland for their helpful comments on the penultimate draft of this essay. The final version is dedicated to Amelia.

NOTES

1. "Uerum apud tegumenta fictionum nulle sunt rethorice partes; mera poesis est, quicquid sub uelamento componimus et exquiritur exquisite": *Boccaccio in Defense of Poetry,* p. 36. Translation cited, with minor adjustments, from Osgood, *Boccaccio on Poetry,* p. 39.
2. I wish to thank the Direzione at the Uffizi for its kind permission to examine the painting in June 1994.

3. This etching is reproduced in *Tiziano nelle gallerie fiorentine,* p. 128.
4. Vasari-Milanesi, VII:443: "Sono nella guardaroba del medesimo duca [of Urbino] di mano di Tiziano due teste di femmina molto vaghe, ed una Venere giovanetta a giacere, con fiori e certi panni sottili attorno molto belli e ben finiti; ed oltre ciò, una testa dal mezzo in su d'una Santa Maria Maddalena con I capegli sparsi, che è cosa rara." Vasari's grouping of the *Venere* with a pair of ravishing but otherwise anonymous *teste di femmina,* and the bust-length figure of the Magdalene, whose unbound hair remains potently erotic, is itself suggestive. They form a sensuous female enclave in what is otherwise a manly catalog of famous sitters for the portraits in the duke's collection. The identification of the figure as a Venus is most recently supported by Rona Goffen, who gives cogent reasons for viewing the *Venus*'s iconography as suited to a marriage picture; see Goffen, "Problematic Patronage," and in this volume.
5. Whether or not Titian counted on his viewers' recognizing it, Giorgione's Dresden *Venus* (which was certainly in Venice through the sixteenth century) supplied the crimson drape and the flowery meadow that are conflated in this later mattress cover. Giorgione's white satin sheet and red mantle (with its gold-patterned border) look more like discarded under- and overgarments than like bed clothes. Johannes Wilde, *Venetian Art,* p. 75, suggested that these resonant draperies may have been among Titian's additions to the painting, although Marcantonio Michiel, who saw Giorgione's *Venus* in the Casa Marcello in 1525, specifically attributed to Titian the landscape background and the now-obliterated Cupid, both on the right-hand side of the painting.
6. On close inspection, the dog appears to have been "molded" from a large fold in the sheets.
7. Wilde underscored the significance of this continuity at the level of the painting's pigmentation. See his *Venetian Art,* p. 159: "The nude has been set in an interior of tapestry-like character in which all the main colours of the foreground . . . have been repeated on smaller planes but with the same identity. This is an important fact. It means that, with regard to colour, there is no difference whatsoever between foreground and background." I realize that the gold sky beyond the window (with the raking light casting the standing servant's shadow on the hangings behind her) could denote either sunrise or sunset, but I have chosen to read it as a dawn scene because the garment slung over the standing servant's shoulder appears to have just been unfurled. Admittedly, a plausible argument could be made for an evening setting. The background scene's enticement depends, in part, on its ambiguity, but for this very reason it also invites a narrative projection to account for its relationship with the nude in the foreground.

8. Rosand's are the most sensitive analyses of Titian's pictorial handling; see his *Meaning of the Mark,* pp. 56–88.
9. I have already attempted a similar argument in connection with another – far more demure – female figure of Venetian provenance, painted about a decade before Titian's *Venus of Urbino;* see my "Subject of Savoldo's *Magdalene.*"
10. See my "Artifice as Seduction in Titian." The argument was first presented at a conference held in 1986 at the National Humanities Center in North Carolina.
11. See Arasse's "Le nu couché dans la peinture," pp. 178–81.
12. On Titian's perspectival construction, Arasse recapitulates arguments he first presented in his *Tiziano: Venere d'Urbino,* pp. 20–6. There he concluded that the floor's orthogonals, as far as the silhouette of the sleeping dog's back, converge at a point a few centimeters in from the partition's edge, at the same height as the figure's left eye. The distance point located at the canvas's right edge implies a viewing distance of under 1 meter. A secondary vanishing point for the more steeply receding orthogonals on the right-hand side of the floor lies on the edge of the partition (to judge from Arasse's diagram, at the height of the figure's *right* eye).
13. See Arasse, "Le nu couché dans la peinture," pp. 186–7. Arasse's identification of the *cassone* alcove as private and the garden as public is unconvincing, given the high visibility of such private spaces as the principal bedrooms in the Renaissance palace. The garden, for its part, seems more a liminal than a public space. Admittedly, the available evidence is too scant to disprove the currency in Venice of *cassone* lids with painted nudes. It would, however, seem that Venetian Quattrocento *cassoni* were stuccoed, gilded, and intarsiaed, but not painted; see P. Schubring, *Cassoni* (Leipzig, 1915; rpt. 1923), text vol. entries 156–7, 165–9, 184–5, 289–90, 755a (a Venetian *cassone* of the type found in the *Venus of Urbino,* which Schubring dates to the early sixteenth century). Images of erotic nudes in splendidly appointed beds were very much in fashion during the decade preceding the composition of the *Venus of Urbino,* and although their general format may be traceable back to that of the images in *cassoni,* they constitute an independent genre by the 1530s; see my "Artifice as Seduction," pp. 68–77.
14. Arasse's characterization of Titian's strategy in the *Venus of Urbino* – the transformation of the entire painting into a kind of magical *cassone* interior by prompting the viewer to experience his own viewing as analogous to that of the miniaturized figure shown rummaging in such a clothes chest – bears a curious affinity to an observation by Richard Wollheim. According to Wollheim, Titian's chief purpose is the representation of corporeality, and in this task he often relies on figurative insets in the

middleground or background of his compositions. These are not perspectival markers but "elements that themselves invite being thought of – again metaphorically – as things that can be put away in a container. Elements of the picture assimilate themselves to toys, or to jewels, or to mere odds and ends. Inviting this thought, they compel the prior thought that the picture within whose four sides they lie is a container." The controlling corporeal metaphor satisfied by this expedient is that the body also "will get itself thought of as a container." See Wollheim's *Painting as an Art,* pp. 305–15, esp. pp. 312–15. Arasse and Wollheim clearly have different points of departure, but they pinpoint something that holds true for Titian's use of the space box in the *Venus of Urbino,* which is more like a "thought balloon" than a rational extension of the foreground.

15. Arasse, "Le nu couché dans la peinture," pp. 186–7. See Alberti, *Opere volgari,* p. 47, for Narcissus and painting: "What else is painting but to embrace with art that surface of the pool?"
16. See my "Testo e contesti," pp. 34–40, 43–4.
17. For the Latin manuscript tradition of *De pictura,* which includes several sixteenth-century examples, see Alberti, *Opere volgari,* pp. 301–4.
18. Here and in what follows I translate from Ludovico Domenichi's translation of the 1540 Basel edition of *De pictura;* see [Alberti], *La pittura,* (Venice, 1547), pp. 4–4v.
19. See Cicero, *De Amicitia* 18; Alberti cites this essay in *De pictura.*
20. For this and the following, see [Alberti], *La pittura,* tr. Domenichi, pp. 4v–5v.
21. For this and the following, see ibid., pp. 6v–8v.
22. For this and the following, see ibid., pp. 22–25v.
23. For Alberti's adaptation of rhetorical formulae, see Baxandall, *Giotto,* pp. 129–39.
24. See Baxandall's informative discussion of the periodic sentence in *Giotto,* pp. 20–31.
25. [Alberti], *La pittura,* tr. Domenichi, pp. 22v, 40v–41. The dyeing of the veil parallels the common workshop practice of tinting paper or parchment surfaces for the purpose of creating tonally diversified drawings, enhanced with white body color – an anticipation of pictorial modeling proper. See Cennini, *Il libro dell' arte,* pp. 15–16. According to Cennini, drawing on a tinted ground leads one "step by step to begin to want to find the principle and gateway of coloring (*del colorire*). . . . And you can either make your dyes pinkish or violet or green, or bluish or gray, that is to say muted colors, or flesh-colored, or whatever you please."
26. Could Alberti have in mind the contest between Zeuxis and Parrhasius narrated in Pliny the Elder's *Naturalis historia* 35, 65? Parrhasius was able to

mislead his rival with a painted drape that seemed to conceal a real painting underneath.

27. *Institutio oratoria* IX, iv, 20–2.
28. Baxandall, in *Giotto,* pp. 136–9, discusses the polemic pitting the advocates of the "composed" or periodic style against those of the "dissolute" style at the time *De pictura* was written. As he points out, Alberti adapted the terms of this literary dispute in his prescriptions against "dissolute" composition.
29. For a discussion, with references, of the *integumentum* (the veil of allegory) in medieval poetics and its reverberations in Renaissance painting, see my "Savoldo's *Magdalene,*" pp. 84–7.
30. On the use of gridded transfer drawings in the mid-Quattrocento, see Ames-Lewis, *Drawing,* pp. 24–6.
31. Filarete, *Trattato di architectura,* 2:677.
32. Paris, Bibliothèque Nationale 2038 (hereafter abbreviated as BN 2038), 24r. See Kemp, ed., *Leonardo on Painting,* pp. 216–17. The Italian text is available in Richter, ed., *Notebooks of Leonardo da Vinci,* pp. 260–1, no. 523. On the same page, Leonardo recommends using a sheet of glass for directly tracing *un sito* – a place – which can then be transferred from the glass with tracing paper and pounced onto regular drawing paper.
33. BN 2038, 20v; Kemp, ed., *Leonardo,* p. 215, and *Notebooks,* pp. 259–60, no. 520. Leonardo proposes other expedients for controlling the light effects observable in the studio; these all involve screening the source of light, whether window or candle. See *Leonardo,* pp. 214–16.
34. See Summers, *Judgment of Sense,* pp. 120–1; and Chastel, "L'aria."
35. See BN 2038, 24v; Kemp, ed., *Leonardo,* p. 202, and *Notebooks,* pp. 264–5: "HOW THE MIRROR IS THE MASTER OF PAINTERS. . . . The mirror is to be taken for master – the flat mirror, that is – because on its surface things resemble a painting in many aspects; that is to say, you see painting made on a flat surface displaying things in relief, and the mirror on a flat surface does the same. Painting is but a single surface and so is the mirror. Painting is intangible (*impalpabile*) inasmuch as that which appears round and protruberant cannot be grasped with the hands (*non si può circundare colle mani*), and the mirror does the same."
36. A strong claim for Leonardo's impact on Giorgione's development is made by A. Ballarin, "Nouvelle perspective," pp. 285–6.
37. Paris, Institut de France, MS A, 10v; Kemp, ed., *Leonardo,* p. 57, and *Notebooks,* p. 54, no. 85.
38. For the following citations, see Albrecht Dürer, *Painter's Manual,* pp. 392–3 (a viewing/tracing device using transparent glass, and another using movable strings and a hinged drawing surface) and pp. 430–5

(added in the 1538 edition: a viewing/tracing apparatus with a device for producing the effect of a more distant viewing position; a lattice made up of threads stretched on a frame).

39. For an analysis of Dürer's perspective machines that emphasizes their practicality and technological refinement (in contrast to Leonardo's), see Kemp, *Science of Art,* pp. 170–3.

40. For this and the following citation, see Koerner, *Moment of Self-Portraiture,* pp. 444–5. Koerner points out that the placement of the model has Dürer's draftsman staring into the woman's sex. In this sense, the potted myrtle on the boundary separating indoors from outdoors is another suggestive link between Dürer's and Titian's images because the myrtle, sacred to Venus, had overtly lascivious connotations. See Valeriano, *Hieroglyphica,* book 50, chap. 25: "One should not forget that the myrtle also signifies the woman's shameful parts." The airy land- and seascape in the background of Dürer's image also evokes the association of landscapes with reclining female nudes in Venetian painting of the first quarter of the sixteenth century.

41. In the posing of the model, Dürer's language suggests the freedom of the grid: "Then place the object to be drawn a good distance away [this important bit of advice is not illustrated]. Move it or bend it as you like (*nach deinem willen*) and view it from level o [at the point of the sighting device] to ascertain that it is in the proper position, so as to please you (*und besich das Corpus wie es dir gefall und ob es recht nach deinem willen lig*)."

42. See *Dürer, Schriftlicher Nachlass,* 2:85–6 and 1:280, 302. (*De pictura*'s Basel publisher, the humanist Thomas Venatorious, was an old acquaintance of Dürer and his Pirckheimer, and may have used the very volume in Regiomontanus's bequest as the manuscript source for his edition of 1540.)

43. See *Titian,* pp. 302–4, cat. no. 51.

6 T. J. CLARK

OLYMPIA'S CHOICE

> We shall define as prostitute only that woman who, publicly and without love, gives herself to the first comer for a pecuniary remuneration; to which formula we shall add: and has not other means of existence besides the temporary relations she entertains with a more or less large number of individuals.
>
> From which it follows – and it seems to me the truth – that prostitute implies first venality and second absence of choice.
>
> Ah! I know very well that by thus restricting the scope of the word, we end up reserving all our indulgence for those women-without-virtue who are the most fortunate, the privileged, the inexcusable, and at the same time we sanction the existence of a sort of *proletariat of love* over whom can be exercised with impunity all kinds of harshness and tyranny.
>
> Henri Turot[1]

In depicting a prostitute in 1865, Manet dealt with modernity in one of its most poignant and familiar, but also difficult aspects: difficult because it had already become a commonplace in the 1860s that women of this kind, formerly confined to the edges of society, had more and more usurped the centre of things and

Reprinted from *The Painting of Modern Life: Paris in the Art of Manet and His Followers* (Princeton, NJ, 1984), chapter 2, with permission of the author.

seemed to be making the city over in their image. Thus the features defining "the prostitute" were losing whatever clarity they had once possessed, as the difference between the middle and the margin of the social order became blurred; and Manet's picture was suspected of revelling in that state of affairs, marked as it was by a shifting, inconsequential circuit of signs – all of them apparently clues to its subject's identity, sexual and social, but too few of them adding up. This peculiar freedom with the usual forms of representation was later held to be the essence of *Olympia* (Fig. 2), as Manet's picture was called, and made it the founding monument of modern art; and certainly it was a painting which revealed the inconsistencies of its manufacture and breathed a kind of scepticism at the ways that likeness was normally secured. This went hand in hand, as the critical reaction at the time testifies, with a seeming displacement of the spectator from his accustomed imaginary possession of the work. Like any other picture, *Olympia* provided various places from which the viewer might appropriate its main fiction, but those places ended by being precisely too various; I shall argue that they were contradictory and largely uninhabitable; and to a great extent they remained so for later viewers, so that instead of the fictive body on the bed, a more limited fiction called "the picture" was consumed and imagined – it seemed the best on offer. Yet even this fact is open to contrary interpretations, and eager discussion of "the free play of the signifier" may on the whole be premature. It is true that *Olympia* makes hay with our assumptions as spectators, and may lead us to doubt the existence on canvas of three dimensions, the female body, and other minds; but this very negation is pictured as something produced in the social order, happening as part of an ordinary exchange of goods and services. The painting insists on its own materiality, but does so in and through a prostitute's stare, a professional and standardized attentiveness, with the self reserved from the purchaser's looking; though the possible grimness of that reflection on the painter's task was hardly understood in 1865, let alone approved of. . . .

. . . *Olympia,* as Baudelaire described it in his letter, was a picture of a nude woman with a Negress and a cat. The poet pretended to doubt the latter detail – "est-ce un chat, décidément?" – which might suggest that it was added to the picture after he left for Brussels, or simply that he raised his eyebrows at the thought of such an overtly Baudelairean signature. It was also a picture of a prostitute, we can be fairly certain of that. And in this too it seems to have derived, at least partly, from Baudelaire: Olympia's hopeless, disabused nobility recalls the kind described – and recommended to the modern artist – in *Le Peintre de la vie moderne:*

> Among these women, some, in whom an innocent yet monstrous fatuity is only too apparent, carry in their faces and in their eyes, which fix you audaciously, the evident joy of being alive (in truth, one wonders why). Sometimes they find, without seeking them, poses both provocative and dignified, which would delight the most fastidious sculptor, if only the sculptor of today had the courage and the wit to seize hold of nobility everywhere, even in the mire; at others, they show themselves in prostrate attitudes of desperate boredom, or adopt the indolent postures of the estaminet, with a masculine cynicism, smoking cigarettes to kill time, with all the resigned fatalism of the Orient; there they lie, sprawling on sofas, skirts ballooning to front and back like two fans, or they balance themselves precariously on stools and chairs; heavy, sad, stupid, absurd, their eyes glazed with brandy, and their foreheads bulging with the force of their own obstinacy.[2]

Zacharie Astruc was a friend and admirer of Baudelaire, and his five lines in the salon *livret* read like an attempt to provide Manet's naked woman with some of the same connotations. *Olympia* was Astruc's choice of title: it was on the face of it a dignified name, and its formality was emphasized by the phrase in his poem – the much-quoted, much-mocked description – "l'auguste jeune fille." Part of the critics' mockery had to do with Astruc's talents as a poet and part with their conviction that the appearance of dignity was deliberately flimsy. For Olympia was a pseudonym favoured by prostitutes: it figured in the classic list of names drawn up in 1836 by the trade's first great investigator, Parent-Duchâtelet:[3] the better class of brothel was full of Floras, Aspasias, Lucretias, Delphines, Thalias, Sidonias, Azelinas, Calliopes, Lodoiskas, and – inevitably – Virginias by the score. For readers in 1865 the name Olympia probably also conjured up, as Gautier put it in his *Salon,* "the memory of that great Roman courtesan on whom the Renaissance doted,"[4] by whom he meant La Dona Olympia, villainous heroine of a popular novel by Etienne Delécluze; sister-in-law, mistress, and manipulator of Pope Innocent X; prisoner and harlot, so avid for gold that after Innocent died she refused even to pay for his coffin.[5] Delécluze's romance had been reprinted as recently as 1862; the reference came easily to Gautier, and other critics seem to have echoed it; but even this reference, Gautier argues, is undeserved by the picture itself.[6] For, after all, the great Dona Olympia had been beautiful as well as sordid; Manet's young woman had taken nothing but her predecessor's name, and in that she was one of many. Her title was bogus; and as for Astruc's "auguste jeune fille"! It appeared to the critics a euphemism coined with the same cynical aplomb.

Some of the critics in 1865 were sure that Manet's Olympia was a prostitute and said as much. There was nothing very remarkable in their doing so: it had become an established critical tactic in the 1860s to detect the contemporary, even the bourgeois, *courtisane* beneath the skin of a Venus or Phryne; and in any case, as we shall see, prostitution demanded and received its representations in the salon each year, in forms both ancient and modern. But the words these critics used to indicate Olympia's profession were once or twice less ordinary, the strangeness having to do with their attempt to exceed the concept *courtisane* – its comfortable, general, archaic field of reference – and specify where Olympia came from and whom she could possibly be looking at.

Of course there were writers who did no such thing. Several were happy with the single epithet *courtisane,* and one followed Gautier's lead in calling Olympia "la dame de beauté de la Renaissance."[7] "What is this odalisque with a yellow belly [asked another], ignoble model picked up who knows where, who represents Olympia? Olympia? What Olympia? A courtesan, no doubt."[8] The question was easily answered, in other words. And *courtisanes* came from the Quartier Bréda, the area just north of the Boulevard des Italiens, not far from the railway station and felicitously close to the debtors' prison in the Rue de Clichy. Olympia was no exception: "It was said of Pradier," wrote one critic in 1865, "that he set out for Athens each morning and arrived each evening in the Rue de Bréda. Nowadays a certain number of artists go to the Rue de Bréda direct."[9] Manet was certainly one of them: he could be seen in Fantin-Latour's ridiculous painting *Le Toast* paying homage to Truth "in the guise of a redhead from the Quartier Bréda."[10]

These references are essentially normal. Brief and highly coded, they barely interrupt the critics' main business of aesthetic judgement. The same is true of Félix Deriège in *Le Siècle,* who ends his account of *Olympia* – we shall see later on that it was an exceedingly hostile one – with the inevitable jibe at Manet's claim to be painting the truth: "one can be true indeed, if one is able to paint like Goya, even in representing a *manola de bas étage,* lying quite naked on her bed, while a Negress brings her a bouquet."[11] No doubt the phrase *de bas étage* is a sneer at Olympia's presumed place in the social order, or at least in her chosen profession – she is clearly no *grande cocotte* – but the phrase is elliptical, and the writer sees no need to spell out its unpleasant implications.

Some writers were not so reticent. Postwer, for example, writing in an eccentric journal called *La Fraternité Littéraire,* quoted all five of Astruc's limping lines and proceeded to the following fraternal analysis:

> What verse! What a picture! Olympia awakes, weary from . . . dreaming. She has had a bad night, that is evident. Insomnia and colic have disturbed her serenity; her colour indicates as much. There are two "*black messengers*": a cat which has unfortunately been flattened between two railway sleepers; a Negress who has nothing about her that *recalls the amorous night* unless it be a bouquet bought at the florist's on the corner, and paid for by Monsieur Arthur, which tells me a great deal about Olympia. Arthur is certainly in the antechamber waiting.[12]

Monsieur Arthur's identity is obscure now and perhaps always was, but his purpose could hardly have been made plainer. And it was dangerous to talk at all of the real circumstances of prostitution, even in this lugubrious way, since doing so could lead so quickly to the kind of fact which the stately word *courtisane* was intended to obscure. The *courtisane* was supposed not to belong at all to the world of class and money; she floated above or below it, playing with its categories, untouched by its everyday needs. It was not clear that Manet's prostitute did any such thing. To more than one critic in 1865 she seemed to occupy a quite determinate place in the Parisian class system: she was an "Olympia from the Rue

Mouffetard,"[13] "the wife of a cabinetmaker,"[14] a "coal lady from Batignolles."[15] All of these references were meant to be funny, of course, but the jokes depended on Olympia's being placed, to some extent unequivocally, in the world of the *faubourgs* and the working class.

The same is true – though here the tone is more elusive and ironical – of Jean Ravenel's description of *Olympia* in a paper called *L'Epoque*. It has at its centre the following compacted, staccato sentence or two, in which the writer seems to be casting round for categories in which *Olympia* might begin to make sense. The list he provides is brilliant and unexpected:

> Painting of the school of Baudelaire, freely executed by a pupil of Goya; the vicious strangeness of the little *faubourienne,* woman of the night from Paul Niquet's, from the mysteries of Paris and the nightmares of Edgar Poe. Her look has the sourness of someone prematurely aged, her face the disturbing perfume of a *fleur du mal;* her body fatigued, corrupted, but painted under a single transparent light. . . .[16]

For the moment let us extract from the pattern of phrases the words "petite faubourienne, fille des nuits de Paul Niquet, des mystères de Paris et des cauchemars d'Edgar Poe." No doubt these descriptions are meant to evoke the painting's dreamlike, literary quality, but for the reader in 1865 they would also have suggested that Olympia belonged to Paris in quite ordinary ways. To call her a *petite faubourienne* was simply to say she was working-class; to have her be a character from Eugène Sue's novel *Les Mystères de Paris* was essentially to make the same point; to imagine her haunting the tables of Paul Niquet's was to place her in the lower depths of prostitution, among the women who catered to the porters of Les Halles. (Niquet's establishment in the Rue aux Fers stayed open all night and "was frequented by a quite special clientele of ragpickers, idlers, drunkards, and women whose sex and age were indistinguishable beneath their mass of rags."[17] For a while the bar had been a stopping place for sightseers of the Parisian underworld, but by 1865 it had returned to its normal obscurity.)

These are descriptions of Olympia's class; and I shall end this chapter by arguing that class was the essence of Olympia's modernity and lay behind the great scandal she provoked. But it seems none of the critics in 1865 – not even Jean Ravenel – would have agreed with me. There were over seventy pieces of writing on Manet's picture that year, and they contained, as I have shown, no more than a handful of references to prostitution and a grand total of six attributions of class, all fleeting and formulaic. However one looks at it, this is a strikingly poor haul, and the questions raised by the scarcity can be put as follows: If class was somehow signified in *Olympia,* and sometimes mentioned, what were the signs of it? And why could they not be identified in more detail, even by a critic like Ravenel, who seemed convinced that Olympia was working-class and that he should say so? The critics were certainly offended by *something* in Olympia: What was it, then, that they believed they saw and thought improper?

We have to do with art critics writing salon reviews in the daily press or monthly magazines. These writers would presumably have liked to discuss Manet's picture as an example of a school or a tendency in art, most probably that of Realism. Was not Manet included, along with Astruc, Whistler, the etcher Félix Bracquemond, and others, in the picture Fantin-Latour had sent to the salon entitled *Le Toast* or *Hommage à la Vérité?* Courbet had a painting in the salon of the anarchist Proudhon; Théodule-Augustin Ribot a study of Saint Sebastian, in his best Spanish manner; and Whistler his odd *Princesse du pays de la porcelaine.* The critics could flesh our their account of Realism in various ways: by including a kitchen scene by Antoine Vollon, for example, or a "metallic" Virgin by Albert Lambron,[18] or by giving encouragement to two beach scenes by Claude Monet, the "young Realist who promises much."[19]

This was already a list of eccentrics and anomalies, and perhaps Manet could be added to it. He was the "self-styled Realist, pupil of Courbet";[20] his *Jésus* was "Raphael corrected by a third-rate Courbet";[21] master and imitator were the two "Marquis de Sade of painting."[22] The violence of this final phrase was not necessarily a guide to the critics' overall tone: though Courbet was still condescended to in 1865, his school was an established part of the French scene, and even its enemies wished to discriminate and recognize talent where it occurred. They tried to do so in Manet's case.

Manet was a skilful technician, they quite often conceded. His draughtsmanship had character and originality, his colour was supple and mordant, he had "tempérament," "facultés," "une main d'artiste."[23] His painting was understood to be deliberately bold and experimental, and regularly attained to "a very great truth of tone";[24] it had "the charm of naïveté" it had touch, vigour, and "hardiesse,"[25] it derived (a bit slavishly) from Goya,[26] and even at its worst "one made out passages which were straightforwardly well done."[27]

Yet on the whole the critics in 1865 could not be so charitable as this. There was something about *Olympia* which eluded their normal frame of reference, and writers were almost fond of admitting they had no words for what they saw. *Olympia* was "informe," "inconcevable," "inqualifiable," "indéchiffrable"; the picture "ne s'explique pas."[28] "The least handsome of women has bones, muscles, skin, form, and some kind of colour,"[29] whereas Olympia had none; she was "neither true nor living nor beautiful."[30] The negatives multiplied: "she does not have a human form,"[31] and therefore "I can say nothing about her in truth, and do not know if the dictionary of French aesthetics contains expressions to characterize her."[32] "Not that I dream of examining her, describing her. God preserve me from so doing!"[33] "*Que signifie cette peinture,*" finally, "and why does one find these canvases in the galleries of the Palais de l'Industrie?"[34]

Of course these phrases are partly mechanical. A good salon review was incomplete without its quota of monstrosities, and one or two works each year were consigned to the space outside Art altogether. They were to be compared with the latest popular song or Hottentot Venus, and described as mere sign painting or "images d'Epinal."[35] All of these stock figures were tried out on *Olympia* in 1865; and yet in this case the critics' sneering claim not to be able to see or describe *Olympia* – not to have the least sense of its formal logic – does seem to be close to the truth. There are ways, after all, in which *Olympia* was at pains to disclose its relationship to the great tradition of European art, and by and large the critics seem genuinely not to have noticed that it did so.

For instance, *Olympia* derived – and stated its derivation – from Titian's *Venus of Urbino* (Fig. 1).[36] The pose of the nude is essentially the same, and the nude's accessories seem to be chosen as the modern forms of their Renaissance prototypes: orchid in place of roses, cat for dog, Negress and flowers instead of servants bringing dresses from a distant *cassone.* The nineteenth century believed that Titian's Venus was a courtesan. This was probably too secular a reading, but the sense of the picture's sensuality it stemmed from – the unchasteness of its chastity, the openness of its promise of undress and attentiveness – does not seem much mistaken. Promise, in Titian's case, may have been the operative word: if the picture was painted to commemorate a wedding, it was most likely that of Guidobaldo II della Rovere, who was married in 1534 to a ten-year-old girl, Giulia Varano.[37] That the body represented in the picture is older and more mature, and that the signs arranged round it seem to denote for the most part fidelity and the domestic virtues, may well have carried in the circumstances a quite pointed meaning. In any case, the picture's domesticity is of a special kind: the woman on the bed is Venus as well as wife, and the Urbino records were surely right to name her, bluntly, "la nuda."[38]

For the nineteenth century this painting *was* the nude. Like many another student, Manet had done an oil copy of it in the Uffizi when he was in his twenties, as a normal part of learning the alphabet of art. Salon criticism was supposed in turn to be largely about that alphabet and how well young painters were using it: the writing of a *Salon* was organized around the critic's ability to recognize quotations from older art and say whether they were apposite or not. But in the case of *Olympia*'s relation to the *Venus of Urbino,* for all that the critics were capable of producing the key word *courtisane,* the usual connections did not follow. In the mass of commentary in 1865, only two critics talked at all about Manet's sources, and they did so in a thoroughly outlandish way. "This Olympia," wrote one Amédée Cantaloube in *Le Grand Journal,*

> a sort of female gorilla, a grotesque in India rubber outlined in black, apes on a bed, in a state of complete nudity, the horizontal attitude of Titian's *Venus;* the right arm rests on the body in the same fashion, except for the hand, which is flexed in a sort of shameless contraction.[39]

This should be compared with some lines by Pierrot in a fly-by-night publication called *Les Tablettes de Pierrot*:

> . . . a woman on a bed, or, rather, some form or other, blown up like a grotesque in India rubber; sort of monkey making fun of

the pose and the movement of the arm in Titian's *Venus,* with one hand shamelessly flexed.[40]

Perhaps the other seventy-odd writers said nothing about Titian as a way of registering their contempt for what Manet had done to him; but I am inclined to think that they simply did not see that Manet had done anything. We might compare their silence in 1865 with what they had had to say two years earlier about Manet's *Déjeuner sur l'herbe.* That painting was similarly held to be bizarre and immoral, and it had been shown in the extraordinary Salon des Refusés – to that extent, officially beyond the pale of Art. Critics certainly came to laugh at its mistakes and incoherences, and yet the very way to do so best was to point out what Manet's picture derived from – and how incompetently. The writers whose *Salons* dealt with *Le Déjeuner sur l'herbe* were quick to connect it to the painting in the Louvre then thought to be by Giorgione, the so-called *Fête champêtre;* and one of them even claimed to detect that Manet had quoted – a peculiar, literal repetition it is – from a print after Raphael of river gods and attendant nymphs.[41]

But in 1865 none of this took place. If the revisions of the *Venus* could be seen at all, they could not be said; and if on one or two occasions they were spoken of, it was in Cantaloube and Pierrot's terms. Their violent fantasies of what Manet had done to Titian explain the other critics' silence, I think for if the old arrangement of the nude was present at all in Manet's picture, it seemed there as a sign of everything the actual, latter-day *Olympia* was not. The past was travestied in *Olympia:* it was subjected to a kind of degenerate simian imitation, in which the nude was stripped of its last feminine qualities, its fleshiness, its very humanity, and left as "une forme quelconque" – a rubber-covered gorilla flexing its hand above its crotch.

I shall take Pierrot and Cantaloube's descriptions as licence to say – quite crudely in the end – that the meanings Manet contrived in terms of Titian in 1865 amounted to nothing for most of his viewers. The *Venus of Urbino* was painted out or painted over, and seemed to the public no part of the image Manet had produced. It is as if the work of negation in *Olympia* – and some such work was surely intended, some kind of dissonant modernization of the nude, some pitting of Baudelaire against Titian – were finally done, but somewhat too well. The new Dona Olympia was too much the opposite of Titian's for the opposition to signify much, and the critics were able to overlook those features the two pictures had in common.

NOTES

1. Turot, *Prolétariat,* pp. 107–9: "Acceptons donc, si vous le voulez bien, la définition de M. Emile Richard, qui s'appuie sur le *Digeste* pour formuler sa pensée dans les termes que voici:

   " 'Doit seulement être réputée prostituée toute femme qui, publiquement et sans amour, se livre au premier venu, moyennant une rémuneration pécuniaire, formule à laquelle il convient d'ajouter: et n'a d'autres moyens d'existence que les relations passagères qu'elles entretient avec un plus ou moins grand nombre d'individus.'

   "D'où il résulte – ce qui me parait être la vérité – que la prostitution implique d'abord la vénalité et ensuite l'absence de choix.

   "Ah! je sais bien qu'à vouloir ainsi restreindre la portée du mot, nous arrivons à réserver toutes les indulgences pour les plus heureuses des femmes sans vertu, pour les privilégiées, pour les plus inexcusables, et que nous consacrons au contraire l'existence d'une sorte de *prolétariat de l'amour* sur qui peuvent impunément s'appesantir toutes les sévérités et toutes les tyrannies. . . .

   "Et ce prolétariat est, tout comme l'autre, l'inéluctable conséquence du régime capitaliste."
2. Baudelaire, *Oeuvres complètes,* pp. 1188–9.
3. See Parent-Duchâtelet, *De la prostitution,* 1:134. Its usual French form, Olympe, is given as one of a list of thirty-five common *surnoms* for prostitutes of the *classe élevée.* (Those of the *classe inférieure* preferred Bellecuisse, Faux-cul, Mont-Saint-Jean, La Ruelle, Crucifix, Le Boeuf, etc.) Farwell, *Manet and the Nude,* p. 232, was the first to point out that Olympia was a well-known prostitutes' nickname.
4. Gautier: "*Olympia,* dont le titre réveille le souvenir de cette grande courtisane romaine dont raffola la Renaissance, ne s'explique à aucun point de vue, même en la prenant pour ce qu'elle est, un chétif modèle étendu sur un drap. Le ton des chairs est sale, le modelé nul. Les ombres s'indiquent par des raies de cirage plus ou moins larges. Que dire de la négresse qui apporte un bouquet dans un papier et du chat noir qui laisse l'empreinte de ses pattes crottées sur le lit? Nous excuserions encore la laideur, mais vraie, étudiée, relevée par quelque splendide effet de couleur. La femme la moins jolie a des os, des muscles, une peau, des formes et un coloris quelconque. Ici, il n'y a rien, nous sommes fâché de le dire, que la volonté d'attirer les regards à tout prix."

5. See Pastor, *History of the Popes* 30:32–47. Delécluze's novel was first published in 1842.
6. As far as I can tell, these are the only connotations of the title to which the critics seem alert. There are other tempting possibilities: for instance, the automaton heroine, Olympia, of Hoffmann's story "L'Homme au sable," with which Astruc and Co. would surely have been familiar (see *Contes d'Hoffmann,* pp. 115ff.). There is a similarly named cold *courtisane* heroine in Dumas's *La Dame aux camélias* (see Reff, *Manet: Olympia,* pp. 111–13).
7. Ego: "L'auguste jeune fille est une courtisane. . . ." Leroy, *L'Universel:* O chat de la courtisane Olympia. . . ." Cantaloube, *Le Grand Journal:* "Il s'agit d'une Olympia chantée par M. Zacharie Astruc, et bien différente de la dame de beauté de la Renaissance."
8. Claretie, *L'Artiste:* "Qu'est-ce que cette odalisque au ventre jaune, ignoble modèle ramassé je ne sais où, et qui représente Olympia? Olympia? Quelle Olympia? Une courtisane sans doute."
9. Du Pays: "on a dit de Pradier qu'il partait le matin pour Athènes et arrivait le soir à la rue de Bréda. Aujourd'hui, un certain nombre d'artistes vont à la rue de Bréda directement." This follows a discussion of Fantin-Latour's *Le Toast,* and various apoplectic asides about Manet in previous articles.
10. Challemel-Lacour, in a passage on the "grotesques" of painting: "Leur trait commun, un des symptômes les plus connus dans les Petites-Maisons, est la prétention d'être les seuls vrais amants de la Vérité; on l'adore sous les traits de quelque rousse du quartier Bréda, on se réunit autour d'elle en paletot, en robe de chambre, en chapeau tubuliforme, on lui offre des fleurs, on lui porte des toasts, on appelle, le public à lui rendre hommage, et le public répond à cette leçon par une autre que ces artistes feraient bien de comprendre." Manet's painting and Fantin's are deliberately being conflated. See also p. 89.
11. Deriège: "l'on peut être également très-vrai, quand on sait peindre comme Goya, en représentant une *manola* de bas étage, couchée toute nue sur son lit, pendant qu'une négresse lui apporte un bouquet."
12. Postwer: "Quels vers! Quel tableau! Olympia s'éveille, lasse . . .de songer. La nuit a été mauvaise, c'est évident. Une insomnie, panachée de coliques, en a troublé la sérénité; son teint l'indique. Il y a deux '*messagers noirs*': un chat, qu'une circonstance malheureuse a applati entre deux tampons de chemins de fer; une négresse, qui n'a rien de *pareil à la nuit amoureuse,* si ce n'est un bouquet acheté chez la fleuriste du coin, et dont M. Arthur a fait les frais, ce qui m'en apprend très-long sur Olympia. Arthur est certainement dans l'anti-chambre, qui attend."
13. Geronte: Clark, *Painting of Modern Life,* p. 97.
14. Bertall, *Le Journal Amusant.*

15. Bertall, *L'Illustration,* 3 June.
16. See Clark, *Painting of Modern Life,* ch. 2, pp. 139–40 and note 144.
17. Larousse, *Grand Dictionnaire* 3:11: "Ce cabaret, ouvert toute la nuit, était fréquenté par une clientèle tout particulière, des chiffonniers, des ródeurs, des ivrognes et des femmes dont l'age et le sexe n'eussent pu se reconnaître sous l'amas de haillons qui les couvraient. . . . Grâce à tout ceci, le cabaret de Paul Niquet était connu du monde entier, et lorsqu'un roman d'Eugène Sue eut mis les tapis francs à la mode, ce fut à qui irait visiter celui-là, au risque de s'y trouver en bien mauvaise compagnie."
18. Described as such by Cantaloube in *Le Grand Journal,* in his general attack on the Realists that year. Geronte described him as "un Fra Angelico de pacotille." Lambron was regularly bracketed with Courbet and his followers. Geronte had previously, in an article of 2 June, praised Vollon's *Intérieur de cuisine* as worthy of Chardin, but could not resist a side swipe at Baudelaire in passing: "Il y a, dans cette cuisine, un certain mou de veau, pendu à un croc, qui vaut tout un poème. (Est-ce bien un mou de veau? Je consulterai M. Baudelaire.)"
19. Gallet: "un jeune réaliste qui promet beaucoup. – Ses deux marines: *L'Embouchure de la Seine a Honfleur* et *La Pointe de la Hève à marée basse,* portent l'empreinte d'une main forte, peu soucieuse du joli, très-préoccupée de la justesse de l'effet." Cf. Geronte: "Que dire, par exemple, de cette *Embouchure de la Seine à Honfleur* (no. 1524), où les flots sont figurés par des mottes de terre, les voiles des bateaux par des triangles de bois noir, et qu'on croirait dessinée par un enfant de douze ans sur la couverture de son catéchisme. . . ."

    Among the many critics who discuss Manet in the context of a Realist school, the more interesting accounts are those by Louis Auvray (a bitter attack on the Realists' assault on traditional standards, and the art of Bouguereau in particular), Deriège, Geronte, Jankovitz, Mantz (for whom the Realism of 1850 survives only in Belgium!), and, in a typically bizarre way, Pierrot. One standard tactic was to extract Ribot from the group and declare him the only Realist worthy of the name; see, e.g., Gallet and Bonnin.
20. Ego: "Je ne cite pas le nom du prétendu réaliste, élève de Courbet, qui a déposé cette *Olympia* le long du mur officiel. . . ."
21. Jankovitz: "*Jésus insulté* par M. Manet, je veux dire dû à son pinceau, est un tableau au-dessous de toute critique. C'est du Raphaël corrigé par un Courbet de troisième qualité. . . ."
22. Gille: "Qu'on ne s'y trompe pas, MM. Courbet, Manet et autres font vraisemblablement ainsi, parce qu'ils ne peuvent faire autrement, et j'ai grand peur pour eux qu'ils ne soient que consciencieux en nous offrant ces monstruosités. Ce sont des esprits malades, comme qui dirait des

sortes de marquis de Sade de la peinture, dont le sens artistique est déplacé ou corrompu, et qui ont perdu le chemin lumineux du naturel et du beau; tous deux se heurtant dans l'ombre, y chercheront vainement l'inconnu et le nouveau, ils ne pourront y trouver que des fantômes difformes et hideux." The Baudelairean echoes in the last few phrases – especially the echoes of the close of *Le Voyage* – seem deliberate. Compare the terms of Ravenel's evocation of the same "source."

23. Anon, *L'Autographe au Salon:* "M. Manet a de rares qualités d'originalité et de caractère comme dessinateur, de souplesse et de mordant comme coloriste. On peut s'en aperçevoir rien qu'à ces petits croquis qui semblent faits du bout d'une plume usée avec l'insouciance parfaite et la verve pittoresque de Goya." About uses the words "tempérament" and "facultiés." Drak: "Une main d'artiste guidée par une cervelle bourrée de paradoxes jusqu'à l'indigestion."
24. Compare Fillonneau, "M. Manet expose aussi Jésus insulté par les soldats, où nous voudrions trouver autre chose à louer que des valeurs de tons, témoignages insuffisants d'une certaine recherche," with d'Arpentigny in Martinet's magazine: "M. Manet, entre autres, ariste d'une nature fine, distinguée, est remarquable dans ses oeuvres, par une vérité très-grande des tonalités, par une hardiesse, sans mesure il est vrai, mais qui cédera devant le besoin d'études plus sévères." Aubert, Chesneau, and Du Camp were also well aware of Manet's tonal aims.
25. Gonzague Privat, p. 66: "Eh bien! moi, je n'hésite pas à le diré: M. Manet a le tempérament d'un peintre, l'inspiration poétique, le charme de la naïveté, des tons, des finesses, et un côté vivant que peu d'artistes possèdent." Montifaud: "Nous savons reconnaître la touche de M. Manet au milieu des excentricités qu'il a voulu nous servir, comme son Christ insulté et sa composition d'Olympia, et cette touche dénote une vigueur qui, employée par un esprit plus sain, pourrait produire des oeuvres." Rapinus Beaubleu: "Un peintre de cette valeur devrait se méfier de son extrême facilité qui touche en quelque sorte à l'improvisation. Mais ce défaut prouve une ardeur, une vigueur, un tempérament peu communs à notre époque." (Fillonneau: see note 23.)
26. The Goya link is mentioned in *L'Autographe au Salon;* Cantaloube in *Le Grand Journal* – "Constatons, en effet, des tons dérobés aux Espagnols, surtout à Goya, mais délayés dans je ne sais quelle mixture nauséabonde" – and more cryptically in *L'Illustrateur des Dames:* "Elle [the figure of Truth in Fantin's *Toast*] dirait à l'un, ne démonétisez ou ne barbouillez pas Goya avec vos hideux pastiches à la façon de Barbarie; à l'autre, ne décalquez pas au carreau l'une des estampes de l'album des cinquante femmes du Japon" (clearly Manet and Whistler are meant); Deriège (see note 11 above); Gautier, in discussing the Christ: "L'exécution rappelle, moins l'esprit, les

plus folles ébauches de Goya, lorsqu'il s'amusait à peindre en jetant des baquets de couleurs contre sa toile"; and Ravenel, p. 134 above.

27. Gautier *fils:* "Dans *Olympia* M. Manet semble avoir fait quelque concession au goût public et à travers le parti pris on discerne des morceaux qui ne demandent pas mieux que d'être bons."
28. Aubert: "Eh bien, comment se fait-il qu'il soit l'auteur de cette *Olympia,* qui par courtoisie, par intérêt sympathique pour l'homme, je ne veux pas analyser, mais que je caractériserai en peu de mots en disant qu'elle n'est ni vraie, ni vivante, ni belle (belle, grand-Dieu!), qu'elle est informe, qu'elle a je ne sais quoi de lubrique, que ce corps est sale, que sais-je?" Cantaloube, *Le Grand Journal:* "Nous voulons, ici, parler de certaines ébauches informes ou grotesques qui causent un véritable scandale." Chesneau: "un parti pris de vulgarité inconcevable." Clément: "Quant aux deux toiles qu'a envoyées M. Manet, elles sont inqualifiables." Gille: "Cet indéchiffrable *rébus. . . .*" Gautier; see note 24 above.
29. Gautier; see note 4.
30. Aubert; see note 27.
31. Deriège: Clark, *Painting of Modern Life,* ch. 2, note 72.
32. Dubosc de Pesquidoux: "Quant à l'*Odalisque* que M. Manet a exposée au-dessous de son *Christ,* et dans une pose si honnête, je n'en puis rien dire en vérité, et je ne sais pas si le dictionnaire de l'esthétique française offre des expressions pour la caractériser. . . . On ne peut point parler de tels tableaux, ni en donner l'idée."
33. Merson: "Auparavant, néanmoins, un mot des tableaux de M. Manet, initiateur fameux selon quelques gens. Non pas que je songe à les examiner, à les décrire. Dieu m'en préserve!"
34. Escoffier: "Que signifie cette peinture et pourquoi trouve-t-on ces tableaux dans les galeries du Palais de l'Industrie?"
35. Auvray: "Et voilà pourquoi Olympia est si bien placée. . . . 'Que c'est comme un bouquet de fleurs.' " Compare the captions of the Bertall cartoon in *Le Journal Amusant* and Cham's in *Le Charivari* (in all three cases the reference is to a famous café-concert song by Paulus, "Le Baptême du petit ébéniste," which is quoted and discussed in chapter four); Geronte: "cette Vénus hottentote"; Postwer: "Le tableau peut servir d'enseigne à une maison d'accouchement; l'auteur a une consolation toute trouvée"; Merson: "M. Manet, qui a peint l'enseigne de la *Femme à barbe,* est original," and, "Et aux personnes qui n'ont pas vu ces pièces mirifiques, il suffira d'affirmer que le *Juif errant,* tel qu'Epinal l'expédie à toutes les auberges du globe, est un pur chef-d'oeuvre auprès d'*Olympia* et de *Jésus insulté par les soldats*"; Cantaloube, *L'Illustrateur des Dames:* "Voilà donc ces artistes, comme bien d'autres entraînés par l'abus des improvisations et du métier, uniquement préoccupés d'attrouper le

public selon le mode des enseignes de la foire" (his verdict on Manet, Fantin, and Lambron); Deriège, see Clark, *Painting of Modern Life,* chap. 2, note 72; Geronte (the pseudonym hides Victor Fournel, a special expert in such matters), see Clark, chap. 2, note 70, and a parallel phrase earlier in his article, "ces deux toiles foraines."

36. See Farwell, *Manet and the Nude,* p. 199ff. for full discussion. See also Reff, *Manet: Olympia,* pp. 46–61.
37. See Reff, "Meaning of Titian's Venus of Urbino," pp. 362–3. Hope's more recent dismissal of the Guidobaldo connection (*Titian,* p. 82) seems based on an odd view of Titian's scrupulousness as regards the art market.
38. See Wethey, 3:203.
39. Cantaloube: "Jamais, du reste, on n'a vu de ses yeux spectacle pareil et d'un effet plus cynique: cette Olympia, sorte de gorille femelle, de grotesque en caoutchouc cerné de noir, singe sur un lit, dans une complète nudité, l'attitude horizontale de la Vénus de Titien; le bras droit respose sur le corps de la même façon, sauf la main qui se crispe dans une sorte de contraction impudique. De l'autre côté du lit, une négresse, 'un doux messager noir,' lui apporte, à son réveil, le printemps sous le forme d'un bouquet de fleurs qui n'a guère l'air de flatter l'odorat. On ne sait ce que vient de faire un pauvre chat maigre, d'une couleur de noir animal, car il gonfle piteusement son échine au pied de 'l'auguste jeune fille en qui la flamme brûle' (voir le livret)."
40. Pierrot: "L'autre peintre de ce groupe expose; 1. un Christ. O divin maître, tu n'a jamais été plus torturé; qu'on éloigne de toi ce calice! 2. une femme sur un lit, ou plutôt une forme quelconque gonflée comme un grotesque en caoutchouc; une sorte de guenon grimaçant la pose et le mouvement du bras de la Vénus du Titien, avec une main impudiquement crispée! Une négresse, un chat noir, tout maigre d'échine qu'il soit, n'en faisant pas moins le gros dos, complètent cette vision du sabbat." The nearest thing to another reference in 1865 is the title "la Vénus au chat" given the picture in passing by J. Claretie in *Le Figáro.* Pierrot and Cantaloube are surely one and the same writer.
41. The evidence for the critical reaction in 1863 is incomplete; but of the handful of references to Manet we know, one mentions the Giorgione connection directly – Astruc in "Le Salon," *Le Feuilleton Quotidien,* 20 May 1863, p. 5 (cited in *Zacharie Astruc,* by Flescher, p. 121). Astruc's reference seems to be echoed, quite casually and not approvingly, in Thoré's attack on "ce contraste d'un animal [he means the reclining man] si antipathique au caractère d'un scène champêtre, avec cette baigneuse sans voiles," where the words "scène champêtre" are perhaps meant to remind the reader of the nineteenth-century title of Giorgione's picture (see Thoré, *Salons de W. Bürger* 1:425.) The recognition of the Raphael

source was added as a note to Chesneau's *L'Art et les artistes modernes,* p. 190, which is a reprint of his "Salon" in *Le Constitutionnel* the previous year. Though Chesneau does not say so, one suspects he had been primed, perhaps by the artist.

The evidence is fragmentary and odd, as I say, but what we have of it suggests some kind of contrast between the critical language of 1863 and 1865 along the lines I have sketched.

Bibliography

Adelmann, Howard B. *The Main Currents of Embryological Thought before Malpighi,* vol. 2 of *Marcello Malpighi and the Evolution of Embryology.* Ithaca, NY, 1966.

Agostini, Grazia. "La Venere d'Urbino." In Mina Gregori, et al., *Tiziano nelle Gallerie fiorentine,* pp. 125–35. Florence, 1978.

Alberti, Leon Battista. *De re aedificatoria.* Ed. by Giovanni Orlandi. 2 vols. Milan, 1966.

I dieci libri de l'architettura di Leon Battista de gli Alberti Fiorentino. Trans. by Pietro Lauro. Venice, 1546.

L'Architettura di Leon Battista Alberti. Trans. by Cosimo Bartoli. Florence, 1550.

On the Art of Building in Ten Books. Trans. by Joseph Rykwert, Neil Leach, and Robert Tavernor. Cambridge, MA, 1988.

On Painting and On Sculpture, The Latin Texts of "De Pictura" and "De Statua." Ed. and trans. by Cecil Grayson. London, 1972.

Opere volgari. Ed. by Cecil Grayson. Bari, 1973.

[Alberti, Leon Battista]. *La pittura di Leon Battista Alberti.* Trans. by Lodovico Dominichi. Venice, 1547.

Ames-Lewis, Francis. *Drawing in Early Renaissance Italy.* New Haven and London, 1981.

Amundsen, Darrel W., and Carol Jean Diers. "The Age of Menarche in Medieval Europe." *Human Biology* 45 (1973): 363–9.

Anderson, Jaynie. "Giorgione, Titian and the Sleeping Venus." In *Tiziano e Venezia: Convegno internazionale di studi, Venezia 1976,* pp. 337–42. Ed. by Massimo Gemin and Giannantonio Paladini. Vicenza, 1980.

"The Giorgionesque Portrait: From Likeness to Allegory." In *Giorgione: Atti del convegno internazionale di studio,* pp. 153–8. Ed. by Filippo Pedrocco. Castelfranco Veneto, 1979.

Arasse, Daniel. "La signification figurative chez Titien: remarques de théorie." In *Tiziano e Venezia: Convegno Internazionale di Studi, Venezia, 1976,* pp. 149–60. Ed. by Massimo Gemin and Giannantonio Paladini. Vicenza, 1980.

"Le nu couché dans la peinture." In *Shakespeare et le corps à la Renaissance,* pp. 175–87. Ed. by M. T. Jones-Davies. Société Française Shakespeare, Actes du Congrès 1990. Paris, 1991.

"L'Opération du bord: observations sur troi peintures classiques." In *Cadres et Marges: Actes du colloque du CICADA,* pp. 15–25. Pau, 1993.

Tiziano: Venere d'Urbino. Venice, 1986.

Aretino, Pietro. *Sonetti lussuriosi e pasquinate.* Ed. by Alcide Bonneau [1882]; rpt. with intro. by Guillaume Apollinaire. La Spezia, 1981.

See also Lawner, Lynne.

Averlino, Antonio. *See* Filarete, Antonio Averlino detto il.

Ballarin, Alessandro. "Une nouvelle perspective sur Giorgione: Le portrait des années 1500–1503." In *Le siècle de Titien: L'âge d'or de la peinture à Venise,* pp. 281–92. Paris, 1993.

Barolsky, Paul, and Andrew Ladis. "The 'Pleasure of Deceits' of Bronzino's so-called London *Allegory.*" *Source* 10 (Spring 1991): 32–6.

Bartalini, Roberto. In *Domenico Beccafumi e il suo tempo,* pp. 242–3. Exh. cat. Milan, 1990.

Bataille, Georges. *Manet.* Trans. by Austryn Wainhouse and James Emmons. New York, 1955.

Baudelaire, Charles. *Oeuvres complètes.* Rev. ed. C. Pichois. Paris, 1961.

Baxandall, Michael. *Giotto and the Orators.* Oxford, England, 1971.

Béguin, Sylvie. "Vénus et Cupidon." In *Le siècle de Titien: L'âge d'or de la peinture à Venise,* pp. 494–5. Paris, 1993.

Benedek, Thomas G. "Beliefs about Human Sexual Function in the Middle Ages and Renaissance." In *Human Sexuality in the Middle Ages and Renaissance,* pp. 97–119. Ed. by Douglas Radcliff-Umstead. Pittsburgh, 1978.

Benjamin, Walter. "L'oeuvre d'art à l'ère de sa reproductibilité technique." In idem, *L'Homme, le langage et la culture,* pp. 137–81. Trans. by Maurice de Gandillac. Paris, 1971.

Bernardini, Maria Grazia, ed. *Amor Sacro e Amor Profano.* Milan, 1995.

Bernini, Dante. "Tiziano per i duchi di Urbino." In *Tiziano per i duchi d'Urbino, Mostra didattica,* pp. 17–26. Urbino, 1976.

Bloch, R. Howard. *Medieval Misogyny and the Invention of Western Romantic Love.* Chicago and London, 1991.

Bo, Carlo, et al. *Tiziano per i duchi d'Urbino, Mostra didattica.* Exh. cat. Galleria Nazionale delle Marche. Urbino, 1976.

[Boccaccio, Giovanni]. *Boccaccio in Defense of Poetry.* Ed. by J. Reedy. Toronto, 1978.

Bosch, Lynette M. F. "Bronzino's London *Allegory:* Love versus Time." *Source* 9 (Winter 1990): 30–5.

Boschini, Marco. *La carta del navagar pitoresco* [1660]. Ed. by Anna Pallucchini. Civiltà veneziana, Fonti e testi 7; Serie prima, 4. Venice and Rome, 1966.

Boswell, John. "Concepts, Experience, and Sexuality." *Differences* 2 (1989): 67–87.

Boylan, Michael. "The Galenic and Hippocratic Challenges to Aristotle's Conception Theory." *Journal of the History of Biology* 17 (1984): 83–112.

Brown, David Alan. "Venus with a Mirror." In *Titian, Prince of Painters,* pp. 302–5. Venice, 1990.

Bullough, Vern L. "Medieval Medical and Scientific Views of Women." *Viator* 4 (1973): 493–7.

Callmann, Ellen. *Apollonio di Giovanni.* Oxford, England, 1974.

Campana, Lorenzo. "Monsignor Giovanni Della Casa e i suoi tempi." *Studi storici* 17 (1908): 145–282, 381–606.

Campbell, Lorne. *Renaissance Portraits: European Portrait-Painting in the 14th, 15th and 16th Centuries.* New Haven and London, 1990.

Caulfield, Mina Davis. "Sexuality in Human Evolution: What Is 'Natural' in Sex?" *Feminist Studies* 11 (1985): 343–63.

Cavalli-Björkman, Görel, ed. *Bacchanals by Titian and Rubens.* Nationalmusei Skriftserie N.S. 10. Stockholm, 1987.

Cecchi, Alessandro. "Portrait of Eleonora Gonzaga della Rovere." In *Titian, Prince of Painters,* pp. 220–3. Venice, 1990.

Cennini, Cennino. *Il libro dell'arte.* Ed. by F. Brunello. Vicenza, 1971.

Cecini, Nando. "Cultura e letteratura nei centri maggiori e minori tra Rinascimento e Barocco." In *Arte e cultura nella provincia di Pesaro e Urbino dalle origini a oggi,* pp. 333–62. Ed. by Franco Battistelli. Milan, 1986.

Chastel, André. "L'aria: théorie du milieu à la Renaissance." In idem, *Fables, formes, figures,* vol. 1, pp. 393–404. Paris, 1978.

Art et Humanisme à Florence au temps de Laurent le Magnifique. Paris, 1959.

Cheney, Iris. "Bronzino's London *Allegory:* Venus, Cupid, Virtue, and Time." *Source* 6 (Winter 1987): 12–18.

Chesneau, Ernest. *L'Art et les artistes modernes en France et en Angleterre.* Paris, 1864.

Christiansen, Keith. "Lorenzo Lotto and the Tradition of Epithalamic Paintings." *Apollo* 124 (1986): 166–73.

Ciavolella, Massimo. "Métamorphoses sexuelles et sexualité féminine durant la Renaissance." *Renaissance and Reformation/Renaissance et Réforme,* N.S. 12 (1988): 13–20.

Claretie, Jules. *L'Art et les artistes français contemporains.* Paris, 1876.

Clark, Kenneth. *The Nude: A Study in Ideal Form.* A. W. Mellon Lectures, 1953; Bollingen Series, XXXV.2. Rpt. Garden City, NY, 1959.

Clark, T. J. *The Painting of Modern Life: Paris in the Art of Manet and his Followers*. Princeton, NJ, 1984.

Cozzi, Gaetano. "La donna, l'amore e Tiziano." In *Tiziano e Venezia: Convegno internazionale di studi, Venezia 1976,* pp. 47–63. Ed. by Massimo Gemin and Giannantonio Paladini. Vicenza, 1980.

Cropper, Elizabeth. "The Beauty of Woman: Problems in the Rhetoric of Renaissance Portraiture." In *Rewriting the Renaissance: The Discourses of Sexual Difference in Early Modern Europe,* pp. 175–90. Ed. by Margaret W. Ferguson, Maureen Quilligan, and Nancy J. Vickers. Chicago and London, 1986.

Crowe, Joseph Archer, and Giovanni Battista Cavalcaselle. *Titian, His Life and Times.* 2d ed. 2 vols. London, 1881.

Delécluze, Etienne-Jean. *Dona Olympia.* 2 vols. Paris, 1842.

Del Serra, Alfio. *See* Tofani, Annamaria Petrioli.

Di Monte, Michele, Francesco Mozzetti, and Giovanna Sarti. "Pietro Aretino 1991: Proposte e propositi." *Venezia Cinquecento* 2 (1992): 139–61.

Dolce, Lodovico. *Dialogo della pittura intitolato l'Aretino* [1577]. In *Trattati d'arte del Cinquecento,* vol. 1. Ed. by Paola Barocchi. Bari, 1962.

Dominichi, Lodovico. *See* Alberti, Leon Battista.

Dominici, Giovanni, Bl. *Regola del governo di cura familiare, parte quarta: On the Education of Children* [c. 1405], trans. and ed. by Arthur Basil Coté. Washington, DC, 1927.

Dürer, Albrecht. *Dürer, Schriftlicher Nachlass.* Ed. by H. Rupprich. 2 vols. Berlin, 1956–69.

The Painter's Manual [1525]. Ed. and trans. by W. L. Strauss. New York, 1977.

Dworkin, Andrea. *Pornography, Men Possessing Women.* New York, 1979.

Eiche, Sabine. "La corte di Pesaro dalle case malatestiane alla residenza roveresca." In *La corte di Pesaro, Storia di una residenza signorile,* pp. 13–55. Ed. by Maria Rosaria Valazzi. Modena, n.d.

Fallopio, Gabriele. *See* Falloppii, Gabrielis.

Falloppii, Gabrielis. *Omnia, quae adhuc extant opera, in unum congesta . . . .*Venice, 1584.

Farwell, Beatrice. *Manet and the Nude: A Study in Iconography in the Second Empire* [1973]. Garland Outstanding Dissertations in the History of Art. New York, 1981.

Ferino, Sylvia. [Ferino-Pagden, Sylvia]. "Portrait of Isabella d'Este." In *Titian, Prince of Painters,* p. 218. Venice, 1990.

Ferino-Pagden, Sylvia, et al. "*La Prima donna del mondo*": *Isabella d'Este, Fürsten und Mäzenatin der Renaissance.* Exh. cat. Vienna, 1994.

Fermor, Sharon. "Movement and Gender in Sixteenth-Century Italian Painting." In *The Body Imaged: Human Form and Visual Culture Since the Renaissance,* pp. 129–45, 197. Ed. by Kathleen Adler and Marcia Pointon. Cambridge, England, 1993.

Ferrarino, Luigi. *Tiziano e la corte di Spagna nei documenti dell'Archivio Generale di Simancas.* Collana "Documenti e Ricerche," Istituto Italiano di Cultura. Madrid, 1975.

Filarete, Antonio Averlino detto il. *Trattato di architectura.* Ed. by A. M. Finoli and L. Grassi. Milan, 1972.

Findlen, Paula. "Humanism, Politics and Pornography in Renaissance Italy." In *The Invention of Pornography: Obscenity and the Origins of Modernity, 1500–1800,* pp. 49–108, 345–58. Ed. by Lynn Hunt. New York, 1993.

Flandrin, Jean-Louis. "Sex in Married Life in the Early Middle Ages: The Church's Teaching and Behavioural Reality." In *Western Sexuality: Practice and Precept in Past and Present Time,* pp. 114–29. Ed. by Philippe Ariès and André Béjin. Trans. by Anthony Forster. Oxford, England, 1985.

Flescher, S. *Zacharie Astruc: Critic, Artist and Japoniste.* New York, 1978.

Fort, Bernadette. Review of Jacqueline Lichtenstein. "In Defense of Color": *La Couleur éloquente: rhétorique et peinture à l'âge classique* (Paris, 1989). *Critical Texts* 7 (1990): 75–81.

Freedberg, David. *The Power of Images: Studies in the History and Theory of Response.* Chicago and London, 1989.

Freedberg, S[idney] J. *Painting in Italy 1500–1600.* Pelican History of Art. Harmondsworth and Baltimore, 1971.

Freud, Sigmund. *The Interpretation of Dreams* [1925]. Ed. and trans. by James Strachey. New York, 1958.

Fried, Michael. *Absorption and Theatricality: Painting and Beholder in the Age of Diderot.* Berkeley, 1980.

La Place du spectateur. Esthétique et origines de la peinture moderne. French trans. of idem, *Absorption and Theatricality.* Paris, 1990.

Fry, Edward. "In Detail: Titian's *Sacred and Profane Love.*" *Portfolio* 1 (1979): 34–9.

[Galen]. *Galen on the Usefulness of the Parts of the Body.* Ed. and trans. by Margaret Tallmadge May. 2 vols. Ithaca, NY, 1968.

Gautier, Théophile. *Abécédaire du Salon du 1861.* Paris, 1861.

Gemin, Massimo, and Giannantonio Paladini, eds. *Tiziano e Venezia, Convegno internazionale di studi, Venezia, 1976.* Vicenza, 1980.

Ginzburg, Carlo. "Tiziano, Ovidio e i codici della figurazione erotica del Cinquecento." *Paragone* 339 (1978): 3–24.

Giorgi, Roberta. *Tiziano: Venere, Amore e il Musicista in cinque dipinti.* Rome, 1990.

Goffen, Rona. *Giovanni Bellini.* New Haven and London, 1989; rpt. 1994.

"Giovanni Bellini's *Nude with Mirror.*" *Venezia Cinquecento* 1 (1991): 185–202.

"*Nostra Conversatio in Caelis Est:* Observations on the *Sacra Conversazione* in the Trecento." *Art Bulletin* 61 (1979): 198–222.

Piety and Patronage: Bellini, Titian, and the Franciscans. New Haven and London, 1986; paperback ed., 1990.

"The Problematic Patronage of Titian's *Venus of Urbino.*" *Journal of Medieval and Renaissance Studies* 24 (1994): 301–21.

"Renaissance Dreams." *Renaissance Quarterly* 40 (1987): 682–706.

"Titian, His Donors and Sacred Subjects." In *Titian, Prince of Painters,* pp. 85–93. Venice, 1990.

"Titian's *Sacred and Profane Love:* Individuality and Sexuality in a Renaissance Marriage Picture." In *Titian 500,* pp. 121–44. Ed. by Joseph Manca. Washington, DC, 1992.

"Titian's *Sacred and Profane Love* and Marriage." In *The Expanding Discourse: Feminism and Art History,* pp. 111–26. Ed. by Norma Broude and Mary D. Garrard. New York, 1992.

Titian's Women. New Haven and London, 1997.

"Wives and Mothers: Adultery, Madness, and Marital Misery in Titian's Paduan Frescoes." In *Desire and Discipline. Essays on Sex and Sexuality in Premodern Europe.* Ed. by Jacqueline Murray and Konrad Eisenbichler, pp. 217–44. Toronto, 1996.

Gombrich, E[rnst] H. "Aims and Limits of Iconology." In *Symbolic Images: Studies in the Art of the Renaissance,* pp. 1–25. London, 1972.

"Apollonio di Giovanni: A Florentine Cassone Workshop Seen Through the Eyes of a Humanist Poet." In *Norm and Form: Studies in the Art of the Renaissance,* pp. 11–28. London, 1966.

"Botticelli's Mythologies: A Study in the Neo-Platonic Symbolism of his Circle." In *Symbolic Images: Studies in the Art of the Renaissance,* pp. 31–81. London, 1972.

Goy, Richard J. *Venetian Vernacular Architecture: Traditional Housing in the Venetian Lagoon.* Cambridge, England, and New York, 1989.

Gregori, Mina. "Tiziano e L'Aretino." In *Tiziano e il Manierismo europeo.* Ed. by Rodolfo Pallucchini, pp. 271–306. Florence, 1978.

et al. *Tiziano nelle Gallerie fiorentine.* Exh. cat. Florence, 1978.

Gronau, Georg. "Die Kunstbestrebunden der Herzöge von Urbino." *Jahrbuch der königlich preuzischen Kunstsammlungen* 25 (1904): 1–33.

Documenti artistici urbinati. Italian ed. of "Die Kunstbestrebunden der Herzöge von Urbino." Raccolta di fonti per la storia dell'arte, 1. Florence, 1936.

Gubar, Susan. "Representing Pornography: Feminism, Criticism, and Depictions of Female Violation." *Critical Inquiry* 13 (1987): 712–58.

Heinse, Wilhelm. *Ardinghello und die glückseligen Inseln, kritische Studienausgabe* [1781]. Ed. by Max L. Baeumer. Stuttgart, 1975.

Held, Julius S. "Flora, Goddess and Courtesan." In *De Artibus Opuscula XL: Essays in Honor of Erwin Panofsky*, pp. 201–18. Ed. by Millard Meiss. New York, 1961.

Hoffmann, E. T. A. *Contes d'Hoffmann*. 2d ed. Paris, 1859.

Holberton, Paul. "Antique and Other Figures: Metaphor and Early Renaissance Art," *Word and Image* 1 (1985): 31–58.

Hope, Charles. "A Neglected Document About Titian's 'Danae' in Naples." *Arte veneta* 31 (1977): 188–9.

"Problems of Interpretation in Titian's Erotic Paintings." In *Tiziano e Venezia, Convegno Internazionale di Studi, Venezia, 1976*, pp. 11–24. Ed. by Massimo Gemin and Giannantonio Paladini. Vicenza, 1980.

Titian. London and New York, 1980.

Horowitz, Maryanne Cline. "The 'Science' of Embryology Before the Discovery of the Ovum." In *Connecting Spheres, Women in the Western World, 1500 to the Present*, pp. 86–94. Ed. by Marilyn J. Boxer and Jean H. Quataert. New York and Oxford, England, 1987.

Howard, Seymour. "The Dresden *Venus* and Its Kin: Mutation and Retrieval of Types." *Art Quarterly* N.S. 2 (1979): 90–111.

Il gioco dell'amore: le cortigiane di Venezia dal Trecento al Settecento. Exh. cat. Casinò Municipale di Venezia. Venice, 1990.

Irwin, Joyce. "Embryology and the Incarnation: A Sixteenth-Century Debate." *Sixteenth Century Journal* 9 (1978): 93–104.

Junkerman, Anne Christine. "*Bellissima Donna:* An Interdisciplinary Study of Venetian Sensuous Half-Length Images of the Early Sixteenth-Century." Ph.D. dissertation. University of California, Berkeley, 1988.

Kahr, Madlyn Millner. "Danaë: Virtuous, Voluptuous, Venal Woman." *Art Bulletin* 60 (1978): 43–55.

Keller, Evelyn Fox. " 'The Gender/Science System' " Or, Is Sex to Gender as Nature Is to Science?" *Hypathia* 2 (1987): 37–49.

Kelly, Joan. "Did Women Have a Renaissance?" In *Women, History & Theory: The Essays of Joan Kelly*, pp. 19–50. Women in Culture and Society. Ed. by Catharine R. Stimpson. Chicago and London, 1984.

Kelso, Ruth. *Doctrine for the Lady of the Renaissance*. Urbana, 1956.

Kemp, Martin. *The Science of Art: Optical Themes in Western Art from Brunelleschi to Seurat*. New Haven and London, 1990.

ed. *Leonardo on Painting*. New Haven and London, 1989.

Klapisch-Zuber, Christiane. "The Griselda Complex: Dowry and Marriage

Gifts in the Quattrocento." In *Women, Family, and Ritual in Renaissance Italy,* pp. 213–46. Trans. by Lydia G. Cochrane. Chicago and London, 1985.

Koerner, Joseph. *The Moment of Self-Portraiture in German Renaissance Art.* Chicago and London, 1993.

Laclotte, Michel, and Giovanna Nepi Scirè, eds. *Le siècle de Titien: L'âge d'or de la peinture à Venise.* Exh. cat. Paris, 1993.

Laqueur, Thomas. "Orgasm, Generation, and the Politics of Reproductive Biology." In *The Making of the Modern Body: Sexuality and Society in the Nineteenth Century,* pp. 1–43. Ed. by Catherine Gallagher and Thomas Laqueur. Berkeley, Los Angeles, and London, 1987.

Larivaille, Paul. *La vie quotidienne des courtisanes en Italie au temps de la Renaissance.* Paris, 1975.

Larousse, Pierre. *Grand Dictionnaire universel du dix-neuvième siècle.* 17 vols. Paris, 1865–90.

Lawner, Lynne. *The Lives of the Courtesans: Portraits of the Renaissance.* New York, 1987.

——— ed. and trans. *I Modi, The Sixteen Pleasures: An Erotic Album of the Italian Renaissance.* Evanston, 1988.

Le siècle de Titien: L'âge d'or de la peinture à Venise. See Laclotte, Michel, and Giovanna Nepi Scirè, eds.

Lemay, Helen Rodnite. "Anthonius Guainerius and Medieval Gynecology." In *Women of the Medieval World: Essays in Honor of John H. Mundy,* pp. 317–36. Ed. by Julius Kirshner and Suzanne F. Wemple. Oxford, England, 1985.

Leonardo da Vinci. *See* Kemp, Martin; Richter, Jean Paul.

Lermolieff, Ivan [Giovanni Morelli]. *Kunstkritische Studien über italienische Malerei: Die Galerien zu München und Dresden.* Leipzig, 1891.

Levey, Michael. "Sacred and Profane Significance in Two Paintings by Bronzino." In *Studies in Renaissance and Baroque Art Presented to Anthony Blunt on His 60th Birthday,* pp. 30–3. Ed. by Jeanne Courtauld, et al. London and New York, 1967.

Lichtenstein, Jacqueline. *The Eloquence of Color: Rhetoric and Painting in the French Classical Age.* Trans. by Emily McVarish. Berkeley, 1993.

Lightbown, Ronald. *Sandro Botticelli.* 2 vols. Berkeley and Los Angeles, 1978.

Lydecker, John Kent. "The Domestic Setting of the Arts in Renaissance Florence." Ph.D. dissertation. The Johns Hopkins University, Baltimore, 1987.

Mahler, Margaret S., Fred Pine, and Anni Bergman. *The Psychological Birth of the Human Infant: Symbiosis and Individuation.* New York, 1975.

Mancini, Giulio. *Considerazioni sulla pittura.* Ed. by A. Marucchi and Luigi Salerno. 2 vols. Rome, 1956.

Manfrini, Monica. "La Maddalena." In *Tiziano nelle gallerie fiorentine,* pp. 106–10. Florence, 1978.

Marin, Louis. "Annonciations toscanes." In *Opacité de la peinture: Essais sur la représentation au Quattrocento,* pp. 125–63. Paris, 1989.

"Le Trompe-l'oeil, un comble de la peinture." In *L'effet trompe-l'oeil dans l'art et la psychanalyse.* Paris, 1988.

"Mimésis et description." In *Word and Image: Conference Proceedings,* pp. 25–36. London, 1988.

Massa, Nicolaus. *Epistolarum Medicinalium.* 2 vols. in 1. Venice, 1558.

Mercuri, Scipione. *La comare, o Ricoglitrice.* Venice, 1596.

Michiel, Marcantonio. *Notizia d'opere di disegno.* Ed. by Gustavo Frizzoni. Bologna, 1884.

Notizie d'opere di disegno nella prima meta del XVI. Ed. by Jacopo Morelli. Bologna, 1800.

[Michiel, Marcantonio]. *Der Anomin Morelliano* (*Marcantonio Michiel's Notizia d'opere del disegno*). Ed. by Theodor Frimmel. 2 vols. Quellenschriften für Kunstgeschichte und Kunsttechnik des Mittelalters und der Neuzeit, N.F. 1. Vienna, 1888.

[Mondino dei Liucci]. *Anothomia Mundini.* Venice, 1494.

Morelli, Giovanni. *See* Lermolieff, Ivan.

Moschini Marconi, Sandra. *Gallerie dell'Accademia di Venezia, Opere d'arte dei secoli XIV e XV.* Rome, 1955.

Mucchi, Ludovico. "Radiografie di opere di Tiziano." *Arte veneta* 31 (1977): 297–304.

Mulvey, Laura. "Visual Pleasure and Narrative Cinema" [1975]. In *Feminism and Film Theory,* pp. 57–68. Ed. by Constance Penley. New York and London, 1988. Rpt. in Mulvey, *Visual and Other Pleasures,* pp. 14–28. Theories of Representation and Difference. Ed. by Teresa de Lauretis. Bloomington and Indianapolis, 1989.

Nash, Jane C. *Veiled Images: Titian's Mythological Paintings for Philip II.* Philadelphia, London, and Toronto, 1985.

Nepi Scirè. *See* Scirè Nepi. *See also* Laclotte, Michel.

Noonan, John T., Jr. *Contraception: A History of Its Treatment by the Catholic Theologians and Canonists.* Rev. ed. Cambridge, MA, and London, 1986.

Ortner, Sherry B. "Is Female to Male as Nature Is to Culture?" In *Women, Culture, and Society,* pp. 67–87. Ed. by Michelle Zimbalist Rosaldo and Louise Lamphere. Stanford, 1974.

Osgood, Charles G. *Boccaccio on Poetry.* Indianapolis, 1956.

Ost, Hans. "Tizians sogenannte 'Venus von Urbino' und andere Buhlerinnen." In *Festschrift für Eduard Trier zum 60. Geburtstag,* pp. 129–49. Ed. by Justus Müller Hofstede and Werner Spies, Berlin, 1981.

Panofsky, Erwin. *Hercules am Scheidewege und andere antike Bildstoffe in der neueren Kunst.* Studien der Bibliothek Warburg 18. Leipzig. 1930.

"Iconography and Iconology: An Introduction to the Study of Renaissance Art." In *Meaning in the Visual Arts: Papers in and on Art History,* pp. 26–54. Garden City, NY, 1957.

Problems in Titian, Mostly Iconographic. New York, 1969.

Studies in Iconology: Humanistic Themes in the Art of the Renaissance. New York, 1939; rpt. 1962.

Pardo, Mary. "Artifice as Seduction in Titian." In *Sexuality and Gender in Early Modern Europe,* pp. 55–89. Ed. by James G. Turner. Cambridge, England, and New York, 1993.

"Testo e contesti del 'Dialogo di pittura' di Paolo Pino." In *Paolo Pino teorico d'arte e artista: Il restauro della pala di Scorzè,* pp. 33–50. Ed. by Angelo Mazza. Scorzè, 1992.

"The Subject of Savoldo's *Magdalene.*" *Art Bulletin* 71 (1989): 84–90.

Paré, Ambroise. *Les oeuvres.* 2d rev. ed. Lyon, 1664.

Parent-Duchâtelet, A.-J.-B. *De la prostitution dans la ville de Paris* [1836]. 3d rev. ed. 2 vols. Paris, 1857.

Pastor, Ludwig. *The History of the Popes From the Close of the Middle Ages.* 40 vols. St. Louis, 1891–1953.

Persio, Antonio. *Trattato dell'ingegno dell'huomo.* Venice, 1576.

Petraglia, Clorinda. "Regesto." In *Itinerari rovereschi nel Ducato di Urbino,* pp. 9–16. Itinerari marchigiani 1. Urbino, 1982.

Pignatti, Terisio. *Giorgione.* 2d ed. Milan, 1978.

Pleynet, Marcelin. *Giorgione et les deux Vénus: Plaisir à "La Tempête."* Paris, 1991.

Quintillian. *Institutio oratoria.* Trans. by H. E. Butler. Cambridge, MA, 1966.

Ranum, Orest. "The Refuges of Intimacy." In *Passions of the Renaissance,* pp. 207–63. Ed. by Roger Chartier. Trans. by Arthur Goldhammer. Vol. 3 of *A History of Private Life.* Ed. by Philippe Ariès and Georges Duby. Cambridge, MA, and London, 1989.

Reff, Theodore. *Manet: Olympia.* Art in Context. London, 1976.

"The Meaning of Titian's 'Venus of Urbino.' " *Pantheon* 21 (1963): 359–66.

Reilly, Patricia L. "Writing Out Color in Renaissance Theory." *Genders* 12 (1991): 77–99.

Richter, Gisela M. A. *The Sculpture and Sculptors of the Greeks.* Rev. ed. New Haven and London, 1950.

Richter, Jean Paul, ed. *The Literary Works of Leonardo da Vinci.* 2d ed. 2 vols. London, 1939.

ed. *The Notebooks of Leonardo da Vinci* [1883]. New York, 1970.

Récanati, François. *La Transparence et l'énonciation: Pour introduire à la pragmatique.* Paris, 1979.

Rogers, Mary. "The Decorum of Women's Beauty: Trissino, Firenzuola, Luigini and the Representation of Women in Sixteenth-Century Painting." *Renaissance Studies* 2 (1988): 47–88.

"Sonnets on Female Portraits from Renaissance North Italy." *Word and Image* 2 (1986); 291–305.

Romani, Vittoria. "Flore." In *Le siècle de Titien: L'âge d'or de la peinture à Venise,* pp. 363–5. Paris, 1993.

Rosaldo, M(ichelle) Z. "The Use and Abuse of Anthropology: Reflections on Feminism and Cross-Cultural Understandings." *Signs* 5 (1980): 389–417.

Rosand, David. "*Ermeneutica Amorosa:* Observations on the Interpretation of Titian's Venuses." In *Tiziano e Venezia: Convegno internazionale di studi, Venezia 1976,* pp. 375–81. Ed. by Massimo Gemin and Giannantonio Paladini. Vicenza, 1980.

The Meaning of the Mark. The Franklin D. Murphy Lectures 8. Lawrence, KS, 1988.

Painting in Cinquecento Venice: Titian, Veronese, Tintoretto. New Haven and London, 1982.

" 'So-and-So Reclining on Her Couch.' " In *Titian 500,* pp. 101–21. Ed. by Joseph Manca. Studies in the History of Art, Center for Advanced Study in the Visual Arts, National Gallery of Art. Washington, DC, 1992.

Titian. New York, 1978.

"*Ut Pictor Poeta:* Meaning in Titian's *Poesie.*" *New Literary History* 3 (1971–2): 527–46.

"Venereal Hermeneutics: Reading Titian's *Venus of Urbino.*" In *Renaissance Society and Culture: Essays in Honor of Eugene F. Rice, Jr.,* pp. 335–56. Ed. by John Monfasani and Ronald G. Musto. New York, 1991.

Roskill, Mark W. *Dolce's "Aretino" and Venetian Art Theory of the Cinquecento.* New York, 1968.

Rubin, Gayle. "The Traffic in Women: Notes on the 'Political Economy' of Sex." In *Toward an Anthropology of Women,* pp. 157–210. Ed. by Rayna R. Reiter. New York, 1975.

Rylands, Philip. *Palma Vecchio.* Cambridge Studies in the History of Art. Ed. by Francis Haskell and Nicholas Penny. Cambridge, England, and New York, 1992.

Santore, Cathy. "Julia Lombardo, 'Somtuosa Meretize': A Portrait by Property." *Renaissance Quarterly* 41 (1988): 62–79.

Schubring, Paul. *Cassoni: Truhen und Truhenbilder der italienischen Frührenaissance.* 2 vols. Leipzig, 1915; rpt. 1923.

Scirè Nepi, Giovanna. *Treasures of Venetian Painting: The Gallerie dell'Accademia.* New York, 1991.

Sholes, Robert. "Uncoding Mama: The Female Body as Text." In *Semiotics and Interpretation,* pp. 127–42. New Haven and London, 1982.

Simons, Patricia. "Women in Frames: The Eye, the Gaze, the Profile in Renaissance Portraiture." *History Workshop* 25 (1988): 4–30.

Siraisi, Nancy G. *Avicenna in Renaissance Italy: The "Canon" and Medical Teaching in Italian Universities After 1500.* Princeton, NJ, 1987.

Sohm, Philip. "Gendered Style in Italian Art Criticism from Michelangelo to Malvasia." *Renaissance Quarterly* 48 (1995): 759–808.

Squellati, Fausta Paola. "Venere con Amorino, un cane e una pernice." In *Tiziano nella gallerie fiorentine,* pp. 60–5. Florence, 1978.

Steinberg, Leo. "Art and Science: Do They Need to be Yoked?" *Daedalus* 115 (1986): 1–16.

Stendhal. *Souvenir d'égotisme.* Rpt. in *Oeuvres intimes,* vol. 2. Paris, 1982.

Stevens, Wallace. *The Collected Poems of Wallace Stevens.* New York, 1954.

Summers, David. "Form and Gender." *New Literary History* 24 (1993): 244–71.

The Judgment of Sense. Cambridge, England, 1987.

Michelangelo and the Language of Art. Princeton, NJ, 1981.

Talvacchia, Bette. " 'Figure lascive per trastullo de l'ingegno.' " In *Giulio Romano,* pp. 277–80, 283–6. Exh. cat. Ed. by Sergio Polano. Milan, 1989.

Tervarent, Guy de. *Attributs et symboles dans l'art profane 1450–1600.* Geneva, 1958–9.

Thoré, Théophile. *Salons de W. Bürger, 1861 à 1868.* Paris, 1870.

Thornton, Peter. *The Italian Renaissance Interior 1400–1600.* London and New York, 1991.

Ticozzi, Stefano. *Vita dei pittori Vecellj di Cadore.* Milan, 1817.

Tietze, Hans. "An Early Version of Titian's *Danae:* An Analysis of Titian's Replicas." *Arte veneta* 8 (1954): 199–208.

Tietze-Conrat, Erica. "Titian's Workshop in His Late Years." *Art Bulletin* 28 (1946): 76–88.

Titian, Prince of Painters. Exh. cat. Palazzo Ducale, Venice, and National Gallery of Art, Washington, DC. Venice, 1990.

Tiziano e Venezia: Convegno internazionale di studi, Venezia 1976. Ed. by Massimo Gemin and Giannantonio Paladini. Vicenza, 1980.

Tiziano nelle gallerie fiorentine. See Gregori, Mina.

Tofani, Annamaria Petrioli, Antonio Natali, and Alfio Del Serra. *La "Venere di Urbino" di Tiziano restaurata.* Gli Uffizi, Studi e Ricerche. I pieghevoli, 30. Florence, 1996.

Trexler, Richard C. "Florentine Religious Experience: The Sacred Image." *Studies in the Renaissance* 19 (1972): 7–41.

Turot, Henri. *Le Prolétariat de l'amour.* Paris, 1904.

Twain, Mark. *A Tramp Abroad.* Toronto, 1883.

Urrea, Jesus. "Venus with an Organist and Dog." In *Titian, Prince of Painters,* pp. 294–7. Venice, 1990.

Valazzi, Maria Rosaria, ed. *La corte di Pesaro, Storia di una residenza signorile.* Modena, n.d.

Valcanover, Francesco. "Madonna and Child with Saints Catherine, Dominic and a Donor." In *Titian, Prince of Painters,* pp. 162–4. Venice, 1990.

"Portrait d'Eleonora Gonzaga." In *Le siècle de Titien: L'âge d'or de la peinture à Venise,* pp. 524–5. Paris, 1993.

"*Vénus à sa toilette.*" In *In Le siècle de Titien: L'âge d'or de la peinture à Venise,* pp. 534–5. Paris, 1993.

Valeriano, Pierio. *Hieroglyphica* [1556]. Lyons, 1602.

Valéry, Paul. "The Nude." In *Degas, Manet, Morisot.* Trans. by David Paul. Vol. 12 of *The Collected Works of Paul Valéry.* Ed. by Jackson Matthews. New York, 1960.

Varese, Ranieri. "Tiziano e i Della Rovere." *Notizie da Palazzo Albani* 5 (1976): 15–29.

Vasari, Giorgio. *Le vite de' più eccellenti pittori, scultori ed architettori* [1568]. Ed. by Gaetano Milanesi. 9 vols. Florence, 1878–85; rpt. 1973.

Vasari-Milanesi. *See* Vasari, Giorgio.

Watson, Paul. "*Virtù* and *Voluptas* in Cassone Painting." Ph.D. dissertation, Yale University, New Haven, 1970.

Wethey, Harold E. *The Mythological and Historical Paintings.* Vol. 3 of *The Paintings of Titian, Complete Edition.* London, 1975.

The Portraits. Vol. 2 of *The Paintings of Titian, Complete Edition.* London and New York, 1971.

Wilde, Johannes. *Venetian Art from Bellini to Titian.* Oxford, England, 1974; rpt. 1981.

Wind, Edgar. *Pagan Mysteries in the Renaissance.* Rev. ed. Harmondsworth and Baltimore, 1967.

Witthoft, Brucia. "Marriage Rituals and Marriage Chests in Quattrocento Florence." *Artibus et Historiae* 3, no. 5 (1982): 43–59.

Wollheim, Richard. *Painting as an Art.* The A. W. Mellon Lectures in the Fine Arts, 1984. Princeton, NJ, 1987.

Zecchini, Maurizio. "La Bella." In *Tiziano nelle gallerie fiorentine,* pp. 110–15. Florence, 1978.

Zeri, Federico, and Elizabeth E. Gardner. *Italian Paintings: A Catalogue of the Collection of the Metropolitan Museum of Art, Venetian School.* New York, 1973.

Ziliotto, Baccio. *Raffaele Zovenzoni: La vita, i carmi.* Trieste, 1950.

INDEX